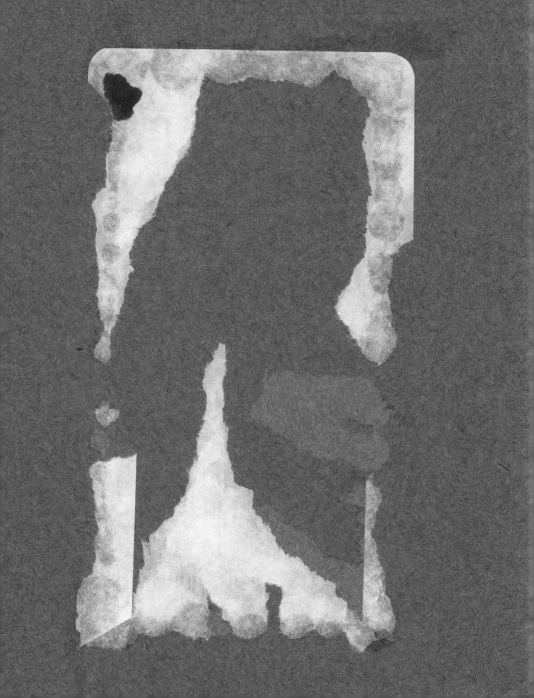

The Complete Singer-Actor:
Training for Music Theater

To Barbara
and
To Janis, Vern, and Yale,
the founding ensemble

The Complete Singer-Actor: Training for Music Theater

by
H. Wesley Balk

University of Minnesota Press, Minneapolis

Preface

Why should a person who comes from an unpretentious, small-town, rural Midwest environment find himself deeply involved with opera, an art which, of all the arts, is the most elevated, cosmopolitan, aristocratic, and stylized (or phony, snobbish, pretentious, and sterile—depending upon one's point of view and frankness)? And why should this encounter of contraries resolve itself in amity and devotion? In answering the latter question—why the integration of opposites not only happens, but *must* happen—one is led to an exploration of the fundamental yin-yanging of life itself, and in the present case to the writing of this book. But the first question—why a form with such enormous potential for aesthetic disaster and human boredom should fascinate in the first place—has continued to intrigue me. The first chapter of this book explores some possible answers to that question, but an experience that occurred after it was written suggests still another.

I have directed a series of opera training programs based on the philosophy described in this book. The most recent of these institutes for singers, conductors, and directors culminated in an enormous outpouring of emotion by the participants, who realized the growth and enlightenment they had achieved. Some of this emotion was the result of the open-endedness of the work, the honesty of it, the freedom to explore without fear of failure, and the sheer fun of creative play—all of which are stressed in the following pages. But the intensity of the experience transcended such factors; they are evident in a great many exploratory theater sessions not connected with opera which have never achieved an emotional experience on the scale encountered in our exercising for music-theater.

The difference, I believe, lies in the nature of the form itself, in the very totality of the demand opera makes on the human performer. In effect, we say to the participants in our institutes and training programs,

We are here to fulfill the demands of the operatic art. It involves a human commitment of physical, vocal, and emotional energy which is out of the ordinary; which is, in fact, the most extreme combination of these energies in the performing arts. The way you deal with these demands as a person and as a performer cannot be separated. Habitual personal tensions which interrupt or impede the maximal flow of energies required for good performance will have to be attended to, along with those tics and tensions which occur, or seem to occur, only in performance. Although performance tensions arise only in the context of performance and may not seem to relate to personal life, any habitual energy interferences on a personal level *will* affect your performance. The two are related on an organic level, for life itself is a form of continual performance, however well practiced and natural it may seem. We will ask you to perform exercises that diagnose these interferences in personal and performance energy, as well as exercises that correct or strengthen the organic flow of physical, vocal, and emotional energies on both a personal and performance level. All this will be done, however, with one basic goal in mind: your growth as a performer of the demanding and rewarding art of music-theater.

Having made this clear—never, of course, stating it quite so explicitly—we release the participants from the self-consciousness and fear which so often plague sensitivity courses or encounter sessions. They are allowed to forget themselves in the pursuit of art, and as a result they attain a more complete sense of themselves than if they had gone for it directly. Personal growth training often demands artificial emotional stimulation; rage and joy have to be aroused and dealt with, for maximal emotional energy situations create most of our life problems because of either *stoppage* of energy flow or *bad usage* of energy flow. It is not enough to talk about these emotions; they must be experienced. But the arousal

of these energies can feel artificial, self-conscious, and deeply threatening.

Much of this can be avoided by concentrating on a different goal, but only if that goal embodies indirectly the very problems that must be experienced. Opera permits this in extraordinarily objective ways. It is the essence of high emotional situations: people are forever dying, loving, hating, agonizing, rhapsodizing, and generally tearing a passion to tatters. This emotional intensity is opera's greatest strength and, as we are reminded in thousands of cartoons, its greatest weakness. For intense emotional situations enacted without total commitment can appear ludicrous, boring, and all the other pejoratives with which unfulfilled opera is favored by the world at large. But the emotional potential is there and offers the precise objective challenge needed to bypass the obstacle of self-consciousness. The challenge demands flexibility of response and freedom from tension of all kinds as well as a sustaining strength of emotional commitment. The absence or blocking of that emotional commitment will be more effectively revealed and diagnosed by music-theater exercises than by those in any other performing art. Effective as theater games and theater therapy can be, their emotional and stylistic range is simply not as all-encompassing as that of music-theater.

This is not to say that opera therapy is our goal, but simply to suggest something about the fascination of the form. The totality of human abilities and experiences demanded by opera makes it, potentially, not only the most pompous and absurd but also the most exhilarating and rewarding of all performance activities. Opera training shares the dichotomy: it can be either the most rigidifying, authoritarian, tension-creating, puppet-making indoctrination, or the most freeing, joyous, open, thrilling kind of personal growth activity. It is the purpose of this book to help move both the training process and the performance product closer to the positive experiences they can be.

Integrating opposites—person and performer, words and music, theater and music, process and product, singer and actor—is perhaps the fundamental issue in music-theater[1] training and performance, as well as the thematic basis of this book. If this is true, the best way to achieve such an integration may be a life-long movement between the various opposites that create the essential artistic tension in the form. Unfortunately, the number of young artists— whether singers, conductors, or directors—who accidentally acquire training of this seesaw nature is limited (and accidental training seems to be the only kind that can be acquired at present). There are even fewer who have the foresight to *plan* a life of rhythmic alternation between the polarities of the form.

Leaving out singer-actors[2] —for their problem is the subject of the book itself—the available *useful* training for stage directors and conductors of opera is strictly limited. This is not to say that there are not a great many fine directors and conductors who manage to accomplish the fiendishly difficult task of creating totally unified music-theater (a polite lie—there are few who do). But unusual circumstances are required to develop a conductor-director team dedicated to integral music-theater, each member of which is able to maintain a separate but unflinching devotion to her or his own half of the art. Ideally, each partner in such a team should have worked in both music and theater in depth before becoming committed to either side of the music-theater tug-of-art.

It is perhaps a peculiar accident of my own career that I have crossed the music-theater boundaries often enough to have become deeply aware of the necessity for an integrated aesthetic. I began with acting, then moved to singing, then to singing-acting, then choral conducting, then theater directing, then opera directing, then professional theater training at the Yale Drama School, along with opera directing at the Yale Music School. To understand how rarely anyone moves between the two fields and explores that virgin territory, witness the subject of my doctoral dissertation: *The Director and the Mozart Operas*. Where else but in the dilettantes' stamping ground called opera could such a broad topic be accepted for advanced work?

The research for that dissertation began in Germany with the special stimulus of Walter Felsenstein's astounding work in East Berlin and ended in New Haven a year later. After completing the dissertation I began directing for the Minnesota Opera Company (then called the Center Opera Company), which presented a unique opportunity to continue my exploration of music-theater, especially through a series of experimental workshops initiated by the

Company. At the same time I began teaching directing and acting at the University of Minnesota and occasionally directed University plays as well, thereby continuing my involvement with theater as well as with music-theater. In succeeding years the Minnesota Opera Company established a resident ensemble as the basis of its work, allowing further development of the training and techniques begun in the workshops. This in turn led to the establishment of the Minnesota Opera Studio, an adjunct to the Company which is focused on the training of the young singer-actor. All these experimental and training activities went hand in hand with the Company's growing international reputation for the production of new works and for the development of new performance and production techniques.[3]

The work with the Minnesota Opera Company, combined with my University teaching and directing, provided the most fertile possible ground for a continuing exploration of music, words, and their interrelationship in the action-crucible of performance.[4] But it was not until I directed the opera training program at the Aspen Music Festival that all the pieces—professional and educational, musical and theatrical—fell into place, and a coherent training program began to emerge. That program (and this book) evolved out of the two years at Aspen and two at the Wolf Trap Farm Park for the Performing Arts. During those four years I worked with young professionals from nearly every noteworthy academy in the country, encountering in the process virtually every kind of problem it is possible to allow a young singer-actor to develop.

In retrospect, all those years of moving between theater and music-theater, between directing and teaching were probably the best of all possible postgraduate courses in training the singer-actor, however unplanned it may have been. It kept me moving serendipitously between a great many music-theater opposites until I realized the necessity for doing so purposely. Whether this process can become a part of the institutional training of singer-actors (*and* of conductors and directors) remains to be seen. In any event that is the reason for this book's existence: to make the training of the singer-actor measure up to the magnificent potential of the music-theater form.

The Use of the Book

The book is divided into three main sections which deal generally with the philosophy of the music-theater form, an analysis of the skills required by the form, and a series of exercises to better those skills. Although it is important that the philosophic basis for the exercises be clearly understood, some readers may be familiar with the content of the first two sections. They may wish to sample the exercises before concluding the first two sections. They are encouraged to do so as long as the basic point of view is understood. Many of the exercises in the third section were created in the turmoil of practice before the philosophic principles of the first and second sections were derived. There is no reason why a similar process should not be followed in using the book. It should be stressed, however, that the point of the exercises can easily be misconstrued without a complete reading of the first two parts, particularly if one is using them to work with singer-actors. But as long as practice and philosophy are finally integrated, the book may be used according to one's interests and needs.

H. W. B.

Table of Contents

PART ONE
The Implications of the Form

Without the organic union of words and music there is no such thing as the art of opera.

Konstantin Stanislavski
Stanislavski On Opera

Whatever different opinions may be entertained concerning the contemporary interpretation of opera, no doubt exists that the focal center is the singing human being.

Walter Felsenstein
*The Music Theater
of Walter Felsenstein*

Chapter

1

Exploring the Territory

A. The Disputed Boundaries

Let us begin this exploration with a parable. It concerns two ad-jacent kingdoms whose borders are in dispute. The kingdoms are called Musiconia and Theatrylvania, with their capitals located in the cities of San Techniko and Feelitopolis respectively. A tourist visiting these countries would find their laws and customs to be a fascinating study in contrasts for such close neighbors. Their na-tional slogans, for example, suggest opposing views about ultimate authority; Musiconia's is "In Score We Trust" and Theatrylvania's is "Honor That Which Communicates." Accordingly, our tourist would quickly learn that the way you *sound* as you communicate is of prime importance in Musiconia (and a good phrase inflection book is a necessity), but how you *feel* as you communicate is more vital to Theatrylvanians. The tourist who can relax and "let it happen," as they say in Theatrylvania, will have no problems.

Theatrylvanian life is a bit more permissive and freewheeling (some of its most valued citizens are notorious rule-breakers), and tourists may prefer life in Musiconia where there is a stronger emphasis on law and order. The two countries' relationship to au-thority is also reflected in the status of their kings. The Musico-nian monarch, known as Il Maestro, is regarded with almost super-stitious awe by his subjects; fortunately it is only occasionally that

3

his almost absolute authority corrupts absolutely. On the other hand the ruler of Theatrylvania, known as Il Directorio, has a prime minister (Il Producerista) who has great power as well, and who has been known to depose Theatrylvanian kings on occasion, thereby promoting a more liberal political climate in Theatrylvania.

Other tourists will be most fascinated by the disputed territory between the two countries where their borders overlap. In that unofficial third country, called Operania by its inhabitants, there is great confusion and split loyalties, and no end to the questions facing the troubled subjects residing there: To which king should they pay homage? On which of the king's ministers should they attend? Which kingdom's laws should they obey? Which kingdom's customs should they adopt? Which kingdom's language habits should be dominant? With these questions and others providing daily dilemmas for Operanians, it is no wonder that there is continual bickering in the land, a kind of permanent social cold war which is waged on all levels, from the hybrid language itself (with the "feelers" and the "sounders" snubbing each other) to the question of which king is the *real* authority figure.

It is, in short, a land of contention where opposing forces, external and internal, seek supremacy. The very name Operania is looked upon with scorn by the parent kingdoms, both of whom make special demands on the disputed territory. For example, the Theatrylvanian legislature strictly enforces their construction and clothing codes in Operania (even though Musiconians are generally indifferent to such things), while periodic National Sounding Examinations are imposed on all inhabitants by the Musiconian legislature, with exemptions granted only to certain bureaucratic functionaries. There are many other specific instances of this problem, but the twin imposition of national duties demands extra time from all Operanians, making time one of the territory's most valuable commodities. There is never enough of it, and schemes abound to compensate for the lack of it. There are commercial firms advertising solutions (Instant Operania, Inc. is the best known of these), but seasoned observers of the bifurcated culture agree that the answer lies in the Operanian educational system. It has been shown that Operanian children can be taught to adjust to the dual responsibilities with an ease and flexibility impossible for their Musiconian or Theatrylvanian parents. Efforts are under way to achieve the "New Integration"—as the approach is called—but like all reforms, it will probably be slow. There are simply too many patriotic Musiconians and Theatrylvanians in the system who oppose an integrated Operanian culture.

But the OLF (Operanian Liberation Front), which is the primary force behind the struggle for an Integrated Operania, continues to gain power, and we may yet see its vision realized.

One may draw any number of morals from this parable, but one lesson is clear: any situation that requires genuine cooperation and collaboration is bound to be in trouble much of the time. Forget territorial relations between disputatious neighbors; even marriage, which has the supporting advantage of a biological urge, fails in a remarkably high percentage of cases. Opera, the obvious subject of our story, is the most collaborative art form ever conceived, involving the cooperation of more artists of different kinds than any art has a right to expect or a reason to tolerate. Is it any wonder that it has even greater problems than either a failing marriage or a territorial dispute, lacking counselors, ministers, and ambassadors to negotiate a settlement, cement the relationship, or ease the divorce?

Why does the operatic form persist? Why should an art that seems hopelessly boring, eccentric, and elitist to the majority of the population continue to live and grow from year to year? Many musicians despise it as a vulgar, bastard entertainment beneath the dignity of pure music; an equal number of theatricians avoid it as a pretentious and lifeless kind of outdated pageantry. What is there at the source of this unlikely collaboration, this impossible venture in cooperation, which allows it to exist and, even more astonishingly, to thrive?

If one calls the form music-theater instead of opera, one has made the first step in understanding the polarity suggested by our parable. This polarity and its integration has always been the basis of the music-theater form, from the very beginnings of our dramatic and literary heritage, which originated in the combining of words and music. It has been said of Aeschylus, the first and perhaps the greatest of the Greek librettists and composers, that "his thought . . . sought not so much some golden mean as the vision large enough to encompass and reconcile the most diverse extremes. In this he perhaps shows his closest affinities to the romantics—Blake, Coleridge, Hegel, Hugo, Nietzsche, Yeats—who have repeatedly insisted that the highest truth is a synthesis of contraries."[1]

If the highest truth is found in this synthesis, then the song form contains the potential for such truth and the operatic form carries the challenge of such a synthesis to its ultimate limits. William Irwin Thompson has said that "human culture is a complex field in which a value is defined and achieved in conflict with its opposite." Substitute the word *opera* for *human culture* and one has an equally valid definition: "Opera is a complex form whose values are defined and achieved in conflict with their opposites." Thus opera is a synthesis of contraries which can convey an experience of the profoundest truth and significance.

But operatic contraries are more than abstractions: they involve people. More than any other art, opera is a collaborative form, an artistic paradigm of human culture. Because it does depend upon the interaction and cooperation of more different arts and artists than any other performing medium save civilization itself, the *training* for such a medium should also be based upon the problems of collaboration and cooperation rather than avoiding them.

One might suggest that this collaborative effort, this mingling of opposing impulses, began even before the literary-dramatic origins of Western civilization, at the beginning itself which, it is said, was the Word. But that Word was surely sung if the Speaker on that occasion had any sense of drama, and thus the original blending of modes, the divine combination of Apollonian reason and Dionysian feeling, was initiated as a paradigm for all future creation (if we may mingle theologies as well as modes). At one end of this all-encompassing continuum we have music, which refers to nothing, argues nothing, describes nothing, and exists for its own sake. At the other end, we have the word, which refers to everything, argues about everything, attempts to describe everything as literally and logically as possible, and exists for the sake of a reality separate from itself. Music relates most strongly to pure feeling, idealistic longings, and irrational but Godlike arousal. Words relate most strongly to rational thinking, logical perception, dissection, and analysis. Thus the two modes relate to opposed tendencies in the mind of man or, according to current psychophysiological understanding, to the right and left hemispheres of the brain. And although no pair would seem less likely to meet and marry than words and music, we have been joining them through the act of singing since the very beginning.

The weakness of each mode, of course, derives from its greatest strength. The earthbound rationality of words can be seen as either a strength or a limitation, and so may the soaring abstractions of music. How can one elevate one and channel the power of the other? There are many ways of allowing words to achieve a transcendent mode, including poetry and song. But song is the most compelling way of seducing the word away from its concern with an ungenerous reality to a more deeply felt ideality. To have the best of both worlds, to combine the clarity of reason with the turbulence of feeling, is to sing. The most popular kind of music is always sung, which is to say, it is word-connected, grounded in rationality even as it endeavors to soar. And in attempting to channel the abstract power of music, we go so far as to impose verbal content on music which was not intended by its composer to deal with the rational world of description.

There seems to be a veritable compulsion in man to fuse the worlds of reason and feeling, logic and passion, by combining verbal and musical modes. The popular song and musical comedy are two enduring examples of the impulse. And opera? The impulse is the same but the attempt is larger and more demanding in its thrust toward an ultimate, transcendent mingling of modes. Richard Wagner spent much of his life explaining this need to integrate the opposing aspects of our being in a totally unified work of art. Today, Stephen Sondheim watchers are aware of his search for a more demanding form, a higher plane of achievement in unifying those twin forces. Wagner's roots were primarily musical, and Sondheim's have been primarily theatrical, but the intent is the same for both. What Sondheim really wants, one feels, is to write an opera, a *Gesamtkunstwerk* without the concessions which seem to be an integral part of the musical comedy form. His problem (and the problem of every opera composer) is to find the right words, the right book, and the right rationale; for the words must in some way contain the seeds of the very music that will elevate and transcend them.[2]

Based upon what we have said thus far, let us derive some of the laws and basic assumptions governing the overlapping territory of Operania, that land which so badly needs to declare its independence and define its identity.

B. The Territorial Imperatives

The first and most basic assumption to be made is that music-theater is an art form in which music and theater are equal partners and not, as in the musical comedy tradition or the grand, grand opera tradition, inferior servants of one another. Music-theater is an art form with different judgmental criteria than either music or theater, although certain standards from each of them form a necessary foundation for their effective combination. This is not to imply that the relationship between the musical elements and the theatrical elements of music-theater is always equal. The balance may shift from moment to moment and either one may dominate at any given time. But there must always be some kind of organic relationship between them, especially within the singer-actor, who is the very core of music-theater. The organic relationship between the two arts must be maintained *at that core at all times*. The theatrical energies of any music-theater piece must always be in contact with the musical impulse, and the music must always, in some way, vitalize the theatrical statement.

An opera production in which this balance is not sought may be either a concert with theatrical effects or a theater piece with incidental music, but neither of these is our direct concern.[3] It is also true that surpassingly inferior work may be enthusiastically applauded on the operatic stage. There is not a person in the profession who cannot relate grotesque and hilarious stories of dreadful performances, backstage incompetence, and onstage fraudulence, which were all rewarded with ovations. That music-theater has this power to deceive is to its credit, but this neither justifies nor rationalizes inferior or uninvolved work. Music-theater at its best, that is, fulfilled in all its aspects, is the most vital, stimulating, and meaningful experience one can offer an audience.[4] And it is the singer-actor to whom one must inevitably turn to achieve this goal. No matter how stunning the sets, how splendid the costumes, or how superb the orchestra, the performer contains the true life of the piece and without the full realization he can provide, the production may be many things, but it will not be fulfilled music-theater.

In addition to that basic assumption about the nature of music-theater, there are four special conventions that differentiate it from both theater and music. The first and most important of these is the alteration of time by music. In music-theater the real time of theater and the ideal time of music mingle and span the complete continuum of time flow from accelerated time to real chronological time to total suspension of time. The other conventions are related to this time-altering power. The second is all situations in which a performer is left alone on stage to sustain the action for five or ten minutes. This rarely happens in theater, but is a common occurrence in music-theater: it is called the aria. The third convention is simultaneous singing by two or more characters for extended periods of time. This never happens in theater, but is a commonplace in opera—the ensemble. The fourth convention requires that a singer remain on stage without singing during the introductions, interludes, postludes, and spaces when the orchestra plays. Actors never pause as often or for as long as singers must do regularly during their performances. And although singers are aided by the fact that there is music filling the pauses, their psychological and physical processes must fill the pauses as well without the aid of that primary weapon, the voice. We will deal with these four conventions at length below, but for the moment we can simply note that, although they create most of the performance problems for the singer-actor, they are integral to the potential excitement of the music-theater form. .

C. The Challenge of the Territory

If music-theater is potentially the most exciting and fulfilling of the theater arts, it may be fair to assert that singing-acting, when completely realized, is the most complex aesthetic task a human being can be called upon to perform. A realized singing-acting performance requires a believable portrayal of character, an enormous expenditure of physical energy, an extremely complex, taxing, and technically difficult vocal delivery, and the comprehension and coordination of a musical score which is staggeringly complex to a nonmusician. In addition, the rhythms of the psychological events portrayed must be expanded and compressed according to the fluctuating flow of time. The singer-actor must also relate to fellow performers, to the conductor, and to the sounds of the orchestra while acting in a physical style that is unlike customary behavior and that must also relate to the musical alteration of time. Whether or not the sum of these problems equals the most difficult task in the performing arts, it is clearly a formidable one[5] — so formidable that it is easy to understand the operatic bum approach.[6] "Memorize the music and the blocking, and let instinct take care of the rest; just remember to cheat out so you can be heard, every man for himself. If you get in trouble, wing it. All that music will cover it anyway and will make it seem as if something is happening whether it is or not. Opera has so much going for it there's nothing to worry about." One can understand this point of view—given the appalling conditions of rehearsal and performance—without condoning it. The fact that opera has so much going for it only increases our responsibility to fulfill its potential, however difficult that task may be.[7]

And there is no question about its difficulty. To attain surpassing heights in combining words and music, one must first find voices of unusual quality and size. Next, the possessors of those voices must become true singer-actors, i.e., beings who *sing* the *words*, beings in whom resides the ultimate fusion of the two forces.[8] Such beings are the living embodiment of the impulse wedding reason and feeling. The singers of songs, the performers who best unite words and music, receive more adulation and sheer worship in our society than any other kind of artist. Sills, Jagger, Janis Joplin, Callas, Sinatra, Caruso, Streisand, no matter what the style, the human being who is able to fuse the energies of words and music touches the very core of our collective being. And those singers who do justice to *both* words and music even while integrating them totally are the most adulated.

If the act of singing a song is the ultimate implosion of the real and the ideal which reveals us to ourselves, the song must make great demands on the singer, physically and emotionally. The words must be personally felt on the deepest level and the voice must cry out to us. However beautifully controlled the song may be, the emotions must be palpable. The popular singer uses electronic technology to satisfy this need; the opera singer depends upon the unassisted voice. The point is that the total emotional commitment of voice to the singing of words is what makes the art compelling for the audience. Pure sound, whether nakedly unaided or electronically cosmeticized, is not enough. The word must affect that sound; the cry, the scream, the shudder, the whimper, the sob, the sigh must be there, must be felt, must be part of the total blend of music and words.

Our concern is for the singer-actor who depends upon the voice alone, who wants to become an opera singer, who wants to make a commitment to the art, and who wants to deal with the emotions, the words, and the music as a single unified work of musical-dramatic art. She or he is the core of music-theater. The song and the words are unified within the performer and with them we are all elevated as we watch and listen. The task we have set for the singer-actor is surpassingly difficult. What about the training for that task, the preparation for its fulfillment? Have we been doing an effective job in preparing the singer-actor to face such a challenge?

The very existence of this book implies a negative answer to that question. But there is a special qualification to make before we probe the sore spot of singer-actor training in this country. Individually, it is hard to point an accusing finger at any aspect of the young singer's training, for the teaching of the separate skills involved is generally on a very high level. Collectively, the view is quite different. If the assumptions we have made thus far are valid, we have the basis for a broader view of the training of the singer-actor. All the skills previously mentioned, and more, many of which are at opposite ends of the performance spectrum, must be combined and integrated to create the total music-theater performance.

It is this fact that creates the special implications for operatic training. Beginning with the opposites underlying the form—music and theater, singing and acting—one must deal with a constant process of integration and unification. The form is neither musical nor theatrical, it is both; the operatic performer is neither a singer nor an actor, but a singer-actor. These may be truisms, but the implications of these truisms are seldom acted upon nor is the logic deriving from them often obeyed. The fundamental task in opera performance, then, is the integration of all the opposites basic to the form, beginning with the functions of singing and acting.

In the past decade exploration of the different functions of the right and left hemispheres of the brain has given us an interesting validation of this view. In the nineteenth century, it was established that the left hemisphere of the brain governed not only the right hand, but also verbal logic, sentence construction, and other rational and structural use of functions. But it has taken another century for continued experimentation to suggest that the right hemisphere governs the use of the left hand as well as aesthetic, intuitive, imaginative, and musical functions. One particularly interesting experiment focuses directly on the singing-acting problem, furnishing "dramatic proof that speech and music are lateralized to different sides of the brain."[9] The researchers injected an anesthetic in the carotid arteries on either side of the neck, thus putting one half of the brain to sleep. This was done while a subject was singing, with the following results: if the right half was anesthetized, the subject forgot the tune, but not the words; with the left half of the brain asleep, the subject could continue the melody, but forgot the words.

Thus, in order to keep singing the complete song—both words and music—it was necessary to have both sides of the brain awake and coordinated. This process of integrated coordination is vital to life as well as to music-theater; but when it is lacking in music-theater, it is more directly evident than it is in life. One might suggest that man's fundamental problem as a human being is to effectively integrate within himself the right and left hemispheres' functions. The ideal human is perhaps one who has best integrated the creative, intuitive, imaginative, and musical capacities with the rational, logical, structural, and verbal capacities.

If that is so, it may not be too far-fetched to suggest that truly integrative music-theater training is the best possible kind of *human* training because, as we have suggested, it deals directly with coordination of these diverging functions. This would help explain the paradox discussed in the preface: the more our training has focused on opera, the greater its impact has been upon human growth. For our work is the reverse of the experiment described above: we must enliven each half of the brain rather than numbing it, and we must increase the coordination between the two rather than diminishing it. This, then, is still another way of viewing the challenge of music-theater training.

We can also make our question about the singer-actor's preparation more specific: if integration is so clearly the fundamental task of operatic performance, how successfully have we trained our young singer-actors to accomplish that task? Putting the question in this way emphasizes the fact that it is not a question of the quality of any *single* aspect of singer-actor training, but rather a question of improving the relationship *between* the various teachers, trainers, and authority figures. If integration is to take place in the mind of the singer-actor, we must not prevent the process from taking place by insisting on the priority or supremacy of what each of us has to offer individually. That may mean giving up the individual guru-hood that we are each accorded in our work with the young singer-actor—whether as voice teachers, acting coaches, musical coaches, conductors, or directors—and acknowledging the fundamental need that each of us has for our music-theater "opposites." We must integrate with one another in working with the singer-actor before any changes can take place in the results of that training.

Assuming that there are no personal reasons for avoiding this kind of integration with one another as participants in singer-actor training (an assumption that is admittedly dubious), what are the factors that prevent it from happening on the academic level? One of them is the administrative game of chair-upmanship—or who's the boss?

D. The Bureaucratic Dilemma

In a professional opera production, there are always two directors:

the music director and the stage director,[10] who form a working partnership. It is not always an amiable partnership and is often characterized by psychological warfare rather than cooperation. Because the technical preparation of music always precedes the integration of musical and theatrical skills in rehearsal, the conductor usually has the advantage in a power struggle; and because many conductors have misplaced aspirations as stage directors, the problem is exacerbated.[11]

This ego-based struggle could be left to the chronicles of backstage scandal were it not for the fact that it affects the training of literally thousands of young singer-actors in this country. For the initial imbalance which promotes such struggles for dominance exists on the academic level where there is no loyal or disloyal opposition: a single chairman (usually a musician, for the reasons suggested above) is the invariable rule for any opera department. And since opera departments are also opera training programs, any theatrical training is simply grafted onto the musical program without genuine integration as music-theater training. If the head of the opera program happens to be a theater-trained person without a good background in music, the problems can be even greater. It is a dilemma for which there is no easy answer. Although the idea of two directors in an academic situation seems to be anathema, the music-theater form, as professionally practiced, has dual leadership from the beginning. The training for that form must also involve some kind of partnership. One director is not enough.[12] The education of the young singer-actor requires a program in which two artistic directors, each devoted to one art, maintain the tension in a cooperating, collaborating, artistic tug-of-war. But the rules of this tug-of-war differ from the familiar version in one crucial way: each person pulls as hard as possible *unless the opposite person gives way*. In that instance, the first director must simply hold the ground in the hope that the opponent will again take up the slack and create the maximum tautness. The ideal situation is a performance (or training) rope of sizzling artistic tension, ebbing and flowing between opposites, each person pulling as hard as possible without disrupting the balance, with no thought of winning in the usual sense. For a winner creates a loser, and if either side loses, the ultimate goal of creative interplay is sacrificed. To reverse

Coach Lombardi's famous dictum, not-winning isn't everything, it's the only thing in the potential ego-warfare of opera. Unless each partner-antagonist lives by this rule, opera can and often does degenerate into a series of petty, self-indulgent struggles in which each individual victory signals a defeat for the total product.[13]

Whoever grasps theater's end of the music-theater rope should be musically sensitive, musically involved, musically knowledgeable, and, if possible, musically trained, even while preserving an essential commitment to theater. It should be stressed that one's basic instincts and strongest artistic talent should be theatrical. One's background should reflect the duality of thought and training inherent in opera. It is not enough to be a teacher of acting, a director of theater, and the possessor of theatrical skills. One must have begun the serious integration of those skills with the demands, restrictions, and freedoms of music-theater. Unfortunately, most theater artists are trained under the same kind of one-director situation that musicians are, and thus in both areas a self-perpetuating system is created which produces musical *or* theatrical artists, unequipped to integrate with their opposites, and who in turn train future artists similarly unequipped.[14]

Since formalized training for true music-theater integration does not exist for conductors or directors except in rare circumstances, it is left to the individual to accomplish it. At present there seem to be very few such self-integrated artists in academia, and understandably so. There are random efforts at cooperation between music and theater departments, but it is rare indeed to hear of a case in which both sides are not unhappy with each other. And since the academic stage director seldom understands the problems of music-theater any better than does the music director (those of you who *do* understand, *know* you are the exception), the final experience for singer-actors is anything but integrated. They are left to fend for themselves, and if they have superb instincts, the results will be effective within limits; if not, we all lose.

All those involved with music-theater at the present time must do their own integrating of opposites, crossing the no-man's-land between music and theater as often as possible, extending their sense of the boundaries from both sides until the two begin to overlap. Where this overlap occurs, where our parable located the disputed country of Operania, we will find genuine music-theater, a new land with laws and assumptions based on a combined and altered heritage from the other two lands. To better understand the complexities of that transformed dual heritage—the legacy of Musiconia and Theatrylvania—let us look separately at what goes on in each country so far as the training of the singer and the actor is concerned.

2

The Legacy of the Past?

A. The Musiconian Heritage

Even before the *production* of opera on an academic level, we encounter the phenomenon I call supermarket training. The singer-actor can pick up just about any individual skill from the excellent offerings on the curricular shelves at our academies. But, like a shopper in the finest supermarket, a student purchasing ingredients for an operatic performance recipe will be at a loss without knowing how to put them all together. For that you need either an operatic cooking course or an operatic cookbook unless you have the intuitive skills of that rare creature, the instinctive singer-actor cook. And there are such people, there are performers who can prepare and serve a gourmet operatic meal under any circumstances, who can put all the ingredients together on their own without help or instruction. But at most they make up only 5 percent of the total and will do well regardless of what is given them. The fact that 5 percent is able to survive and thrive, however, does not justify a system that leaves the operatic performance kitchens of the other 95 percent a mess. The vast majority of our young singer-actors have a great need for integrative training, for training that helps them effectively combine their separate skill ingredients. Until they receive such training on a continuing basis, the superb gourmet items with which we provide them will continue to furnish a greasy spoon menu.

What factors besides the unintegrated curriculum impede the process of singer-actor integration? One of them is the vocal requirement itself. A voice of operatic size and quality is a *sine qua non* for performance of opera. The voice is the singer-actor's greatest strength (and therefore the source of greatest weakness), and it is in the initial strengthening and refining of this tool that the imbalance in training begins. This initial training in the form of voice lessons is necessarily weighted on the musical end of the music-theater continuum. Unfortunately, years of obligatory (although not always good) vocal training may create inadvertent habits and tensions that have nothing to do with the vocal process itself, but that nonetheless cripple the theatrical energies of performance. The integration of music theater and singing-acting must begin in vocal training without, of course, imposing an undue burden on the voice teacher or interfering with that foundation laying process. If the voice teacher is aware of the problem, much can be accomplished without imposition or interference. If, for example, at every voice lesson the teacher makes certain that the student eliminates *all* unnecessary physical tensions while singing (and there are no *necessary* tensions for any performance activity) along with all poses and mannerisms (both of which are based on tension), the labors of everyone else in music-theater would be eased. At present one encounters innumerable voice students who have been allowed and even unconsciously encouraged to develop unnatural poses, postures, and hand positions, all of which are based on tension, and all of which have to be released before any effective performance growth can occur. It may take months, even years, to relax a bodily or facial tension that has been permitted to develop during the formative years of vocal training. One can only reiterate the most fundamental rule: there is no such thing as useful physical tension in performance. Flowing intensity, readiness to act, or force applied to a specific task have a place, but generalized, held tension does not.

It should also be evident that the possession of a fine voice does not guarantee the presence of all the other skills necessary for total music-theater performance.[1] In most cases these skills must be developed, and they will often require as much training as the voice does to become functional.[2] And like the voice, they must be exercised with integration in mind; they must be made a part of total music-theater training from the beginning. As a bonus, such training in nonvocal physical and psychological skills will often improve the singer's vocal work, a commonly observed occurrence when working with the music-theater exercises we will describe. Each improvement comes about, I suspect, because of the release of various kinds of nonvocal performing tension that have been impeding a free use of the vocal apparatus. This, again, is simply another fortunate by-product of the training and not its goal.

Still another problem in the early training of the singer-actor is performance in foreign languages that the singer does not understand. It is a rare singer who sings only in English; all the others spend hours mouthing what are for them little more than nonsense syllables. This situation not only permits, but encourages the fatal music-theater habit of generalization. It is extraordinarily difficult to sing with genuine nuance and expression in English, let alone in a language which is not one's own. And when one spends most of one's time learning repertoire in a language one does not truly understand, memorizing sounds with generalized meanings, one is learning how *not* to sing with specificity. The intensely human experience of an operatic aria or ensemble becomes instead an unspecific ritual. The student may know that the aria is about the loss of love, or some such gloss of the overall meaning, but that vital second-to-second, word-to-word understanding essential to communication, to drama, and to music is absent a great share of the time.[3] We encourage one of the worst mental habits the young singer-actor can acquire by our tolerance of unintegrated, unincorporated work in a foreign language. This is no place to get into the "original tongue vs. the language of the audience" argument. It is important to note, however, that opera *training* demands not only a specific knowledge, word by word and phrase by phrase, of what is sung, but a thoroughly imagined analysis of what is happening before, behind, and around the words and how they can be colored and inflected to convey all their meanings. What is the psychological experience of the aria in detail? To answer this vital question takes time, thought, and imagination, but it must be answered. It is better for a student to master three arias in real depth than to learn twenty in the superficial, generalized way which seems to be the norm of current preparation.

Beyond such specific problems of singer-actor training, there is the more general question of the different views of life which musical and theatrical training produce. The training of a musician is necessarily authoritarian and highly disciplined, requiring continual conformity to other people's wishes: to the score, to the coach, to the voice teacher, to the conductor, to any number of external imperatives. A lifetime of such discipline leads inevitably to a temperament that is conservative, careful, and correct. The training of a theatrician, on the other hand, requires more personal expression, more volatility, more interpretative freedom and encourages a looser, more liberal temperament.

Yet singing is one of the creative, imaginative activities controlled by the right hemisphere of the brain, and one would expect singers as a group to reflect an uninhibited, nonconservative, freewheeling attitude. Although this theory is contradicted by the conservative bent of singers, recent experimentation suggests a reason. According to this work,[4] musicians transfer their music-making, right hemisphere skills to the management and control of the left hemisphere where the logical, disciplined, reason-oriented capacities can guide the musical-fantasizing energies. Perhaps, like all attempts to control freedom, creativity, and fantasy, a system of overcontrol sets in. The logical and, in this case, repressive left half of the brain overcompensates in its control efforts and stifles the rest of the right half functions to some extent even as it controls the musical capacities.[5]

The actor, on the other hand, is a simpler case. The element of discipline which is so necessary in music, and which presumably creates the need for right hemisphere subordination, is lacking (some might say *sadly* lacking) in theater. In acting, there does not seem to be the same need for a complex, controlled discipline, and so there is no need for the left hemisphere to exert its control.

These are generalizations, it is true, and the best performers in each profession partake magnificently of the characteristics of their opposites. But the observation tends to hold true, particularly for the beginning singer who is suddenly thrust into a music-theater situation after years of relative inhibition. In this new context the singer grasps for quick techniques, most of which are based on tension, imitation, gratuitous posing, or retreat from the demands of committed performance. As the tension increases, the masks become inflexible, the repressions ache for release, and the result is unfulfilled music-theater.

The existence of the prima donna, male or female, makes perfect sense in this light. Anyone whose training dictates subservience to the often contradictory whims of those in charge, who is seldom called upon to make a decision, but for whom decisions, good and bad, are made, is not a person properly trained for the responsible exercise of artistic authority. When that power is given a singer by reason of artistic talent and popular appeal, it should be no surprise that he or she imitates the authoritarian manner of opera mentors. The prima donna is the unbalanced product of an unbalanced system: because there was no organic relationship between the forces of music and the forces of theater in the singer's training, the resulting lack of knowledge about energy, performance, and music-theater technique leads inevitably to dysfunctions within the system. The prima donna as a type is fading, but we have a long way to go in correcting the imbalance in training which creates the phenomenon.

Another dilemma commonly faces young singer-actors beginning stage rehearsals for opera. Although they must perform in the most highly stylized theatrical form in existence, they are unequipped to deal with the problem of unusual performance styles (a problem that very few *actors* are equipped to solve). The result is tension. Unable to trust their natural instincts, yet having no set of trained skills with which to tackle the problem, the novice singer-actors are caught in a state of tension which is neither natural nor appropriately stylized. This syndrome recurs endlessly, and it invariably prevents singers from either using their vocal and physical energies effectively or attaining a useful level of stylized energy. The stylization that opera requires can *only* exist if it is firmly grounded in the singers' *relaxed* sense of their own being: in their natural state, if you will. Singer-actors, *available* as persons in a relaxed but *ready* fashion, capable of letting power flow freely, can soar to fantastic stylistic heights. But if this initial relaxed readiness is short-circuited by a posture-set, an artificial pose, a performance stance, or a physical tension that attempts to simulate emotion, the energy will be blocked instead of released as powerful stylization.[6] The singer must be comfortable with herself or himself before taking flight as someone else.

The old-time operatic ham, lacking the inhibitions which, depending on one's view, curse or bless the contemporary singer-actor, simply charged in with a series of splendidly overdone gestures and poses, and got away with it. And in making those gestures, the ham primed the pump a bit, and thereby activated the feedback process, receiving some useful emotional energy. Today we worry intensely about the emotional impulse, but we do not allow ourselves to prime the pump physically and get the feedback process started. That is an unfortunate limitation, because it is objectively easier to perform an external action and accept whatever emotional response it evokes than it is to arouse a specific manifestation by means of an emotional impulse. A strong physical movement is far more likely to evoke automatic emotional feedback than is a thinking process to evoke a desired physical response, especially a response that is specifically stylized.

We will deal with the question of style at greater length when discussing the Theatrylvanian heritage, but for the present we can simply note that of all the challenges of integration facing the singer-actor, this is one of the most imposing. To make a formal style seem like a personal expression and to allow one's personal energies to flow freely into a style that is not personally natural are the twin challenges of music-theater style integration.

But if the integrative process is part of the singer-actor's training from the beginning, such integrative challenges become part of the normal developmental process rather than creating unexpected and traumatic obstacles. This integrative training can (and therefore should) begin at the initial voice lesson and continue through every coaching session, acting class, music rehearsal, and staging rehearsal of the singer-actor's career. This may require some special generosity on the part of those of us in charge of these various activities; we must give up the demand that the singer-actor be able to execute a single, "correct" interpretation (at least in nonre-hearsal situations) and concentrate instead on teaching the student to execute *any* interpretation with ease and flexibility. We must understand that there can be no superfluous tension, or sustained tension of any kind, in good music-theater performance, and that it is *everyone's* problem to keep habitual tensions from becoming part of singing-acting. It is necessary to undo or not create the au-thoritarian, judgmentally frightened performance habits which give rise to not only the prima donna but to all performers whose minds have been locked into rutlike inflexibility. We need to be-come aware of all the problems attendant upon total music-theater performance, and to relate to them *through* our own spe-cialties, not in spite of them. We do not have to solve those prob-lems immediately; we must simply be aware of them and make our singers aware of them so that on an unconscious level the singers may work on their solution.

These requirements may imply to some a relinquishing of con-trol over their special slice of the operatic pie. In fact, it gives each of us a more important kind of control over the final product, a performer who has good vocal technique *and* who sings with musi-cal sensitivity *and* good diction *and* dramatic understanding *and* who acts well, projects emotion well, moves well *and* gestures well *and* is physically *and* emotionally sensitive *and* who is imaginative *and* flexible *and*, most of all, who can combine all these skills in a single coordinated act of total music-theater. It is obvious that to achieve these skills, the singer-actors with whom we work should at some point in their training practice the integration and coordi-nation of the total act. It is equally obvious that this total coordi-nation is only practiced at present under the impossible conditions of actual rehearsal. In opera, especially in opera, rehearsals imitate the product-oriented conditions of performance so closely that the majority of singers, who desperately need a process-oriented, growth situation, are incapacitated. The problem of providing that kind of situation is thrown back in the laps of those of us who do the training. The nature of the music-theater form dictates the de-mands on the singer-actor which in turn define the unusual nature of our responsibility.

That responsibility, like the training of the singer-actor, has as much to do with human factors as operatic ones. Adding to our list of requirements for conductors and directors, we must submerge our egos for the greater good of the performer and the art; we must develop genuine cooperation where relationships traditionally have been stand-offish; we must approach the performer's training in an open-minded and flexible way rather than adhering to a monolithic idea of correctness. Beyond this list of exhortations, all of us must increase our sensitivity to the skills and difficulties of singing-acting, whether physical, vocal, or emotional, and whether they fall within our particular area of expertise or not.

B. The Theatrylvanian Heritage

Although it may seem redundant to keep stressing the necessity for integration of the worlds of music and theater in achieving music-theater, the distinctiveness of each form is so seldom given its due, and it is so basic to the problem of music-theater *training*, that repetition is unavoidable. The aesthetic standards of the three forms are different, and these differing standards must be taken into account when training for performance in each of the forms. For example, it is no denigration of acting classes to say that they are very often of little benefit to the singing actor, for they deal with the rules of theater,[7] not the rules of music-theater, and singers may emerge from them even more confused about the problems of *singing*-acting. This is not the fault of the teachers of acting, and I hope that the ideas and exercises in this book may encourage them to apply their theater expertise to the problems of music-theater and singer-actors.[8]

Theater directors making a first expedition into operatic no-man's-land might also benefit from a consideration of some of these ideas. Most theater directors unfamiliar with the music-theater form take one of two approaches when first directing an opera: they are either apologetic foreigners careful not to infringe on the prerogatives of the citizens of the land they are visiting, or boorish tourists who impose their own standards on the natives without understanding the customs and traditions of the land. When directors talk about opera directing, they are really speaking of *theater* directing;[9] useful literature on the subject of opera direction is almost nonexistent, and the total literature is little greater.[10] Admittedly, operatic no-man's-land is a confusing place: choreographers are often delegated to deal with large pieces of territory, and the guidebooks to the area are simplistic, disdainful, or naive. As for competent *critics* of the literature on opera direction, those sufficiently knowledgeable to criticize it are either writing about it themselves or doing it.[11]

Another factor affecting the integration of music and theater is the fact that the interpretive style of each is in a constant state of unsynchronized flux. For example, over a period of time the interpretive aesthetics of music swing between the poles of a lush, subjective romanticism and a dry, objective classicism. Theater, although moving between similar interpretive poles—between a subjective, personalized realism and an objective, extended stylization —moves at a different rate from a different point than does the musical cycle. The law of opposites would suggest that each end of these pendulum swings needs to partake of the other for maximum vitality, but when one is also trying to synchronize the separate pendulums, both swinging at different speeds, the problem becomes more complex. Let us isolate the theatrical pendulum for a moment, and examine one complete swing. The past thirty years take in a complete cycle, beginning with a firm commitment to a representational form of subjective realism (Arthur Miller-Tennessee Williams), moving through a more presentational form of objective stylization (Edward Albee, Sam Shepherd, the Absurdists, the Open Theater et al.), back to a new realism (reflected in the nostalgic revivals of realistic classics as well as in new forms of social and documentary realism). I became aware of the cycle somewhere in the middle of that swing when I began to teach acting.

It was then that I came into direct contact with another set of music-theater opposites, the popular American view of what acting *is* as opposed to what music-theater demands that it *be*; or, in briefer terms, Stanislavski vs. Style. Anyone teaching acting in America, whether for singers or for actors, must finally come to terms with Stanislavski, or, more correctly, with the naturalistic doctrine based on his teaching.[12] Every young person in our country seems to have acquired either educationally or osmotically an unconscious but voracious appetite for realism-naturalism, whether from films, television, or acting classes. The confusion that exists about the terms *realism*, *naturalism*, and *believability* has created a swamp of acting systems and jargon surpassed only by the morass of religiosity and terminology surrounding vocal pedagogy.[13] The average person in this country finds the technique and stylization of opera difficult to deal with precisely because of a trained appetite for realism, and that realism can be traced directly back to Stanislavski and his influence on actor training throughout the world. If Stanislavski had not existed, the American acting tradition would have invented him. His point of view, however distorted by his disciples, swept the country in the 30s and 40s, and his first book, *An Actor Prepares*, has been the fountainhead of American academic actor training ever since. Stanislavski's idea of inner honesty as the prime virtue in theater was compatible with the egalitarian, antiaristocratic tradition in America. No phony, pretty, high-falutin speechifying—just plain unvarnished talk, flowing directly into the already established stream of literary and dramatic naturalism. Anyone could be a star like Marlon Brando, who happened along at just the right time to solidify the public's fascination with the Method Establishment. All one had to do was be *honest, natural*, and *show what one felt*! No special training was necessary, no voice work, no body work, no acting technique—just unvarnished truth. Down with aristocratic notions of special talent and training—express youself openly and art would be born.

Although this is an oversimplification of the situation, these impulses, in broad form, were and are there. Our error has been to go to one end of the performance continuum and not to the other—to do what one feels and neglect learning how to feel what one is obliged to do. Stanislavski was a supreme integrator of opposites, and this may be a major reason for his greatness. His aphorisms abound with explicit injunctions to integrate opposites, such as "find the art in yourself, yourself in the art," and "feel the role in yourself and yourself in the role." He is not to be blamed for the present overemphasis on feeling, naturalism, and personal idiosyncrasy as the basis for performance, and the underemphasis on technique, stylization, and characterization. If one is to work with the theory of opposites — and it is essential for the singer-actor to do so — one must be able to live with insecurity and without definite answers, and to be ready for constant here-and-now readjustments. Perhaps it is because Stanislavski realized that his theories had been pushed too far in one direction by his adherents — especially those in America — that his second and third books deal largely with technique. These books, of course, have largely been ignored in America, along with Stanislavski's later work, which concentrated almost exclusively on externals. Today we are finally recognizing approaches to acting which draw upon the rest of the explosive Russian heritage — Meyerhold, Vahktangov, Tairov, and the rest — upon theories of later experimentalists from Europe — the Dadaists, Artaud, Grotowski, Brook — and Indian and Oriental acting theory, as well as the techniques of the Open Theater, the Living Theater, the Bauhaus, and the many Viola Spolin improvisatory offshoots in our own country. But the basic Stanislavskian concern with inner truth has established itself as an unintegrated opposite in the mass psyche of this country, and has been reinforced by overuse in cinema and television.

Having said all this, one must acknowledge that inner truth *is* vital, as much so as external truth. Stanislavski oversimplified does not invalidate Stanislavski. The best thing one can do is follow his example: that of a lifelong search for ways of achieving total artistic truth in the theater, knowing that although the goal will never be attained, it is the process of searching that is important.

With that thought in mind, I plunged into the morass of scholarly and popular acting systems, looking for ways to help the young actor achieve that special quality of the shared-personal. At the same time, I was teaching *singing*-acting, which complicated the problem. It was evident that the actor and the singer-actor faced problems which were similar but which were also strikingly different. It was important to identify the problems common to both arts as well as the problems peculiar to each.

The powerful performances given by total-immersion film actors, in which the actor and character seem to merge, cannot be ignored as a vital and important dramatic experience. Theater is more stylized than film, however, and opera is still more stylized.

As the imitative mode becomes more stylized, this kind of simplified, Stanislavskian, feeling-the-part way of work becomes less and less useful. For example, imitation of the natural rhythms of laconic Americanese does not lead to a feeling for anything rhetorical, poetic, or sustained, unless one is mocking the characters as Tennessee Williams sometimes does (and of course his powerful gift for poetic and rhetorical language flows from the same source he mocks). "Long-winded, fancy, and wordy," the boy next door would say about any kind of stylized language. The terseness of American naturalism may be a virtue, but if it is the only "natural" standard in the theater, then all musicality of language becomes suspect, and those playwrights—from Aeschylus to Shaw—who depend upon genuine and deeply felt musical language are simply not understood. A playwright who has written words to be spoken cannot be understood without the proper music of language; and if that music is not captured because of rhetorical, poetical, and musical incapacities or prejudices on the part of the actors, then the playwright cannot be *heard* in the truest sense of that word.

The naturalistic bias of our schools and our popular entertainment often interferes seriously with the young actor's ability to handle the essentially musical language demands of Shakespearean, Restoration, Georgian, and Greek drama. Similarly, the young singer-actor is seldom able to feel or appear comfortable performing opera because the degree of stylization in the form feels unnatural.

Had I been teaching only acting, this problem could have been resolved in the usual manner: by reducing the musical language demands of Shakespeare and the rest to fit the requirements of individually felt psychological meanings.[14] But constant work with the problems of music-theater and an increasing awareness that if "you don't get the music, you don't get the meaning," forced me to apply the theory of opposites. For example, unless one deals with the *music* of the language, sustaining the phrasing and outlining the thought as it is spoken, one doesn't communicate the meaning.[15] The meaning (*and* the psychology) is *in* the music, the music is *in* the meaning. The technique is required by the content, and the content requires the technique to be clearly communicated.

These are, of course, aesthetic commonplaces, but to confront them, work with them, and relearn them in actual practice was a far cry from academic note-taking. There is no place like reality for learning *what* and *how* things mean. A great many other artists were relearning the same thing in the 1950s and 60s, and, as we have seen, the ideas of theoreticians other than Stanislavski grew in influence.[16]

Although the awareness was slow in coming, all these diverse approaches to theater were strongly concerned with one thing: the relationship of style, technique, and feeling. That controversial set of terms was part of my own experimental work, and I encountered it daily in my singing-acting classes. Technique, at least external technique, had long been a dirty word in the American theater,[17] but suddenly we were forced to confront it and deal with it. It was about time. Technique became a resource to be developed rather than a mannerism to be avoided. Its opposite—spontaneity, inner truth, the feeling of the first time—had ruled the American theater for decades, despite the fact that capable naturalistic, seemingly spontaneous actors will be the first to acknowledge the immense amount of technique underlying their performances. Nevertheless, we seemed to face an either/or proposition: either we chose inner truth, or we chose external technique. The sense of necessity about this choice may have come from another aspect of the American ethos: the Immediate Results Syndrome or, It Has to Happen Now or It Never Will. If an action looks or feels artificial the first time around, it is rejected out of hand. The idea of working with an action until it feels comfortable and natural and can be judged on the basis of its aesthetic suitability rather than on its naturalness was and is resisted strenuously by the majority of American actors and directors. Instead of trying to unify the opposites of technique and feeling, the American theater clutched the latter to its bosom as if threatened with seduction, rape, or worse by the Demon Technique.

Fortunately, the times were changing, and with the more balanced view afforded by a return to theatrical stylization, old truths became useful coin once again: there is good technique and bad technique, good and bad use of externals (as well as good and bad use of internal processes), and if an action appears artificial, inorganic, or overly technical, it is because the technique itself is badly handled, either externally or internally. All the ancient quarrels about form and content collapse with the renewed awareness that one cannot exist without the other. The problem is to balance the equally valid demands of the external and the internal, and not to choose one over the other.

With this recognition it became possible to deal with singing-acting in new terms. In the prevailing theatrical view (which I had shared), great stress was placed upon a naturalistic mode of operatic acting. This seemed to follow logically from the audience's desire to *believe* in the characters and to eliminate all the stiff wooden behavior for which the operatic stage has become famous.[18] Unfortunately, striving for a naturalistic result places singers in a very strange situation. There they are in the midst of one of the most highly stylized dramatic forms known, and they are asked to be *natural*? (Has anyone ever asked of a ballet that it be stylistically natural?)[19] Natural, implying a realistic series of physical and psychological events in a realistic time scheme? Occasionally the approach succeeds, and although it is usually to the detriment of the musical values, at least the audience is given a performance that does not violate a sense of the dramatically believable. But there is always something missing, even with the seemingly successful efforts. Thinking about this deficiency, I realized that the idea of technique, which had become a useful part of my acting classes, became equally meaningful in teaching *singing*-acting.

The question became: what must one *do*, externally or internally, to make the given action *seem believable* (which is different from *feeling natural*) despite the fact that the mode of performance is highly formalized (i.e., unnatural) and technical? The singer-actor must ask in all situations, "what might the *character* do in that highly unusual situation, how would he or she do it, and how can *I* make that action believable? instead of the reductive and style-defeating question, "what would *I* do if I were in that situation?" (which implies that if I were to do what *I* do, it would seem natural.) Singer-actors must, of course, practice the action until it *feels* as natural as if they had used it all their lives. This, again, requires the absence of tension.

We have discussed the feedback energies which can assist the internal, feeling process through the use of external techniques. And although it is clear that *doing* it doesn't always lead to *feeling* it, anymore than *feeling* it always leads to *doing* it, the former process, if exercised properly, can be far more useful, more evocative, more liberating, and ultimately more stageworthy than reliance on the feel-it-and-hope system alone. This is not difficult to understand. Human feelings do not change greatly from century to century. Aristotle and I experience the same range of emotions. But the human mode of expressing these feelings does change: as a result of nature and nurture, Aristotle and I have different ways of displaying the feelings we experience. The feelings, the internal impulses, are constant, but the externals are in stylistic flux. If we have not practiced the full spectrum of external manifestations of emotions, our feelings will dictate a behavioral response that is in accord with our personal habits and with those of our society. It is not possible to achieve an eighteenth-century physical style by depending upon twentieth-century feelings alone, but it is possible to link up an eighteenth-century physical style with those same twentieth-century feelings. Feeling is the constant, external style is the variable; ergo, the variable is what must be rehearsed and practiced, while one remains receptive to energizing by the constant. We must never be satisfied with half; when working with externals, we must constantly search for the internal link that will make the combination an integrated, organic whole.

There is nothing new here; merely a combination of many old and true ideas. But it is surprising how tenaciously the inner-truth-first approach will resist all work with an external-first, or even an external-at-the-same-time approach. The demand for immediate results will not allow the time for integrating the twin demands. It takes great patience to learn a technique, practice it, explore it, learn to love it, and then find the inner resources to support it before we judge it. To complicate matters, directors and actors who *do* make a practice (sometimes a fetish) of working with technique (the "pace" school, the "get-it-out-fast-with-a-smile-I-don't-care-how" school) are defensively impatient with those who insist that externals be grounded in a careful search for inner justification. From whichever end of the continuum one begins, one can never avoid the responsibility of incorporating the opposite end. Any stage action must be perceived, must be dealt with in terms of its physical use of space, its pace, its flow, its external rhythms (and in opera, its relationship to the music), but it must also seem to proceed from and be a part of an inner process. Which comes first is not the question, but rather how the two processes can achieve simultaneity, how they can interrelate to each other so that a mutually enforcing feedback process is established. We do not think and then speak, nor do we speak and then think; we do both at once. And although physical action will always be prompted by thought, we must learn to think and, more important, to *feel with our bodies.* We must work constantly with the vital feedback process between the physical and the mental. Most of all, we must learn to *practice* the coordination of externals and internals rather than discarding whatever cannot be immediately assimilated. The internal and the external are true opposites in that each requires the presence of the other for maximal vitality. The only way to achieve that simultaneity of process is to exercise both separately with the awareness that they must finally interrelate simultaneously. The feedback process connecting the internal and the external may be the most important relationship one can arouse in the singer-actor.[20] The fact that the internal approach has been so dominant in this country will probably mean that a bit of additional stress must be laid upon an acceptance of the external; but neither must dominate the other.

Technique, however, *is* the basis for most of the musical training singer-actors have received. Their trained willingness to execute actions without relating them to human response may be the reason that academically trained singers are so often accused of being stiff when they act. External technique has dominated their artistic life; they have been strictly trained to prevent human behavior from interfering with or affecting their musical work in any way. Although music-theater training must deal with this problem, it must not counteract it with a strong diet of internal naturalism, for this simply emphasizes the gap between feeling and technique. Instead we must find exercises that emphasize the *relationship* rather than the *separation* of the opposites and that stress their interdependence rather than the gulf between them.

When one experiences the vitality inherent in the blending of opposites, the artificial barriers between the external and the internal disappear, and the approach to training on which this book is based becomes clear. One perceives the clashing of inappropriate styles in music-theater, whether it is the artificial grafting of kitchen-sink realism to the elegant stylistic demands of opera, or the imposition of an equally stultifying concert-in-costume style upon a potentially vital piece of music-theater. This book proposes a third point of view which incorporates both demands, a view which combines the need for the believable with the need for the stylized, and which deals with the fundamental realities of music-theater: the fluctuating flow of time, the blend of linear development and lyric expansion, and the unique interplay of aria and ensemble. In short, we want to deal with music-theater on its *own* terms and not those of its less complicated parents, music and theater.

Chapter
3

Commitment to the Present

A. The Declaration of Capability

Responding to the demands of music-theater and singing-acting is automatically a more complicated task than dealing only with singing or acting. It is so complicated, in fact, that it is not surprising that the process of integrating them has been neglected for the relative simplicity of working on their separate parts. But I suggest that a program of exercises will strengthen these neglected integrative skills by exploring the range of opposites at all levels of singing-acting performance—from the most stylized to the most natural, from the most planned to the most improvised. Let us attempt to help young singer-actors create within themselves a balanced field of opposing forces that can work in partnership for a purpose beyond what any force could achieve separately. Let us set singer-actors free: not free to become prima donnas or to exercise undisciplined individualism but free to do whatever is necessary to fulfill their art. This is the freedom of capability—the capability of doing whatever one wishes as a performer, whether those wishes come from a director, a conductor, or from one's self. The goal of every training program should be: to enable the performer to execute any action desired and to make sense out of that action physically, psychologically, and musically. If asked by a director to undulate the pelvis while singing a melancholy ballad and projecting at the same time exuberant joy, trained performers should have the craft and technique to accomplish it convincingly. It is not necessary to agree with the concept, for one will seldom be in total agreement with anyone else's conception. But performers should be able to give themselves completely to any performing problem and to make stylistic sense of it, even while understanding that what they are doing and how they are doing it may not be to their taste. This is true singer-actor liberation, and achieving it is one of the primary aims of this book.

Most vocal and musical training has precisely this aim in mind. It attempts to create singers capable of doing whatever they wish to do musically and vocally, with maximum vitality and understanding. But their theatrical training, let alone the *integration* of their musical and theatrical training, is treated in a haphazard manner at best. There exists no body of technique which prepares young singers for the special performance problems of music-theater or for the monumental integrative challenge of the form itself. That task becomes less complex and formidable if we treat it as we have treated other difficult problems: by separating it into component parts, exercising those parts individually, and then putting them back together. This approach is familiar to teachers of singing; from the Renaissance onward, singers have performed separate exercises for the voice to prepare to sing a song. Finally, at some point determined by the teacher, the pupil is actually allowed to sing a song. Some teachers have kept their students working on vocal isolations—scales and the like—for as long as six years before allowing them to sing a song.[1] This calls to mind the six years of preparation in *Zen and the Art of Archery*, before the bow, the arrow, and target finally became one. The length of time to be devoted to exercise alone is an individually determined affair, of course, but the principle of isolating parts before reassembling the whole is clear. The same approach is suggested for other aspects of the art of singing-acting. It is useful to compare it to athletic training such as that for pole-vaulting. The pole-vaulter who pole-vaulted constantly would never improve beyond a certain point. Instead, the act of pole-vaulting is broken up in practice into its component parts—the sprint, the pullup of the body by the arms, the strong thrust upward of the legs and the lower body, the push-off of the body by the arms, and the flexible curl of the body over the bar. To develop the skill and/or strength of each of these separate functions, the pole-vaulter does pushups, pullups, weight lifting, situps, leg raises, flexibility exercises, wind sprints, and other exercises, all of which will improve the total act to an extent otherwise impossible.

The analogy is precise. The singer-actor must exercise the isolated skills of the art to improve power and precision and sensitivity so that the total act may attain the highest possible level. The singer-actor should never spend all singing-acting practice time simply singing-acting—rehearsing a specific performance—any more than she or he should spend all singing practice time singing arias. Specific problems must be solved, and specific skills must be strengthened separately. There is no place for self-consciousness or inhibition in the singer-actor, and therefore exercises must be devised which help eliminate these obstacles. The singer-actor must be able to concentrate with unusual power, to project emotion strongly, to create psychological progressions which relate to their musical analogues, to respond emotionally to the accompanying music, to physicalize the dramatic and musical impulses, to characterize effectively, to deal with physical and emotional problems of style, to relate to fellow performers musically, psychologically, and physically, and to be as flexible and coordinated as possible in integrating the musical and dramatic action. All of these skills must be exercised separately before they are reunited in music-theater performance.

We seek a highly energized, strongly projected performance from a relaxed but ready base of self-acceptance. Operatic performance is potentially the most romantic, volatile emotional experience in the performing arts. To achieve that almost outrageous outpouring of energy, we must subject the performance problem to the kind of analysis suggested by Robert Pirsig in *Zen and the Art of Motorcycle Maintenance*. Comparing romantic and classic modes of understanding, Pirsig says that the former sees things primarily in terms of immediate appearance and the latter studies the underlying form. "The romantic mode is primarily inspirational, imaginative, creative, intuitive. Feelings rather than facts predominate. The classic mode proceeds by reason and by law—which are themselves underlying forms of thought and behavior."[2] On the surface opera belongs to the romantic mode; but as Pirsig demonstrates, and as we have discussed at some length, these opposites, like all the great contraries, require each other for their deepest fulfillment. When dealing with the care and maintenance of the singer-actor, it is necessary to apply the classic mode of breakdown and analysis to elicit to its fullest the thrilling romantic product we seek. At the same time we must recognize that the young singer-actor has grown up in a distinctly unromantic milieu and, in order to adjust to the dazzling, inspired exterior of opera, needs all the support that a careful buildup of underlying technique can provide.

B. The Bill of Opposites

Because the music-theater aesthetic is firmly grounded in the blending of opposites, its nature is largely determined by the blending process. Let us examine a brief list of opposites and suggestions for their potential synthesis by the singer-actor. We are in pursuit of a balanced field, a situation in which the tightrope performer holds the balancing pole at the center, shifting it only as required to remain on the wire. If the pole is held too near either end, the performer either will be pulled off the tightrope entirely or will panic, drop the pole, and cling to the rope. But if it is balanced properly, there is freedom and security.

MUSIC	The demands of theater have received less attention in the average young singer's life. Exercises are called for that bring the needs of theater into creative interplay with the demands of music.	THEATER
VERTICAL LYRIC EXPANSION	In all music-theater the flow of time fluctuates from moment to moment. Sometimes it proceeds at a realistic pace, at other times the action flow virtually stops. The singer's understanding of this convention and the acquisition of techniques with which to handle it are absolutely basic.	HORIZONTAL ACTION DEVELOPMENT

REASON | Because the young singer's training has | FEELING
LOGIC | probably involved some subjection | EMOTION

of feelings to the reason and logic of teachers and coaches (as well as the subjection of the creative and musical processes of the right hemisphere of the brain to the structural and logical demands of the left hemisphere) exercises are needed that emphasize the personal creativity of the singer and the choices that can and must be made in order to integrate these energies with the external demands of score and situation.

MEMORIZATION | The young singer's artistic life has been | IMPROVISATION

based in large part on the memorization of scores, which, again, is doing what others dictate. Exercises based on improvisation that utilize as well already memorized material help restore the necessary balance between energies of expression and requirements of the score.

ART | The stylization of singing may suggest | LIFE

that it is divorced from the processes of life. The *singer* and the *person* need exercises that allow them to explore the interrelationship of life and performance energies, and get these to operate from the same center.

EXTERNAL | The memorization and performance of | INTERNAL

a musical score can be seen as a series of external acts. These acts, however, must seem to come from an internal motivation. In order to "seem to come" they must interrelate on an organic level and provide modifying feedback to each other. The singer must exercise the skills of this relationship.

LIMITS | In a great performance we feel that the performer is totally committed to daring her or his limits. At the same time the performer must never reach or exceed those limits. Exercises that stretch and exceed our performing capabilities are necessary both to increase our potential in all areas of music-theater skill and to understand precisely where those limits are so that we may use them effectively in performance. | COMMITMENT

SELF-CONFIDENCE | There is no substitute for a vibrant sense of self-belief in performance. To grow *beyond* that in which we feel confident, we must subject it to analysis, but analysis can undermine confidence. The exercises practiced by the singer-actor must serve both functions: to keep the energies of self-confidence flowing even as they clarify and strengthen areas of undeveloped skill. | SELF-ANALYSIS

DISCIPLINE | The intense discipline of mastering the complexities of a musical score must allow freedom for personal expression once that mastery is achieved. But the freedom must be nurtured even as the discipline is developed. Exercises that build personal freedom into the drills of discipline will help accomplish this. | FREEDOM

SERIOUSNESS | In every artistic activity of value there must be seriousness of purpose. But every artistic activity must also be a higher form of play. We must care deeply as we play, and we must be aware that we are playing even when our art is at its most intense. Music-theater exercise games can develop the skills and the joys of this vital duality. | PLAYFULNESS

CAREFULNESS | In every great performance there is a sense of danger, a feeling that the performer may destroy the role and violate the artistic structure that is being created. The sense of "I don't give a damn!" on the one hand must be balanced by "But I care as deeply as it is possible to care!" on the other. | RECKLESSNESS

RE-CREATION | For the performer this is a basic pair of opposites; one must seem to be creating even as one re-creates. The creative processes of the composer and librettist and the re-creative processes of the singer-actor must merge in the act of performance. To aid this merger the singer-actor must perform exercises which help her or him get inside the minds of the composer and librettist, and go through the same processes they did, confronting the problem of making choices. | CREATION

REPOSE | In moments of physical or emotional stillness, as in the poised, sustaining of the line of an introspective aria, there must be a sense of potential, available energy. In moments of great physical or emotional activity there must be a stillness, a base, a solid point of repose from which the energy springs. Perhaps more than any other pair of opposites, these two must reside in each other. The singer-actor must do exercises which will heighten the awareness of the repose in energy and the energy in repose. | ENERGY

DIFFERENCE | In every character one plays, there is something different from one's self, and there is something like one's self. Thus every portrayal must deal with the integration of these two factors: How am I like the character? How am I different from the character? This | LIKENESS

gives rise to another set of opposites
that demands integration by the singer-
actor, namely:

MYSELF   CHARACTER

NATURAL   Operatic style runs the gamut from the   FORMAL
           realism of dialogue to the formalism of
           singing; yet each sequence of natural-
           seeming dialogue has a definite formal
           structure, and the most classically
           formal singing must seem to be natural
           for the performer-character in that
           situation. Exercises that increase the
           singer-actor's ability to move along
           the full range of this continuum are
           essential to music-theater work.

C. The Integrated Citizen

Although many other opposites could be listed and similarly analyzed, one final set that has to do with singer-actors and their
growth as performers should be noted.

WHAT AM I?   WHAT CAN I BECOME?

In many ways this set of opposites sums up the point of this
book for singer-actors: if they know their present capabilities
intimately, and if they want to grow as performers, all that is lacking is a specific goal and the means to accomplish it. The goal is
defined by singer-actors themselves as they select the qualities they
wish to acquire. But the magnitude of the goal is not nearly so
important as the existence of the goal itself. There is literally no
image-goal which cannot provide a means to growth if it is based
on honest self-analysis and if there is a genuine desire to reach it.
The means to accomplish the goal are the exercises in this book
and other exercises that promote the process of music-theater
integration. It only makes good sense for singer-actors to devise
their own specific exercises as well, once they understand the
principles involved.

Searching for ideas and exercises in a territory as wide-ranging as
music-theater is greatly facilitated by some sort of map. Drawing

upon two sets of opposites relating to the style and the preparation of music-theater, we can create a music-theater mandala which will serve as both a guide to the territory and a definition of its boundaries.

The pair of opposites that relates to the stylistic nature of the product—natural to formal—creates a continuum including all the possible styles of performance from the naturalistic imitation of everyday life to the most formalized kind of ritual: from television intimacy to ritualized Wagner. The pair that relates to the process of preparation—memorization to improvisation—forms a continuum which includes all possible kinds of preparation for performance, from the totally spontaneous flow of everyday life to the most meticulously planned and choreographed musical presentation: from "Candid Camera" to choreographed Mozart.

At the core of our mandala-map we will define music-theater as any performing act that involves words, action, and music. This means we cannot exclude any form of theater from consideration as music-theater.[3] Viewing the problem in this manner we see that training for music-theater must incorporate to some extent all varieties of spoken drama as a means of increasing awareness of two more opposites:

THE LANGUAGE OF MUSIC   and   THE MUSIC OF LANGUAGE

Singer-actors must sensitize themselves to the emotional meanings of the musical shapes and sounds they sing. By increasing their awareness of how spoken language can be shaped musically in communicating meaning more clearly, they will assist this sensitizing process.[4] From whichever end of the sung-spoken continuum one begins, it is necessary to integrate the music and the meaning: to give spoken language its maximal expressive range, consistent with the style of the piece in question, in communicating its meaning, and to seek out the meaning implicit but disguised in the formal intricacies of music.

With the seminal trio of words, action, and music radiating from the center, and the pairs of opposites forming perpendicular axes, we can construct our music-theater mandala (see illustration). The large circle encompasses all possible kinds of music-theater performance in four quadrants: sung planned (memorized), spoken planned (memorized), spoken improvised, and sung improvised. Two more concentric circles divide these quadrants into the solo and ensemble opposites that, as we have seen, are unique and integral to the music-theater form. These quadrants will be used as a reference for the exercises to be practiced by the singer-actor, and each quadrant will furnish exercises to alleviate a specific set of music-theater problems. A singer-actor may never be called upon to improvise an opera but improvised singing can be the most productive way of getting at the singer's traditional performance problems.[5] Each quadrant should itself be thought of as an opposite, and the skills developed by exercise in one quadrant should inform and augment those in other quadrants.

D. Tapping the Power

Let us conclude this examination of the implications of the music-theater form with a final visit to Operania to take another look at one of the many disputes peculiar to the territory. If there is one issue on which the Musiconians and the Theatrylvanians differ most widely, it is on what is meant by "true communication." We discussed previously the conflict between the "feelers" and the "sounders," but the dispute goes deeper than that. In Theatrylvania the *meaning* of the language is the most important aspect of communication, but in Musiconia it is the *music* of the language. Theatrylvanians throw up their hands at the Musiconians' love of the sound they make, which is often divorced from specific meanings. When two Theatrylvanians are conversing, any eavesdroppers could easily agree about what was said. But put two Musiconians together (or three or four or more, for they love to "sound" en masse) and there would be as many opinions about what was said as there were listeners.

Translating this extension of our opening parable into music-theater terminology, we arrive at the opposites of specificity and generality applied to words and music. Words *mean* in a *specific* way, but music *means* in a *general* way (that is, its intellectual meaning is elusive, however clear-cut its musical sense is). We can usually agree about the general meaning of words, but we often have different opinions about the meaning of any given piece of music. It was probably Stanislavski who said, "Generalization is the enemy of theater!" If this is the case, and the meaning of music is generalized, then music must be the enemy of theater. These are Theatrylvanian word games, of course, but the meaning of music has long been a favorite debate topic among music aestheticians. And although the audience can ignore the problem and enjoy the music of opera—or the drama of opera, or both—without worrying about what these mean separately or together, the director and the singer-actor have to face head-on the question of the two kinds of meaning and how to deal with them.

The words in an opera have specific meaning, and so does the action that flows from those words (at least it can and should). It would probably be useful to know more specifically the meaning of the music that interrelates with the words and the action. In my happily expansive dissertation on the Mozart operas and the director, I pursued this question of the meaning of music. The search led from the seventeenth century to the present day, but was largely in vain. The message from music theorists was clear: pure music is its own meaning. A symphony does not mean—it simply *is*; music accompanying a text or a situation simply acquires and modifies the meanings of the text and situation. That is the distillation—or the dregs—of the search. It was not and is not satisfying.

I next decided to pursue theories outside that rather dogmatic mainstream. The result was a metaphorical view that is helpful in dealing with the problems of music-theater. Conceive of music as a current of energy comparable to electricity or cosmic energy, but energy that is simply there as a result of the music's existence. Such energy exists in an untapped form, generalized, until something transforms it and makes it specific. That *something* may be the listener's mind—a thousand minds will transform the general power of symphonic music into a thousand meanings—or, in programmatic music, the story, which is also aided (or denied) by the minds of the listeners. But in music-theater the *something* that transforms and makes specific the power of music is the singer-actor, who is aided in his or her transformational effects by the settings, the costumes, the lighting, the direction, the conducting, and the audience. The singer-actor makes specific the musical meanings of the score and the dramatic actions suggested by the libretto, and provides the connecting link between the theatrical reality and the musical transcendence of the work. The energies of the music infuse and vitalize the theatrical body of the piece primarily through the efforts of the singer-actor. The more specifically and continually the singer-actor transforms those musical energies, connecting them integrally with the theatrical energies of the piece, the greater will be its impact as music-theater.

These specific connections can be musical, theatrical, or both. There are occasions when a bit of brilliant vocal technique becomes its own meaning, and a transforming connection is achieved in that way. There are other instances in which compelling acting will channel all the energies of the moment. But the greatest moments occur when one cannot assign credit: when music and theater become one in the person of the singer-actor, aided and abetted by a composer of genius, by the librettist who inspired him or her, by the orchestra, the conductor, the settings, and the costumes, as well as the hidden portions of the vast operatic iceberg. As a director I had always tried to help the singer-actors make the acting in opera as believable and convincing as possible, but this concept clarified the problem for me. One must find specific transforming connections for the energy of the music in any music-theater piece, whether by use of words, actions, acting, settings, props, or costumes. Baldly stated, it sounds like Axiom One in Beginning Opera Direction, and perhaps it is. But I suspect that all opera directors have to find their own ways, through practice, to a realization of the same basic truth. In any case, the best conductors and coaches I have been privileged to work with have always asked for a specific meaning-sound for each word as it was sung, for a way of singing the words that is not only beautiful but also dramatically meaningful. It is the director's task to do the same, from second to second, for all the other aspects of performance as well (displaying at the same time a coachlike commitment to vocal meaning). No moment can be accepted that does not connect the words and the action with the music in a way that taps its power maximally.

The commitment to a true and all-encompassing specificity necessitates giving up all previous answers in search of the only one appropriate to the situation. It means living in the present in the most fundamental way and not depending upon what has worked in the past (although that may offer helpful hints), but dealing instead with this singer, these words, this music, this situation, and the values these have. It is the same challenge we offer singer-actors when we ask them to improvise, to *live* as they perform. That can seem terrifying, but once experienced, it is not. It is rather the only way to deal with an art that moves through time, for if we deal with either the past (how *did* we do?) or the future (how *will* we do?), we have not given our total attention to how we are doing *right now*. And we—no less than the singer-actor—must be total performers. We must give our total attention to the moment, knowing that the past is only helpful if the future is now. If we are to ask for a total performance from the singer-actor, we must reflect the same characteristics in our teaching and directing: openness to new experiences, flexibility, and courage.

The idea of opposition, of struggle, of internecine warfare has been an underlying theme of everything we have discussed, from the disputed boundaries of Musiconia and Theatrylvania to the Bill of Opposites. The sustained cold war that has taken place in Operania for about 350 years shows little sign of abating. But it is time for a change, a reexamination of all our mutually oriented functions. We are like an army whose battalions have become separated; instead of conquering the whole land, we are occupying separate sectors, and in our confusion we are defending them from one another rather than joining forces to rule the land in harmony. Every few decades one of the occupied sectors asserts an unhealthy domination over the others, causing them to divert their energies even further from the real task. Sometimes it has been the conductor battalions, sometimes the prima donna battalions, sometimes the composer battalions, and most recently it has been the director-designer battalions driving all others into a state of defensive inflexibility. Such separatist views are myopic, nonintegrative, and ultimately detrimental to the greater good of the art. Now that each of the battalions has had a chance to dominate, perhaps a new era of unification and collaboration can begin. That, however, is not up to any *one* of us; it is up to *all* of us. And the process must begin with the integration of the core battalion: the singer-actor battalion. Only singer-actors can provide a proper basis upon which the form can be built; and that can happen only if the rest of us join forces to unite with them in their process of integration.

PART TWO
The Skills of the Form

The unity of music and theater is equivalent to the unity of expression and technique in a singing actor's performance. Accomplishing it is a matter of neither genius nor coincidence; it is learnable for any singer who is musically and dramatically gifted and has a beautiful voice.

Walter Felsenstein
The Music Theater of Walter Felsenstein

Chapter

4

Creating the Energy

A. The Six Basic Skills

In analyzing a performing art as complicated as opera, one may isolate the component skills in a number of ways. I have chosen to categorize these skills as energizing, concentrating, structuring, stylizing, imagining, and coordinating. Although I originally included relating and improvising as skills, I now consider them — and their opposites, solo exercise and memorization — techniques to be applied in practicing the six skills listed above. These skills, practiced both solo and ensemble in each of the four quadrants of the music-theater mandala, using both improvisation and memorization, will exercise virtually every possible performance skill required by the singer-actor.

B. Energizing: the First Basic Skill

1. The Three Energies: Physical, Psychological, Vocal

Before a sculptor can sculpt, he or she must be capable of altering the marble; before a projector can project, it must be turned on. Before anything can happen artistically in any form, the energies must be available. For singer-actors the material is themselves and their vital energies, both psychological and physical. The first task

51

of singer-actors is to call forth these vital energies in as free and powerful a way as possible. In strictly vocal terms this may have been their study for years. We will assume that this is the case and will concentrate on bringing physical and psychological energies to the same level of skill and power possessed by the voice.[1] All human energies interrelate, of course, and there is an inevitable relationship between the release of physical and emotional energies and the release of vocal energy. Our attention to the emotional and physical energies will often aid the vocal process as well.

The use of one's emotional resources is the most familiar and the most easily misunderstood of the singer-actor's tools. Because they are so much a part of our personal lives, we sometimes hesitate to examine the processes by which we project emotion and feeling. In addition, the cult of be-yourself-do-your-own-thing-no-affectations-allowed inhibits both the idea of exercising the emotional processes and the use of techniques that may convey emotion even though they may not *feel* emotional. Again, we will approach the problem by applying the law of opposites: the emotional energy must grow from a natural base, but it must be projected by whatever means are necessary, no matter how artificial those means may seem at first. The personal experience must be communicated in a public place.

The *physical* mode of energizing, as well as the voice itself, relates to the external aspects of the personal-public continuum. Among the externals we will exercise are the physical stance, the use of gesture, the projective power of the face, and movement in and through space. Great attention to detail is necessary to avoid the common mistake of equating energy and tension. Tension will be our greatest adversary as we try to increase our energizing capacity. The slightest physical tension can block what would otherwise be a free flow of communicating energy. The block may come about because of an emotional withdrawal of some kind, a cautious inhibition, or a slight, habitual physical tension; but the smallest interference, like the precipitating twig in a log jam, can create an obstruction far larger than its cause. Our purpose will be twofold: to identify as many of these obstructing tensions as possible, and to explore various mechanisms by which the human energies can be released.

2. Charisma: Natural or Acquired?

Every person has a different degree of ability to communicate feeling, emotion, or energy in a public performance. The ability to project energy can be thought of as charisma, which may be defined in unorthodox terms as a powerful output of high-intensity physical or psychic energy. Charisma is usually thought of as a quality one either does or does not possess. But if we define it as physical or psychic energy flow, we can *exercise* the energies and thereby increase the flow. We must, of course, make certain there is nothing impeding the flow in the first place. Whatever inhibits the flow of energy interferes with one's charisma; remove the interference and the charisma will increase. Once that is accomplished, we need only isolate the elements that contribute to the flow of energies and exercise them separately before recombining them. This is the same logic we follow in other aspects of singing-acting: remove the obstacles, isolate the skills, exercise them separately, then put them back together into a more completely realized whole.

If a student does not project powerfully, must he or she simply accept a less charismatic way of being? To help the student, we separate charisma into its components. We find intense concentration, extraordinary technical skill, great personal confidence, and an openness (vulnerability) which allows all these abilities to flow outward. Some of the components can be exercised directly, but others depend upon combinations of other components. Confidence, for example, depends upon the knowledge that the technical skills—both mental and physical—are available, can be executed, and therefore make success likely. This in turn depends to some extent on the student having practiced those skills successfully a number of times in the past, the factor of experience. At the same time we must continue to watch for all tensions and inhibitions that create resistance to the flow of the isolated skills. Emotional inhibition, fear of failure, and physical tensions must be diagnosed and eliminated.

Finally we put all the components of charisma back together again. Although we cannot say with certainty that there will be an increase in charisma—for the quality is both real and mystical—

there will always be a change for the better. The performer, having concentrated on the parts rather than the sum, on the specific rather than the general, will inevitably produce a strikingly improved whole which is truly greater than the sum of its parts.

3. Style and Self

It is difficult to predict whether a performer will have the dedication necessary to continue to develop charismatic projective power. We have mentioned how easy it is to recognize the obstructive power of tension and the excitement the realization creates: "Incredible! I have always tensed my shoulders and lowered my head when singing, and it creates a mental block about showing emotion!" But we also noted the enormous difficulty of *changing* one's habits and mannerisms — of *doing* something about those shoulders and that head. There will always be an initial, noticeable improvement because of realization. But old habits will reassert themselves, and performers will reach plateaus quickly. Many of these habits prevent one from giving a fully energized performance, have developed over a period of years, and the length of time one has had them is proportionate to the difficulty of breaking them.

Without old habits, one is free to use one's energies in other characterizations and styles; to be *more* than one's self, one must first be firmly grounded *in* one's self. This is another pair of opposites, transcendence and reality, that is related to the fundamental set of music-theater opposites between which every music-theater production must navigate. The musical experience — an abstract sequence of sound, with its own laws — combines with the more realistic theater experience, transcending reality. At the same time, the theater experience acts upon the music experience, channeling its power into a passionate and moving sequence of human events. When the relationship between the two experiences achieves a flow and tension, true music-theater emerges, transcendent yet human, real yet fantastic.

This tension of opposites begins with the actor-singer. To leap to transcendence without a firm grounding in the reality of oneself can lead to the grandiose and the pompous — "operatic acting." Although a realistic approach to all actions may on the other hand seem a welcome relief from the grandiose, it fails similarly to fulfill the polarized demands of the form. One cannot soar without a firm base from which to depart, but if one never *leaves* the base, one is just as unlikely to soar.

Music-theater moves in unusual stylistic realms; it transforms the "empty space" of theater into a charged realm of potential fantasy: *anything* can happen, depending upon the imaginative skills of the individual performer. The external techniques are stylized, unusual, and extreme; the inner feelings must relate to and support the external stylization in the most natural way possible. Time must be stretched, but is must seem to be natural; the physicalizing of psychological meaning must relate to the music, but it must seem natural; whatever is strange, wonderful, and mysterious about the form must also seem personal and believable. Energizing, our present concern, involves both the external and internal. Although we will exercise the two separately, the ultimate goal is always unification.

In music-theater, the projection of emotion places a special burden on the singer-actor. Music-theater deals more lavishly with pure feeling than does any other dramatic form. Actors become actors chiefly because of their ability to project physical and emotional energy. Singer-actors become singer-actors chiefly because of their ability to sing. The chance is slight that they will also have a natural ability to project physical and emotional energy, and this chance is further reduced by the inhibiting effect of their training. The stylization of the form and the convention of time-alteration further increase the difficulty of acting in music-theater: the challenge for the singer-actor is monumental.

4. Vocal Indicating: Tension or Intensity?

Because a great deal of emotion is projected vocally, it is important to connect properly the expression of emotion and the technique of singing. A proper use of one's emotional resources should alter the feeling and sound of one's singing, and should communicate more effectively with the listener than would an uninvolved reading of the score. Yet so little is done to coordinate technique and emotion in singing that the majority of young performers either sing with physical and vocal tension in order to simulate emotion (thereby doing damage to themselves vocally and dramatically) or retreat from the problem into a studied neutrality. Other singers employ a bag of calculated gestural tricks and vocal sobs which may leave the voice unharmed, but leave those who admire dramatic validity dismayed. But such a free use of energy, however hammy, is more admirable and far more useful as a place to begin work than is a tense, inhibited performance. One can always work with energy that flows freely, but if it does not flow, nothing can be done until the impediments are removed. It would be a healthy thing for all young singer-actors to experience early in their training the uninhibited release of their energies in a wonderfully hammy, full-flowing surge of melodramatic passion—fear of phoniness be damned!

The cautionary and spurious argument that is often used to justify inhibition is: "you can't sing and cry at the same time, you've got to be under control." It is always used by performers who are simply defending their own inhibitions and who are no more capable of crying than flying while singing. Very few actors speak and cry simultaneously for any length of time (unless they are unskilled or indulgent), but a great many emotional statements, both subtle and broad, can and should be conveyed while speaking *and* singing. How to blend the two is a problem we must solve, not sidestep by posing either/or questions. I have observed that when those who profess to be concerned about crying actually take the risk and release the emotion they say will make them cry, they sing more freely and with greater feeling, *but they do not actually cry*. It should be remembered that the muscles that prevent one from crying are opposed to the singing process. So it may be that those who say they cannot cry and sing are really saying that they cannot *not* cry and sing, that they cannot arouse the emotions to that pitch, then inhibit them and still sing. What they need to do is *not* to quell the emotions (quelling them for the sake of the art may be the rationale that leaves so many young singers dreadfully uninvolved in performance) but to channel and freely transform those emotional energies into song—which is what singing is all about in the first place.

The singer must sing with great emotion, but the vocal mechanism must be left free. A common problem in American acting is a technique I call "vocal indicating." I coined the term to describe a phenomenon I observed constantly, but for which I knew no identifying description. The term refers to the actor's use of tension in the vocal apparatus to modify the sound of the voice so that it sounds or *feels* "angry," "sad," "joyous," or whatever. It is the vocal equivalent of facial indicating (mugging), the technique of an actor who is doing more than is necessary or true to communicate what is happening. The indicating prevents *true* facial communication. Just so vocally: the performer is adding something to the voice that is not necessary or true, that is based on tension, and that interferes with the communicative process. It is a sign that the actor does not trust the simple truth of the role but gives the audience or the director superfluous "proof" of his or her involvement. So we see a series of facial grimaces and we *hear* a series of vocal grimaces. Neither one is true.

The process almost always involves some form of sustained glottal tension. The abdomen, diaphragm, and lungs compress air against a partially closed glottis. This creates both an altered sound —a sound produced under tension—and a feeling of internal physical pressure which simulates the feeling of actual emotion for the performer.

Of course, strange and wonderful things happen to the face and voice in an emotional situation, but they follow from a *free* flow of energy, however tense or intense the situation. The angry man does not modify his voice, it happens by itself. The chemistry of the blood makes the angry person *feel* differently, the adrenalin charges him up and alters his feeling-state. I am convinced that it is the attempt to duplicate physically this chemically induced state of emotion that causes vocal and physical tension when young actors try to be emotionally "real" or "honest." To "feel it," they tense their bodies and voices, hoping to produce the intense feeling of the emotional state. In so doing they effectively block the flow of real feeling. In a physical sense it is simply bad acting, but it can cause great damage to the voice if practiced over a period of time. This can be prevented if someone notices it, points it out, and helps the performer eliminate it.[2]

Vocal indicating is similar to Wilhelm Reich's concept of body "armoring," the habitual tensing of parts of the body to stop the flow of emotions. The tensing of deep throat and chest muscles, for example, prevents one from expressing and therefore feeling deeply the emotions of grief and sorrow; as most American males know, these muscles are part of the trained inhibitory mechanism that prevents them from crying easily. It is possible that singers who maintain that they become physically tense when they are feeling emotion in life are correct in one respect: when they feel an emotion in life they *do* tense up in order to *block* the feeling rather than experience it. When they do the same thing in performance, they are twice-removed from the original experience—once by the performance situation, once by the tension block; and they are simply displaying onstage a problem they need to attend to offstage.

We observed in the preface that when performers release the tension blocks they have used to cope with emotion, this affects not only their performance lives but their personal lives as well. They find themselves releasing physical tension in their lives in the same way as in performance, and feeling emotions with new intensity in life as well as in performance. Ultimately, the person and the performer are inseparable.

A situation of great emotional stress is not characterized by physical tension, but by readiness to act. There may be great *psychological* tension involved, but the person feeling that tension is ready to act physically—ready to run, ready to attack, ready to plead, ready to embrace, ready to repulse. There are situations, of course, in which the person under tension is physically frozen with fear; in which case the person is comic, impotent or both. But these are the rare instances which define themselves easily and are easy to play because they feed into the syndrome we are trying to correct. Situations of emotional tension are situations of physical readiness; any equation that connects emotional energizing with physical tension is a false one. If physical tension is associated with emotional tension, it will increase and be held as the emotion increases. And it is the *holding* of tension that is the problem, not the initial energy which, for example, causes one to slam the fist into the palm; only if that impacting fist is *held* does the gesture become tense and become a problem. Readiness, then, and not tension, is the useful response to high emotion in both life and performance.

The same problem can occur with the singer who is trying for genuine emotional expressiveness. Instead of allowing the emotion to flow into the music on its own terms, the singer blocks the flow with various kinds of tension, the stress of which he or she has learned to equate with feeling. To change this pattern the instructor must be aware of the use of vocal tension and glottal pressure tricks as false expressive devices, and point it out whenever it occurs. Singer-actors must be able to play a wide gamut of emotions without impairing the vocal process. The ability to isolate vocal production from emotional feelings is absolutely necessary; singer-actors must draw upon their emotional memory banks and let those emotions affect them as they sing in the stylized manner of music-theater. It is a matter of "translation," of using the metaphor of music as stylized and symbolic but real and valid emotion. In a fundamental way, this is what stylization involves: the ability to give to the most abstract and formal actions a human validity, to find the equation that can make a passage of brilliant coloratura an expression of pathetic human madness or a towering human rage. Our job is to help the performer make this kind of connection without needless vocal, psychological, or physical interference.

A vocal interpretation of high emotion does not require vocal tension, but vocal readiness to sing a high note, a coloratura passage, a scream, or a whisper. There is a fine distinction between the sound made as the result of emotion and sound in which a slight glottal or throat tension-interference attempts to duplicate it. But it is a vital distinction, for the destination to which the subtlest vocal-indicating tension leads is a dead end.

Some of this interference, this tension, comes from a mistaken idea of the relation of music to emotion. A well-known theater director has said that the way to move from speaking to singing in a musical comedy is to increase the emotional intensity of the scene until there is nothing left to do but sing; if timed properly, that point is reached just as the dialogue ends and the song begins. But the power of music is not, as this example suggests, purely quantitative. The important contribution of music to words and action is *qualitative*. If this director's theory is true, no play could ever reach the summit of emotional intensity unless set to music. The notion that Hamlet's emotional intensity would be greater if he sang, "O what a rogue and peasant slave am I!" instead of speaking it is absurd. The change wrought by singing the line would be qualitative. Quantitatively, in volume and pitch, it might well be diminished. If we insist upon the idea of a quantitative increase in emotional intensity when a person is singing, we are simply begging for physical, mental, and even vocal tensions. Instead we must stress the ability of music to alter time and emotional quality and the singer-actor's capacity to make imaginative connections between their native emotions and the stylized, public communication of the music. Not tension, but translation.

5. Honesty and Dishonesty: How vs. Why?

When a group of singer-actors is in training for performance, it is important that all members be as honest as possible in telling each other whether the projection of emotional energy functions well or whether it seems facile, insincere, blocked, or stagy. It will take time and care to develop an openness within the group, but it is vital to the growth of all concerned. Only with that awareness of "how I am," can one develop beyond that state.

The next step is to determine the origin of any problems that are apparent in a singer-actor's performance. It may be that personal involvement is lacking, or that inhibition or tension is present, but it is often true that external habits are contradicting what is genuinely felt. If, for example, a singer-actor has made it a life habit to conceal emotional response, the most *honest* thing he or she can do is to show no response when it is called for. This is one of the essential problems of performance: if the most honest thing one can do is essentially *dis*honest, then one must acquire a new concept of what performance honesty means. One must either learn to communicate the emotion that needs to be communicated, honest or not, or find techniques which convince *us*, the observers, that one *is* feeling and communicating it.

Another common error in dealing with one's own emotional resources—which are all one has, after all—is to reduce all the characters one portrays to self-replicas. This is the pattern of many film actors who portray themselves in every role. The star system in opera is based on the same kind of thinking: who really cares about characterization or what happens dramatically so long as Madame X, be she Callas, Sills, or Sutherland, is there *as* Madame X? And when Madame X actually gives herself to the *role*, as all three of the above do frequently, it is cause for critical ecstasy. This kind of involvement, however, should be the rule, not the exception.

It is amazing how many young singer-actors will use a variation of the same reductive reasoning: "*I* would not do something like that, ergo the *character* would not." But obviously what *I* would do, how *I* would act, what *I* would think might be light years from the character's thought and action. The singer-actor (and the director) must ask not only "what would *I* do?" (which can be a useful and stimulating question if it is not the *only* question) but also "how would the *character* do the required actions?" and "how can I make *those* actions as natural as if they were my own?"

Character actions cover a much broader range of possibilities than we at first realize. To take a farfetched example: if the singer-actor playing the part of the Countess in Mozart's *Marriage of Figaro* were asked to leap up on her bed, how wonderfully exciting it would be to have the challenge accepted, and for the singer-actor to decide *how* the Countess would leap up on her bed and do it before determining *why*. Such a request would probably produce a questioning glance (at least) from the most dedicated singer-actors and a barrage of questions, arguments, and refusals from the rest.[3] The true skill of the singer-actor lies not in the ability to ask why something must be done but in the ability to make sense of it. Whether one agrees with the concept is immaterial; how to make it work for one's self and for the audience *is* the point.

Let us look at the opposites of self and character from this vantage point. Our personal energies must be engaged as directly as possible in whatever role we play, but those energies must connect with any number of possible physical or emotional characterizations and actions. Once a variety of these possibilities have been explored, one can select from among them rather than taking whatever comes first. This is one of the differences between a performing artist and a performing victim of habitual responses. It is possible, of course, to return to the first choice as the best of many, but it will not be quite the same as it was before other choices were considered.

6. Sensory Stimuli: Specificity vs. Generalization

I have learned a great deal from working with both acting for theater and singing-acting for music-theater. Like the confused citizens of Operania, I have been confronted with laws of one land which were simply not applicable in the other. Playing of attitudes, for example, is against the "rules" in theater. An actor who plays attitudes is found guilty of generalizing, of playing an emotional wash instead of the specifics of the scene. In spite of this, I assigned arbitrary attitudes to singers performing arias, and it has proved to be an extremely useful exercise. Instructing a singer to assume a sequence of arbitrary emotional attitudes (drawn from the list on p. 132) during an aria almost invariably lends a useful specificity to the aria regardless of the correspondence of the attitudes to the aria. But when I decided to try the same thing with an actor delivering a soliloquy, the result was precisely what might have been expected: a generalized wash of emotion, often accompanied by vocal indicating to "show" me the attitude.

The reason for this difference in response is, I think, that the score is provided in the one instance and is created by the actor in the other. The musical score is already highly specific; the attitudes simply color it and give it nuance in various ways. Because the statement of the score is so strong, it can absorb virtually any set of attitudes one might choose. The soliloquy, on the other hand, has no score; the score must be created by the actor. If the actor plays emotions rather than creates a "score" based on the specific moment-to-moment meanings of the scene, the emotions will wash out the specifics, and generalization, the enemy of good performance, will result. The actor will *sound* "angry" all the time, or "happy," or "annoyed," or "tearful," rather than allowing the feeling in question to be expressed *through* and *with* the words. Continued work with the problem made it clear that this, too, was an awareness which could be usefully cultivated in the actor as well as in the singer-actor. If the actor knows how the scene works as a language-meaning structure, she or he can use the *words* of the scene to make the specific emotional statements rather than using vocal indicating, which is almost always the result — or the cause — of generalized playing. One must allow language and the way it is used to begin the feedback process, the essential link-up of external and internal that guarantees specificity.

Another point should be stressed: one cannot *make* oneself feel an emotion; an emotion is aroused in a person because of circumstances. This is not to contradict all the self-help, positive-thinking books which stress the importance of doing things that make one feel better about one's self. But none of them try to *deny* feelings; feelings, good or bad, must be accepted as real. They are aroused by actions and situations. Most of us accept positive feelings with gratitude; they present few problems if we are able to arouse them, and they also create fewer singer-actor problems in performance. But negative feelings, however we deal with them in life, must be characterized and played in performance. In life there are only two harmful things about negative feelings: if we are responsible for the situation that led to the negative feelings or if we indulge in the negative feeling, cling to it, become increasingly negative as a result, and refuse to do anything to change the feeling. In playing negative feelings in performance, we need only be aware of these traps. If the character we are playing is caught in them, we simply allow that to happen. And feelings can, of course, be changed by new actions and new situations. The feelings were created by the actions or reactions that aroused them, and they can be molded or modified by the conscious choice of further actions or reactions.

Emotions must be aroused indirectly, by dealing with specific sensory stimuli. For example, if one wishes to draw upon a personal event, one must not think about the event itself. Instead one must concentrate on those things about the event that can be sensed; if one can visualize it, hear it, smell it, and taste it, the emotions connected with the event will return of their own accord. If they do not return, they do not return; but they cannot be forced. One can only lure them with sensory stimuli.

In the same fashion, one can use the voice and body to create immediate sensory stimuli that are as valid as past memories. Such sensations are more tangible, more present, and more powerful than memories. If, for example, one speaks loudly or rapidly or softly, one acts upon oneself in a very direct way; if one rounds the shoulders, slouches on one's hips, or holds one's head very high, a sensory message is sent to the mind and to the feeling centers. Speaking or acting in *any* specifically defined way may connect with *any* emotional trigger the scene may contain—it all depends upon the feedback-connecting skills of the performer. Therein lies the importance of technique for the speaking actor, who is too often taught only to listen to the inside rather than to send an occasional message from the outside requesting internal feedback. The least we can do is make the performer aware of the two-way process and its uses. Sense memory is one of the hallmarks of internal "method" acting, and yet method proponents often stop with the remembrance of things past, of time-buried stimuli, rather than utilizing the vast number of physical and vocal stimuli that the actor can bring to bear upon present circumstances. Speaking well, speaking with an accent, speaking with various types of musical energies can provide all kinds of specific emotional feedback if the sensitivities and skills are aroused; physical movements and gestures can accomplish the same result.

The singer-actor has an additional source of stimulation in the music itself. Extended work with young singers has convinced me that their training has desensitized them to the intensely evocative accompaniments of their own arias and ensembles; they have spent years concentrating on everything *but* the emotional energies of the score. Proof of the desensitization process can be seen in most singers' responsiveness to the accompaniments for other singers' arias. They have not become immune to other singers' music.

This numbing process extends from the musical response to the physical and emotional responses, all three of which are inextricably interrelated. It is not difficult to re-arouse a sensitivity to the music: simply calling attention to its importance and doing exercises which stimulate it will help. It is of vital importance to the singer-actor and should be developed.

7. Music-Theater Isolations

The energizing powers of the emotional, the physical, and the vocal can, as we have seen, become locked in a triangle of tension. It is very useful to exercise the capacity to isolate the three. Isolating them will allow the physical and emotional energies to work *with* each other and not *against* each other. Such isolations can be practiced by playing opposites, combining, for example, the emotional attitude of anger with a soft, sensuous sound and a caressing gesture. To isolate the physical, the vocal, and the emotional in a way that allows the three to continue to interrelate is absolutely fundamental to music-theater performance. The singer-actor is constantly called upon to play an attitude without being permitted to alter the music to fit that attitude; the singing can never follow the naturalistic impulse of the emotion. Singing, as we have pointed out, is an unnatural act. The singer-actor must be able to sing independently of the emotional and physical events which occur simultaneously. The singing must always be nuanced and colored by the emotional impulses, but tension cannot be a part of the process. We have discussed the temptation for vocal, physical, and facial tension-indicating to intertwine in conveying emotion, and the closer in kind the various factors are, that is, the more they reflect one another dynamically, the harder it is to sense and understand the necessary isolation. This is why exercising with attitudes and physicalizations that contrast strongly with the vocal is so useful: it makes the necessity of the isolation unmistakable. And the more the attitudes and physicalizations stretch the singer-actor in performing arias or ensembles as exercises, the more flexibility she or he will acquire. As a dividend of this kind of exercise, attitudes that are seemingly contrary to the apparent meaning of the text and the music will often prove to be more effective than those that simply underscore what the text and the music are already saying.

Focusing and Structuring the Energy

A. Concentrating: the Second Basic Skill

1. Using the Energy

We have begun the energizing process. We have turned on the current, physically and psychologically. Our energies have been made available for use. This is the most fundamental requirement of music-theater work: the availability of physical and psychological energy in the service of the music-theater experience. In this state of availability our concern will be to learn to *use* that energy, how it can be focused, structured, transformed, stylized, characterized, and coordinated.

2. Exclusion and Incorporation

Let us approach the skill of focusing or concentrating from the opposites of soliloquizing and relating. At one end of the continuum is the concentration of exclusion, at the other, the concentration of incorporation. When a singer is *soliloquizing* (singing an aria), the concentration is on the internal process, on the musical and psychological *experience* of the aria. When a singer is *relating* (and it goes without saying that one is always relating to something external even in the midst of the most internalized experience), the concentration is on the surroundings—fellow singers, the stage action, the conductor, the set, the props. The problem is how many of these external stimuli to incorporate.[1]

3. Sustaining the Moment

Concentration is, of course, a prerequisite to the successful performance of any difficult task, but it has a special function in musical performance. As Stravinsky once put it, music is the art of altering time. When time is extended by music, it follows that the performer of that music must sustain her or his concentration for the length of that extension. In teaching musical composition, Nadia Boulanger was said to stress the importance of the "grand line," the feeling of connectedness in a musical piece from the first note to the final cadence. Such unity must exist despite pauses, despite the number of movements, and despite the length of the piece. This in turn demands an awareness of the "connectedness" on the part of conductors and performers. Achieving this awareness requires concentration: the ability to make sustaining connections between separated events over an extended period of time. As the length of time increases, so does the demand on the powers of concentration.

The reason for Mme. Boulanger's insistence on the grand line was that music, in its alteration of time, must guard against the intrusion of real time. The musical equivalent of the willing suspension of disbelief in literature is the willingness to believe in the altered, ideal time of music, and a willingness to forget the "real" time of the clock. The burden of maintaining this suspension, this balance, this grand line of concentration, falls upon both composer and performer; but the performer must maintain it audibly, musically, for all to hear, not merely in his or her head or in the score.

When the time-altering power of music is *combined* with the chronologically ordered world of words and events, the balance is delicate, and the musical suspension of disbelief more difficult to sustain. In music-theater there is more fluctuation of time flow than in either music or theater, and there is more movement back and forth between the opposites of real time and musical time. The burden is on the singer-actor to maintain the balance between the poles of real time and musical time, a balance that is constantly shifting. The singer-actor must be prepared to move from one extreme to the other without losing concentration on either the music or the ongoing drama. In short, music-theater stretches the performer's powers of concentration to their utmost.

Let us look at an example of this problem and the singer's response to it. It is common in music-theater for six seconds of real time to be extended to six minutes or more of musical time. The singer is alone on stage: if dependent on the psychology of real time, he or she will be forced into a series of naturalistically oriented actions which will be repeated, with slight variations, over and over: a busy, realistic bird in the gilded but confining reality of music-theater. If the singer retreats from the realistic end of the spectrum and stands in place making few gestures, he or she fulfills the expectations of those who complain about dull, static acting in opera. The singer-actor is faced with what seems to be a choice of negatives: busy repetitiveness at one end of the scale and monolithic stasis at the other. In straight theater, with rare exceptions, this particular set of opposites is not a problem, because actors do not remain alone on stage for the length of time of an average aria.[2] The extension of time which underlies the convention of the aria is music-theater's most powerful weapon and its greatest potential glory. Like all weapons, time extension can be a terrible burden for its possessor, the performer. But if it is grasped firmly by the performer, *owned*, controlled, and understood, the weapon of time extension can be a power and a joy. The skill of concentration can achieve such control.

Sustaining the dramatic moment is the first step in the process, and this depends at first upon one's capacity to concentrate for a given period of time. The fact that one is concentrating, however, is not automatically projected to the degree necessary in music-theater. Focus, the external *communication* of concentration, is a key to the problem. The use of focus provides the external *signs* of concentration, but how are these signs connected to its internal workings? The signs are the external aspects of concentration; let us first isolate them, then trace our way back to their unseen genesis in the internal impulse.

4. Eye Language: the Reflection of Thought

The eyes, more than any other part of the body, reveal the mental process: if they wander, we feel the mind is wandering;

if they search, we feel the mind is searching; and if they focus strongly, we feel the mind is focused strongly. That focus may be on the actual object of the mental process, or it may be on an object which has nothing to do with that process. A man may stare intently into space, or at a building, but actually be thinking about his beloved or about a plan he is devising. When someone is staring intently at something with which they are not concerned, such as a tree, the wall, or the floor, we say, "A penny for your thoughts," because we know the person is thinking about something specific, other than the tree, the wall, or the floor. When we are concentrating on a thought, we try to eliminate all the meaningless visual stimuli that interfere. We focus on one spot for a time, the length of time depending upon the intensity of concentration and the movement of the thought process. When we are bored, on the other hand, we seek out visual stimuli, and our gaze moves continuously. This phenomenon can be translated into useful music-theater technique. The externals tell the story: if the eyes are wandering, so is the mind; if the eyes search, so does the mind; and if the eyes focus strongly on something, so does the mind. We want to find a focus-language that reflects as clearly as possible the way the mind is functioning.

Most arias and songs do not contain a great number of verbal ideas. In most instances there are two or three intellectual ideas which are repeated and expanded upon musically. It may be the idea of one's beloved or one's mission that is repeated and varied, and that fills the expansion of time created by the music. The fact that the ideas do not follow one another in linear, plot-developing fashion, but are expanded upon vertically as time stops, is the crucial stylistic problem. The physical focus of the singer must relate to and convey a sense of this time extension. If the focus shifts realistically, randomly, there is a substantive stylistic clash between it and the music. This creates immediate problems for the audience: how are they to *perceive* the piece being performed, how are they to understand it stylistically? The singer-actor who lacks musical continuity of focus, who does not delineate the music-theater event by use of focus—or, at the other extreme, adopts a fixed focus—is not properly sharing the experience with the audience. Audience concentration will follow the lead of the performers. If the focus of the performers wanders, or is self-conscious, the mind of the audience will do likewise, whether consciously or not. Wandering, uncertain, or generalized focus is eye-body-mind language that says there is nothing of sufficient interest to think about.

Perhaps we can apply the concept of charisma to this idea. Charisma is usually assumed to be based on the intuitive, and is essentially unteachable. But it must consist of external signs as well as internal magnetism, and these external signs can be isolated and exercised individually. One of these external signs, for example, is a sense of concentration, of focus on the task-at-hand, that conveys to the audience that the *total being* of the performer is involved in the act of performance. This relates directly to the performer's powers of concentration. If the power and projection of concentration is increased, perhaps the charisma will increase as well. We have discussed energy as a component of charisma, but we can now turn to how the energy is focused, concentrated, and structured. One can guarantee nothing in this area, but one can certainly work on the external concomitants of a charismatic performance, and the skill of concentration is among them.

The simple act of pretending to look at something which is not there may seem so simple as to need no practice. But it does. There are a remarkable number of singers who have advanced cases of wandering eyes and yet are unaware of the disease. Seeming to see something that is not actually there can be astonishingly difficult at first. Sometimes the best way to learn to do it is to look at something specific in the rehearsal hall, or through the window at a tree in the distance, or, if on stage, at an exit light or a pillar. Once the singer is comfortable with the act of focusing on something, the idea of focus can be used as a working tool.[3]

5. Focus: The Energy Transformer

It may be argued that one cannot work on focus or concentration without having an actual scene in mind, or even a correct interpretation of the scene. It seems, however, that *whatever* one does feeds into whatever focus is attained, and, perhaps surprisingly, it also seems to make little difference what the *object* of concentration is as long as it energizes the concentration and the focus. The object must be of great importance to the performer, but it need not connect logically to the substance of the scene. If it does connect, fine; if it does not, the audience will make the connection. The important thing is that there be energy to be focused.

At the same time, focus must always feel to the observers like a *thought process*. It is not enough to stare blankly at a given point; the mind must be working and must project that sense of thought process. The energies of attitude and physicalization must fill the focus. We have energized, and now we must keep that energy alive even as it submits to necessity of concentration.

One of the most telling experiences I have had as an audience member illustrates this principle perfectly. It was during a concert version of *Fidelio*. There was no set, no lighting, and the tenor who created the experience in question had had very little operatic training. Under the circumstances, the evening promised to be, at best, a reasonably stimulating *musical* event. But after intermission, the tenor stood up to sing Florestan's magnificent aria. It was superbly sung throughout, but when Florestan saw the vision of Leonore[4] the experience encompassed more than fine singing; it became absolutely riveting and emotionally overwhelming. The tenor's focus and concentration were mesmerizing, and the *music-theater* experience was staggering. There were tears running down his cheeks, he was *in that dungeon*, he *saw* Leonore, he was *there* in every way. It seemed like a perfect verification of the principles of internal belief: if one *believes* in a given dramatic situation, the perfect external indications of that belief will follow naturally. I went backstage after the performance and told the tenor just that. The next day I wrote him a letter describing my experience of the performance, how moving I had found it, and asked him if he could tell me the process by which he had achieved the effect. He wrote and thanked me for my compliments, but apologized for his inability to identify with the performance I had described because, and here is the crucial point, *he was thinking so hard about what he had to accomplish musically that none of the thoughts I had assumed were in his mind were actually there.* This, of course, was far more interesting to me than a discussion of "what Stanislavski has done for me." The singer focused on something vital to him, and his concentration was so intense that we, the audience, converted it into the equally intense dramatic situation with no problem whatsoever. The tenor, of course, knew the dramatic situation, and felt deeply about it—the tears *probably* came from that source, although one can never make definite statements about the origins of deeply felt emotions—but he was not concentrating upon the situation. If he had been, his performance might have been less effective than it was, because he did not have the necessary acting technique.

Concentration, then, is of value regardless of its content. It may be important for the object of concentration to resonate in a sympathetic manner with that of the aria being sung, but even this "rule" will have exceptions. There has been far too little exploration of unlikely combinations of actual subject matter and imagined subject matter. Singing about one's beloved and thinking of a wonderful swim one has had may be a more stimulating combination of ideas for the singer and for the audience than a simple equation of the dramatic beloved with a "real" beloved. Once this is accepted, the possible combinations become limitless. It all depends on the mind, the imagination, and the flexibility of the singer.

6. Focal Movement: The Outlining of Thought

Just as there are many kinds of arias, and many kinds of experience making up these arias, so there are many ways of dealing with focus. Focus, again, is simply the performer's eye-body language which tells the viewer that concentration has been achieved. The different kinds of focus, and the movement of the focus, reveal the varieties of internal experience. As a starting point, we can say that a single focus for an entire aria is neither useful, for no aria deals with only one thought, nor feasible, because keeping it "alive" for that length of time would demand unreasonable energizing powers on the part of the singer. There must be shifts in focus, exactly as there are shifts in the thought process of the aria, and these shifts should relate to both the phrasing of the music and the syntactical phrasing of the subject matter.

Movement of focus is a necessity. The next question is *how* it moves, and how often. There seems to be a relationship between the number of focus shifts and the seriousness of the aria. The focus in a patter song can and should shift rapidly, with great precision and clarity, but the focus of a song of deeply felt emotion, such as the Florestan aria, can and should be maintained for longer periods of time. Whatever the number of moves, they must mesh smoothly, for transitions are at least as important as the ideas themselves. One must focus on something, of course, and as a general rule, the object of focus should be higher rather than lower. A focus that is as high as the most elevated point of the audience conveys an experience more effectively to that audience. If the eyes are lowered, the experience is not shared as effectively. Admittedly, it is easier to lower one's gaze[5] and shut out the audience, but overcoming such habits is simply a matter of practice; focus is thought projection, and thought can be projected anywhere.

For a model of *how* the focus moves, we can simply refer to the mental process itself, for we are trying to project a tangible external parallel to an intangible internal event. When the mind moves from one thought to another, it may move rapidly, as in the "light bulb" effect, or it may search its way. Similarly, the focus may shift suddenly with the musical and verbal thought of the aria, or it may search for the new thought before settling on it. Another way of making a transition from one focus to another is to turn inward. With the eyes closed, one seems to retreat from the power of the idea, conveying the message that this thought is too private, too moving, or too painful to contemplate openly. One can also turn away from the audience or lower one's eyes, but this does not share the experience as powerfully. Sharing the music-theater experience as intensely as possible is one of the principal goals of singing-acting, and the attempt to look natural by dropping the head, which is no more "natural" than any number of other physical attitudes, carries the risk of excluding the audience.[6]

Focus need not be confined to the idea of a single white-hot point of vision. There are two kinds of focus that take a panoramic view of the entire space outside the proscenium. One such focus is environmental; the sky, trees, mountains, or armies are imagined to exist in the mind's eye, and can be seen in sweeping fashion by scanning the entire range of vision. The effect should always be specific even as it encompasses vast areas; the specific elements of the environment should be concretely imagined and responded to. The other kind of panoramic focus might be called a fantasy panorama. The image related to is a giant one, a huge, overwhelming vision of one specific thing: a field of skulls, the massive face of the villain, a vision of heaven, a sky filled with angels. The focus can recede as the vision moves toward and overwhelms the observer, or extend to a vanishing point. And, of course, any specific focal point can be chosen as a reference and returned to whenever the words refer to the same idea.

The idea of focus can be profitably compared to the idea of film projection. If one imagines holding a film projector for the audience, the problem with wandering, skittish focus becomes apparent. If one bounces the images about in random fashion, the audience will soon leave, but one can shift the projected image from one place to another if the movements are clean and sharp. If there is a visual transition or the images are not yet clearly formed, the movement of the projected image may wander (search) a bit. But the shifts should relate to the content of the images projected, so that a change in image signals a shift in direction. Performers are just such projectors, with a special difference: the human projectors provide their own images; they are both the projectors and the reflections of the projection at once. They are the translators of the image they "see," and the audience in turn "sees" it through them. They create the image; by responding to it, they can change it; with a single disinterested flick of the focus they can wipe out the entire imaginary world they have created. It is their private domain to love, hate, curse, plead with, enlarge, scorn, destroy, or be destroyed by, hated or desired by; through their developed ability to transmit the experience to the audience, they make available whole worlds of the imagination that the audience can receive in no other way.

There is invariably at least one young singer who, when the subject of focus-concentration and sharing is introduced, asks, "What is the difference between this and the phony old stand-down-center-and-sing-to-the-audience school of operatic acting which we are trying to avoid?" The differences are subtle, but significant, as we will see ever more clearly in succeeding chapters.[7] The most important difference has to do with feedback. The image or experience upon which one focuses can be manipulated in any way desired; by reacting to it, the performer can make it change and progress, depending upon the needs of the score and the performer. The audience, on the other hand, will give a performer no useful feedback during the course of an aria. They have come to see a person involved in an experience: the music itself is part of the experience, the verbal content of the aria is another part, and the dramatic situation is still another. Taken together these make up the total *experience* of the aria. It is that totality of experience upon which the singer must focus. While the audience sits with nonemoting faces, observing, not acting, the performer can obtain from that total experience whatever is needed to promote the dramatic progress of the piece. Another way of putting it is to see the aria as a dialogue between the singer and the points of focus. This dialogue should clarify the progression of the aria, musically, emotionally, and dramatically, and it should be carried on so that the audience shares the experience fully.[8]

Occasionally, of course, there are music-theater situations that call for addressing the audience directly. Even here, however, the actual audience is not as useful to the singer-actor as a mental image of an *ideal* audience. That perfect audience is situated in the same location as the actual audience, but the ideal audience responds to and feeds the singer-actor in whatever manner the singer-actor desires, for both the ideal audience and its attitudes are the creation of the singer-actor. If the singer-actor wishes that audience to be enthusiastic or incredulous or horrified or hostile—so they are, for she or he simply *acts as though* they were. Thus singer-actors need never be at the mercy of the audience's moods, for they can always play to *their* audience, the ideal audience, which reacts in the most useful possible way.

7. Form or Content: Egg or Chicken

Concentration cannot be forced; it must ultimately, like a poem, *be*. It took Herrigel six years to focus properly on the Zen bow, arrow, target, and himself.[9] Concentration is part of the continuing search for a mental relationship that will unify the person, the destination, and the process of getting there. We can speak of external signs, and one can learn to use these with good effect, but they may remain a form without content for a long time. Nonetheless, the form must be available for filling, which is why one works on externals and internals simultaneously. There is a Zen parable that expresses this chicken or egg, external or internal question very well.

> Skill creates the vessel to be filled.
> But until the vessel is filled, its purpose is not fulfilled.
> And until the vessel is created it has no purpose to fulfill.
> If the grain for the vessel grows before the vessel,
> It has no containment,
> It spills and disperses.
> A vessel without grain is barren;
> Grain without its vessel is scattered,
> and feeds neither mind nor body.
> As the grain grows mysteriously,
> The vessel is prepared.
> The vessel-maker's skill sings the song of the growing grain.
> The grain, filled full of earth and sky,
> Thrusts up to its fulfillment.
> When the grain is ready,
> The vessel must be ready.
> The vessel-maker must not lag behind.

The vessel, for us, represents the external techniques that must be prepared at the same time as the internal emotional forces that support and fill them. "As the grain grows mysteriously, the vessel is prepared." Technique, of course, has "lagged behind" in the theater in this country, and while we encourage the growth of the "grain", we will give special emphasis to the problem of technique, hoping to correct the imbalance so that the internal-external opposites may attain their maximum vitality by feeding each other. Also implicit in the parable is the exercise of each of the techniques separately: one can hoe and water the grain, and/or mold, bake, and paint the vessel, and though the two processes come together eventually, they can be practiced separately.

8. Incorporating: Selective Awareness

Thus far we have been dealing exclusively with soliloquizing— the concentration of exclusion. The other aspect of concentration —the concentration of incorporation—is more readily accessible to the singer-actor because it deals with tangible things outside oneself which one can *see* and *touch*, and which can be made part of the experience. But many singers have learned to shut out awareness of anything that is unrelated to their vocal production or the conductor's beat. Every singer-actor is aware of the glaze that can pass over the eyes of colleagues during a performance as they practice a negative version of the concentration of exclusion. Such restrictive awareness is easier than a totally aware performance and is tolerated and even encouraged by individual members of the music-theater hierarchy. When the frenetic demands of instant opera are felt, withdrawal may be absolutely necessary. But if greater awareness is made a part of singer-actor training from the beginning, it becomes easier, not more difficult.

The available mental energy is there in every singer. One need only observe the uses of superfluous mental energy in opera production everywhere: into the breach left by our inadequate training pour the vacuous games, habits, and defenses of insufficiently challenged singer-actors. Backstage we find singer-actors checking out the audience, trying to break up the other performers, playing catty games onstage, upstaging their fellow performers, or worrying so much about their vocal production that they interfere with it. The existence of such habits and games (and they are common among performers) indicates that there is a great deal of mental energy which can be turned to performance if the proper technique and discipline are learned, but that such technique and discipline are rarely learned except by instinct or accident, because they relate to extramusical, integrative considerations.

But unlike many things that are learned only through instinct or accident, technique and discipline can be learned by anyone. The ability to relate to the actual events on stage (not merely to what one has planned for and *hoped* would occur) is a matter of exercising the atrophied mental muscles in question. Awareness of one's fellow performers, of one's costume and its uses, of one's props and their possibilities, of the lighting and its functional meaning, of the orchestral coloring and one's place in it, of the totality of the piece (not merely one's own part but the interrelationship of all parts), all can be cultivated, and, more important, *used* by the properly prepared performer.

Most of our exercises emphasize the idea of responding to what *actually* happens rather than responding to one's expectation. This is the key to what ensemble performance means: a sense of the many possible choices your fellow performers may make, and the ability to respond to any of them—expected or unexpected.

B. Structuring: the Third Basic Skill

1. The Primary Question: What Happens Next?

The energizing process has been set in motion, the energy has been focused and must now be structured. Structuring determines how the energy ebbs and flows, how it progresses. Of all the skills that hold an audience's attention, structuring is perhaps the most important. The primary dramatic question is, "what happens next?"[10] and that question is answered structurally through the use of changes in process, by moving from event to event, whether these events are emotional or physical.

2. Lyric Expansion vs. Linear Action

"What happens next?" is, of course, a plot-oriented question that relates to horizontal development. But we are working with a form which often says, "let's not worry about moving on for the moment, let's consider the implications of *this* moment before going on." Music-theater is a form that expands lyrically, vertically, instead of moving in a linear progression. This is one of the chief reasons for opera's low public esteem: it willfully *avoids* progression and positively revels in narrative stasis. There is, as always, both truth and misunderstanding in public opinion; although there *are* moments of stasis, they can be opera's greatest glory if properly understood and handled.

In each moment we must find the impulse, however small, that allows and demands progression, to the next moment. We must search out the theatrical movement implicit in the musical verticality. We must nurture the seeds, psychological, physical, or both, that unite the opposites of lyric expansion and dramatic progression.

Horizontal plot development vs. vertical lyric expansion: in the fluctuating relationship between these two lie most of the acting problems of music-theater, especially those involving structure. As a general rule, time will flow in a natural, horizontal manner in ensemble situations and will expand vertically in aria situations.[11] For example, in Mozart's miraculous act two Finale in *The Marriage of Figaro*, a great deal of the text can be spoken to the music at a natural rate with believable effect. The relationship of time flow to events is realistic. In the same opera, the "Porgi Amor" or "Dove Sono" experiences alter time so that it expands vertically, lyrically, before returning to a normal flow scarcely any later than when the singers left it by the clock.

Once again, then, we are speaking of opposite ends of the time-flow continuum. The examples above fall to either side and do not represent absolutes. The glory of opera is its infinite flexibility in altering the flow of time from moment to moment, and any great aria or ensemble can no more be confined to a rigid time-flow equation than can life itself.

Thus the rate of response to the "what happens next?" question varies more in music-theater than in theater. In music-theater we dash onward at one moment, in the next we are lost in exquisite contemplation for minutes at a time. The means by which the singer-actor handles the fluctuating time shifts, both physically and psychologically, is a matter of structure. Following our axiom—for maximum vitality opposites must partake of each other—the singer-actor must find progression in the moments of lyric expansion and a sense of lyric depth in the moments of narrative development.

In exercising concentration we found the greatest difficulty at the stop-time end of the continuum. The same is true of structuring. The problem is to find progression in those moments when time stops or bends back upon itself. The difficulty of filling a moment emotionally is proportionate to the degree that time fluctuates, that the flow of real time is the most altered. When a ten-second real-time experience has been expanded to a five-minute music-time experience, the search for progression is additionally complicated. The words have their own psychological progression which sometimes enforces the musical time extension but more often contradicts it; in certain unusual instances the words that lacked a sense of progression are given it by the music.[12]

This conflict of the musical structure and the verbal-psychological structure gives rise to the two schools of operatic staging mentioned earlier: that stressing the real-time progression, which produces busy, repetitive sequences, and that stressing the extended-time progression, which produces static sequences with neither physical nor psychological progression.

Arias present the greatest challenge here, just as they did in concentrating, and for the same reason: arias extend time more often than ensembles do. But there is no set pattern, only a continual alteration of the time flow. All possibilities must be investigated and exercised, from a complete time-stop to a time-flow more rapid than real time. In exercising concentration we emphasized the problem of sustaining the stop-time moments; here we are more concerned with the flow of time no matter what the speed.

3. The Varieties of Progression

Progression, of course, must not be conceived of simplistically. Progression can be purely linear: event (b) follows event (a), event (c) follows event (b). Or it can be block-style: event (a), event (b) and event (c) are different facets of a central experience and are not caused by one another.[13]

The singer-actor will be concerned with the speed of the progression between events, whether they are related or not. One can make a fast progression or a slow progression between two events. At one end of this speed-of-progression continuum one finds the slowest possible progression; at the other, the sudden, instantaneous change of process. One of the best ways of exercising both kinds of progression is with assigned attitudes. The mind can move more quickly than either the body or the voice, and this capacity can be exercised at both ends of the continuum through the use of attitudes. Sudden or slow changes from one attitude to another can be practiced in both solo and ensemble situations. The sudden change of process is also useful to diagnose tension: if tension is used to simulate emotion, the sudden change of process will take just a beat longer to accomplish than it should; the performer has to release the tension before moving to a new tension-emotion setting.

The essential thing is that the singer-actors' consciousness of the importance of progression be raised and that their skill in making all possible kinds of progressions be increased. In achieving these goals, the singer-actors' awareness of the *musical* articulation of the dramatic structure will also be exercised. Asking questions is useful here, as elsewhere: what does a sudden modulation mean dramatically? what is the dramatic implication of a change in rhythm, a change in instrumental color, a change in tempo, a fermata, a melodic line, or anything that interacts with the words and the dramatic action to form music-theater? Such questions are the tools a good coach uses to get answers from the singer-actor. The difference between our use of the questions and the coach's approach is the difference between specific interpretive needs and general ability to fill those needs. The coach rightfully seeks a definite interpretation (the best coaches adjust the answers to fit the special combination of singer and song), but our purpose is to increase the singer-actor's ability to answer *any* such questions flexibly and meaningfully. Exercised in this way, the singer-actor offers coaches and conductors a range of interpretative skill which will serve them far better than a single interpretive view, no matter how correct that view might seem to be.

We will exercise these, as other skills, with progressions in three basic areas: physical, emotional, and vocal/musical, separately and in combination along the complete time-flow continuum.

Chapter

6

Recapitulation — The Final Three Skills

A. The Fourth Skill: Imagining

1. *The Ascending Spiral*

The final three skills—imagining, stylizing, and coordinating—can be considered advanced parallels to the first three. Imagining, like energizing, draws upon our personal imaginative resources to create internal energy; stylizing, like concentrating, gives an external focus to the energies thus made available, selecting from the surplus of resources created by the imagination those most appropriate to the style of the piece and the individual characterization. Coordinating, like structuring, gives the combined resources a unified form, shaping and interweaving all the various skills and energies into an artistic whole. Thus we recapitulate the sequence and conclude with a final coordination of all the skills.

2. *Imagining Fantastically*

In planning the structure of skills to be exercised, I thought imagination especially pertinent to the training of the young singer-actor. We have already directed so many barbs at the authoritarian nature of the singer's musical training that the reason for this feeling is evident. Imagination is a personal adventure which cannot be confined by rules, dictated by the experience of others, or compelled by any outside force. It is an inner-directed skill and one of the prime opposites: it must vitalize and be vitalized by the *other*-directed skills and disciplines integral to the singer-actor's training.

The term *imagining*, however, did not seem strong enough. A word was needed which would suggest and invite a greater sense of free-flowing fantasy. Although *fantasizing* suggests something important about the mental process, it has many negative connotations as well. So *imagining* it is, but *imagining* in as free and fantastic a way as possible. One can always return to common sense and everyday reality; leaving it, however, is more difficult and more important. To learn to free the impulses of our mind, to use them, and to allow them to enrich the disciplined form within which we work is one of our basic aims. Imagining exercises will be suggested which remove the blocks that prevent a free flow of impulse and keep us from enlivening our performances with the rich vein of fantasy we all possess.

3. Criticism: Attitude Non Grata

Criticism creates as many problems in stimulating the growth of imagination as it does in promoting the process of improvisation. Whether from the instructor, fellow performers, or oneself it simply has no place in the initial process of imagining. Our little critical demons must be silenced until the imaginative flow is free and steady. One cannot permit judgment of imaginative ideas at the beginning. Instead one should substitute description, describing all imaginative ideas as objectively as possible.

In this descriptive process there are two kinds of validation. The first occurs when the objective description of a performance matches the internal intention of the performer. If, for example, the performer imagines that he is very fat as he sings, and the observers get a distinct and genuine sense of the person's "fatness" (assuming he is not already in that condition) that is a plus: not for the strength of imagination, but for the correspondence between intention and projection. The second kind of validation occurs when the performance is clearcut and powerful, but is created by an internal image that seems to have no logical connection to the objective effect of the performance. If, for example, a performer imagines an extraordinary environment which affects her emotionally, imagines further that her hands and legs are growing in length as she lives in that environment, and the observers feel an unusual and powerful sense of physical distress and mental terror, then the performer has gained a new freedom of imagination in using internal images. She has learned that the imaginative process need not fit itself into the pigeonholes defined by text and music. The performer may use any fuel available to ignite the creative energies; these energies, *once they are flowing*, will be shaped and character- ized by the text, the music, and the performer. It is extremely rare to see a genuinely energized performance that is so imaginative it has clearly gone astray; but it is all too common to see unenergized, unimaginative performances that betray the form more completely than overimagination ever could. We need years of erring on the imaginative side before a balance will be attained.

It is important for the instructor to encourage *all* efforts. It is also important to make certain those efforts are specific rather than general: a sense of happiness derived from specific circumstance, not from the general idea of happiness. Special praise should be reserved for anyone who takes an imaginative risk (such as the fantasy of growing hands and feet mentioned above). Encourage- ment of every attempt to free the impulses is vital. To overcome the fear of free impulsive play takes all the positive but honest nurturing we can provide.

If, when a performer projects from the imagination, the group perceives neither objective intention nor an interesting offshoot, despite the performer's insistence that there was one, the learning potential is often greater. The group may analyze what *was* pro- jected, and what the performer would have to do to project what was intended. This approach is also useful to diagnose projection interference. If a performer intends to project a sense of ecstasy and does not, the question can be raised, "What physical or emotional factors prevented that projection?" From then on it is a continual process of performance, observation, objectification, analysis, and re-performance.

4. Creation and Re-Creation

There are three kinds of imaginative acts challenging the singer- actor. The first involves the re-creation of the imaginative creations of others. For example, Mozart has given us the characters and situations in *The Marriage of Figaro*, which we study, learn, and re-create. The second kind of imaginative act involves our special contribution to the imaginative constructs of others. There is only one Countess exactly like the one you create. The power of that creation depends upon your imaginative contribution as well as Mozart's. Finally, there are occasional opportunities for the singer-actor to create the complete product—words, music, actions, everything.[1] We shall work with all these varieties of the imaginative act. But as we attempt to right the personal imbalance of opposites in the singer-actor, the third sort, in which the performer is totally responsible for the work, will receive special attention.

And let us emphasize it once again: that imbalance between imagining and memorizing needs correcting in the worst way. When a young singer-actor says, as many have actually said, "I'm completely lost unless I'm told *exactly* what to do," one feels the depth of that need. But neither that individual nor his comrades-in-need are to blame. We have not allowed them to become participating artists in an enterprise that demands their participation. And participating partners they are, whether any of us like it or not. They *participate* in Verdi's (or Mozart's or Puccini's) efforts regardless of their preparedness to do so. It is the *depth* of that participation which we must exercise. We must increase the extent to which singer-actors can become part of the composer's, librettist's, conductor's, and director's imaginative processes. They can become genuine partners in those processes only when they have flexed and strengthened their own imagining process. Every opportunity singer-actors have to exercise their imagination gives them better access to that ideal music-theater state: perfect identity with the minds of the composer, the librettist, and the character.

5. The Imagination of Incorporation

But perhaps the most important use of the imagining powers is that which enables the performer to make the connection between an external requirement and its internal validation. For example, it takes an act of imagination to incorporate and make sense of a series of arbitrarily assigned emotional attitudes; it takes an act of imagination to incorporate and make sense of the accidents of performance, or an assigned gesture, or a costume, or a prop, or a physical movement, or of the musical score itself. The translation of the technical intricacies of a musical score into stylized but seemingly natural expression by a human being is an incredible act of the imagination, and one that is basic to the music-theater form.

The questions one can ask about a music-theater score—what does that fermata mean to the character's situation, why does he sing in those jerky staccato rhythms, what does that coloratura passage mean emotionally, what happens to the character emotionally during that introduction and the interludes—are challenges to the imaginative processes, as are all the injunctions of a musical coach to the singer-actor. When a coach asks a singer-actor to go faster or slower, to be more staccato or legato, to make a crescendo or a decrescendo, to give special emphasis to a certain word, to push on or hold back rhythmically, to give more or less weight to a passage, to extend the phrasing, or any number of other musical modifications of the score, he or she is asking the singer-actor for an act of imagination which will connect those external requests with personal, validating energies.

This connective skill needs all the exercise it can get; but the way things are, young singer-actors may not encounter even a request for the exercise of the skill until long after training days are over. Then they may meet one of the rare breed of coaches who stress the importance of making that connection (unfortunately, only in the service of a single role). Unless the connecting skill has been exercised frequently or the singer-actor practices it instinctively, it will have atrophied, and the coach will wonder at the stupidity of singers. The singer may learn something in the process, but the next contact with a demand for the connecting skill will depend upon chance. This need not be the case. Any one of us—from either side of the music-theater continuum—can and *should* ask young singer-actors to exercise with any one of the foregoing questions. All we have to do is acquaint singer-actors with the need to make the connection between the external request and the internal validation, then make such a request, and finally listen for the connection-making skill in action, training our own ears as well as the singer-actors' skill in the process.

The important thing is that this connecting, incorporating, sense-making imaginative skill can and should be exercised independently of a "correct" interpretation. The correctness, acceptability, or propriety of our training requests is not the question, but rather what those requests can do to increase the singer-actors' awareness of the skill and their capability of executing *any* possible coaching request that might be made.

B. The Fifth Skill: Stylizing

1. Agreements about Differences

An everyday opera is a rare thing; there are very few that are grounded in the homely familiarities of ordinary life, where artifice seems absent. But all theater, including music-theater, is grounded in convention. No matter how close to everyday life in feeling, no matter how improvised and spontaneous in appearance, we always know that what we are watching is a performance: a series of events governed by conventions or *agreements* between audience and performers. A "Candid Camera" approach may presume to present reality, but even there, life needs amending; various ironies are introduced unbeknownst to the "performers" which make us spectators of a performance rather than observers of life. A "Candid Camera" *opera* could not exist, nor could a "Candid Camera" *Macbeth* or *King Lear*. As the stylistic agreements between audience and performer become more complicated, they demand an increased understanding of the nature of these agreements on the part of the performer and the audience. "Candid Camera" actors use themselves totally and unconsciously; as the agreements become more complex, more of this unconscious behavior must become conscious and controlled. Although very few people speak in iambic pentameter, it is probably safe to say that even fewer sing as they converse, let alone sing operatically. These kinds of skills require technique, practice, and control: in short, an intense awareness of means. One must move from an unconscious, unself-conscious use of natural technique to an equally free, but increasingly aware use of more formalized techniques. In a Jungian interpretation one might say that the goal of singer-actors is to make more and more of their unconscious artistic life available to conscious control.

2. *Children, Old Shoes, and Style*

At the same time, this conscious manipulation of physical, vocal, and emotional language must *seem* to be unconscious and natural, which is not an insoluble paradox but a matter of exercise. We come into the world with few, if any, conventions or agreements about behavior or life-style. But we learn by observation and imitation, or re-observation, correction, and constant practice. Eventually, by blending our own dispositions with those of the environment and the people around us, we arrive at a personal style of life. This is precisely the course we must follow in acquiring the ability to use other dramatic styles. We must first try on seemingly strange ways of being, which will not feel any more comfortable than did our first attempts at imitation when we were children. We were clumsy, we stumbled, and the well-practiced grown-ups found us infinitely amusing. But we kept at it, practicing constantly until the feelings fit, the sounds made sense, and the actions became controlled and graceful.[2] Adults who wish to become singer-actors must again become as children, trying on sounds and movements and feelings which are not immediately comfortable.

In a homelier context, you don't throw away a new pair of shoes because they pinch the first time you wear them. It takes a little discomfort, a few blisters, and some annoyance before new shoes become the old shoes in which we feel so comfortable. Those shoes worth wearing have to be *made* our own by lengthy wearing, some pinching and pain, and stretching and enduring.[3]

We find our life-style in the formative years through interaction between our predispositions and the demands of the outer world. We learn a *new* style by interaction between that life-style (which is a new predisposition) and the altered demands of the outside world, be it the real world or the world of a specific piece of music-theater set in a given place and time. There is a parallel between the original learned naturalness and the artistic process of learning and making natural a new style.

Just as it took time to break in a personal style, it will take time to break in other styles. It requires courage, perseverance, hard work, and a host of other intimidating virtues, but if we can learn to think in the role of *homo ludens*, man the player, rather than *homo faber*, man the worker, the burden may ease.[4] Our work is our play is our work is our play is our work is our play – another set of vital opposites that the artist must integrate.

Another way of viewing the process is through the concepts of extending and imploding. In the first, one takes a natural impulse, a natural sound, a natural feeling, a natural action, and extends it until it becomes abstract without losing connection to its source. In the concept of imploding, one begins with an abstract sound and an abstract action, and allows them to compress, to seek out the natural, to relate concretely to their specifically human origins without losing the freedom and energy of their abstract origin. These two concepts should be part of singing-acting at all times, balanced, so that we are always drawing upon both kinds of energy available to us – that from within and that from without.

Yet another step in the movement between extension and naturalism is from naturalism to internalization. The energy of the original extension is imploded, step by step, first compressing to a naturalistic state, then imploding from there to an internal process with no visible external movement but with a readiness for such a movement. The same process can be followed in reverse, from an internal impulse, through its naturalistic evocation, to its abstract extension.[5]

Extension and implosion can also be applied to the singing and speaking of lines. A sung line can be thought of as the extension of a speaking line (though requiring a different vocal process), and a speaking line can be thought of as the implosion of a singing line.[6] The practice of repeating a spoken line, following various paths to its eventual extension as a sung line (rhythmic structuring, inflective-melodic structuring, word coloration structuring) can help the singer-actor achieve a better understanding of the process a composer goes through in creating from the lines of a libretto the song of the score. Repeating a sung line in a similar way, following it back to its naturalistic spoken source can heighten the personal expressiveness that must be part of good singing. Both varieties of understanding aid total music-theater performance and can be usefully practiced by the singer-actor.

3. Confrontation: Self and Character

Here we have a basic confrontation: the singer-actor and the role. We will never be perfectly matched to the roles we must play. We do not enter any of the many music-theater worlds endowed with all the style habits of that world; the shoe always pinches at first. As performers we must ask consciously what we once asked instinctively: "What must I do to make sense of the character I play?" "How must I act, psychologically, physically, and vocally, to achieve it?" Faced with these questions, we can make several possible replies:

(a) I will make the character as similar to myself as possible and trust my own natural behavior to make sense of it. Therefore, I must act in the part as I act in life. Whatever does not feel truthful (or natural or honest) the first time around is not true to me and must be discarded.

(b) I will do whatever silly thing the director asks for. I will sing as well as I can and not worry about anything else.

(c) I will practice whatever needs to be done, knowing that it will not feel normal at first, and hope that it will come to feel natural.

(d) I will imagine how *I* would act if I were the character; then I will compare that to the way the *character* would act. Once I know the difference, I can translate *my* reasons for acting as I do into the character's *actions*. Thus I will do what the character must do even as I search myself for validating reasons and feelings.

The last of these, of course, comes closest to a healthy interplay of opposites and of finding connections between the outer demand and inner justifications.

Singing immediately removes the character from the realm of the natural; the words and the actions will pull her or him back and suggest other possibilities. The three strands and their interrelationship can be examined in detail by asking questions. Ask a question of your character and you will always get some sort of answer, but until the question is asked the answer may remain hidden. Sometimes a question has to be asked over and over during the course of rehearsals. For example, the question, "how does the character behave in each new situation?" deserves constant repetition until the show closes. But it is not an intellectual question to be answered only in the head. It is a body-and-voice-in-action question which must be answered by physical, emotional, and vocal thinking as well. The answer is never final, but always subject to revision from the first rehearsal to closing night. Each new answer must be acted on with total conviction, for at that moment it *is* the correct one.

Another character question never completely answered is, "who am I?" The answers change as the question is asked, and an answer arrived at changes previous answers and thus itself as well. The validating arena is moment-to-moment life, inside or outside of rehearsal, and the search for the answer is one of the vitalizing forces of life and of music-theater.

The problem of search and naturalize is simplified if one accepts the fact that all ways of being (including our own) are acts of stylization, i.e. selections of patterns and ways of life that are no more natural than any other selection. Solving the problem is a matter of practice: we must exercise with many different styles until the human energies feeding them are no longer inhibited by the shape of the vessel into which they flow, but can be used to energize all vessels with equal freedom. This is one reason why gibberish and sound and motion are basic to our exercise program: they promote stylistic capability by encouraging the use of personal energies within a highly formalized style, and thus make all formalized styles more accessible to one's personal energy.

4. Specificity and Generalization

The term *stylization* refers to the individual characteristics within a period as well as the general style of a given period. The first deals with the manners of an individual living in a different time or place; the second deals with the generalized *sum* of the manners of that time and place. For example, there is not only the personal style of Figaro himself, but also the generalized style of the eighteenth century. The difference between the two is at least as important as the similarity.

Every period had characters who acted in a style unlike that of the period; in fact every individual acts unlike his period in some way. The generalized period style emerges from the combination of all the individual styles within the period, some of which go strongly against the common denominator. At the same time there must be a blend of the styles of all these characters. One cannot neglect either end of the sameness-difference stylistic continuum. Individuality and commonality must blend without calling attention to the blend. A sense of the style of any period, then, is a wonderfully complicated mixture of music, words, actions, descriptions, pictures, instinct, and educated guesses: Finding the key to the style of any period can be a fascinating cross-word-music-action puzzle. Too often, however, it is dismissed as too complicated, phony, and removed from what real life is all about to be worth the effort, or reduced to a token nod in the direction of "style" without finding the indispensable life within. For example, our sense of pre-twentieth century people is dictated largely by posed portraits from those times which probably had as little to do with actual life and movement as posed portraits do today. We can only encourage more questions, more searching, and most importantly, greater risk-taking in the search for style. Every production in search of a style (which is to say, all productions) needs a freedom of search, a multitude of attempts, a toleration of early rough edges, and a good dash of the atypical before arriving at a useful sense of period. To begin with a generalized sense of period is to impose a generalization on all the characters; to begin only with individual styles, on the other hand, might create a period-spread of several centuries. Once again, one must deal with both ends of this particular continuum simultaneously:

THE GENERALIZED STYLE OF A GIVEN PERIOD	THE INDIVIDUAL IDIOSYNCRASIES THAT MAKE UP THE STYLE

Each must feed the other for greatest vitality.

If an attitude of free exploration is to be the rule in searching for style, one must trust in one's ability to make a discriminating selection from a wealth of choices. But those choices come *from* the freedom, and nothing so inhibits free physical and emotional exploration as preformed intellectual judgments (as opposed to *performed* intellectual judgments). Not that such judgments do not exist, but they must be placed in abeyance during exploration.

An idea may be terrible, but the *execution* of the idea may suggest another idea that *is* useful. To test a seemingly ridiculous idea by performing it will always be stimulating, sometimes exhilarating, often surprising, and occasionally usable. It is highly unlikely that the singer playing the Countess will leap up on her bed in performance (see page 61), but trying it a time or two in rehearsal might provide all sorts of things, including a fresh view of her character.

C. The Sixth Skill: Coordinating

1. Music-Theater Juggling

Coordinating is the last of our skills. It not only incorporates all the other skills in various ways, it recalls the theme with which we began: that the coordination of many artists, the cooperation of many egos is essential in creating a whole greater than the sum of its parts. It recalls as well the coordinating and balancing of opposites. From any angle the art of singing-acting is the art of coordination *par excellence*. It is a veritable juggling act, and each of the objects juggled is a different size, a different shape, a different material, a different essence. It is the objects themselves – the words, the actions, the music, the emotions – that define the artistic quality of the juggling act, but whatever the status of the objects – whether they make up light opera or atonal fantasy – the skill and technique of the singer-actor as juggler is what creates the music-theater experience.

2. Shifting Gears in Music-Theater

The primary act of coordination has to do with the feedback process between form and content or between technique and feeling. We have discussed this particular process before, but not with reference to a concept we will call the ratio factor. For a moment let us consider the interrelated areas of energizing – the physical, the emotional, and the vocal. On a normal, nontheatrical level, the relationship between the three areas is roughly one (P) to one (E) to one (V). That is, the emotional energy expended will give rise to a proportionate physical and vocal expenditure of energy. The three quantities tend to be equal, assuming there is no false equating of energy with tension.

When the stylistic demands change, however, we encounter coordination problems among the three quantities. If the physical style becomes larger in scale or more ornate or more sustained or more energized or all of the above, a quantitative change in the vocal or emotional output is not necessarily called for. It is the quality which should change. But if the performer attempts to maintain the quantitative ratio as the physical energy increases, say, to six, tension or oversinging or overemotionalizing will automatically follow.

The performer who deals with style must be able to maintain a flexible ratio among the physical, the emotional, and the vocal. Six to one to one, if that is what is called for. An example of this particular ratio might be a florid Restoration physical style which calls for a low-key emotional accompaniment (depending upon the situation) and a languid, flowing vocal characterization (depending upon the character).

If the second ratio factor, the emotional level, changes, we often find tension interference in the use of physical tension or vocal indicating to justify, motivate, or "prove" that the emotional level *is* being played. This is a trap we have discussed at length, and need only mention it here as part of the ratio-coordination problem. We might also stress that constant injunctions to performers to motivate or justify what they are playing do as much to create this kind of tension as anything. As soon as performers begin worrying about proving their motivations or making them clear to the director, they will be pulled into physical facial or vocal indicating instead of trusting the emotional process to create the necessary results.

But even if actors or singer-actors have learned to trust the efficacy of the emotional process (and many have not), we find in the third ratio factor – the vocal – the greatest coordination problem. This is especially true for actors confronted with the stylized vocal-musical demands of the Greeks, Shakespeare, Congreve, Sheridan, et al. If, as the vocal energies increase, there is an automatic increase of energy in the emotional and the physical, we have a classic music-theater problem. Either tension develops through vocal indicating to justify the heightened emotions, or the energy demands of the language are not obeyed and a monochromatic, hard-to-understand naturalism sets in. If a one-to-one vocal-emotional ratio is too ingrained, the performer will have difficulty moving between stylistic levels without encountering the tension factor, especially if there is the slightest hint of the equation of false energy and tension. For the singer, of course, it is possible to divorce the relationship entirely and let the vocal level increase with *no* change in the physical or emotional levels, rather than battering against the impossible one-to-one ratio demand. With singing, any pretense at a one-to-one emotional-to-vocal relationship is absurd. Giving up the relationship entirely, however, is not a useful alternative. Here the true physical-emotional-vocal imaginative athleticism of the singer-actor is tested. The development of this athleticism is subverted by all those who suggest that the way to move from speech to song is to increase the quantity of emotion. The shift, as we have stressed repeatedly, is qualitative. This imaginative shift demonstrates singer-power in its purest form: the use of emotional energies which are both integral to the singing and have an independent, free-flowing life of their own, and which, while never losing touch with the musical expression or failing to provide musical nuance also have the capacity to make statements seemingly contrary to the implications of the music itself.

A specific example of the kind of flexible coordination this demands is the use of attitude assignments in connection with emotional energizing. An aria can be assigned several different sequences of attitudes, yet each of the sequences may be used effectively, depending upon the coordinating and imagining skills of the singer. Sometimes, in fact, the most effective attitudes are those that *seem* to fight the implications of the subject matter or the music or both. We have discussed the use of images or environments that vary from those suggested by the text to stimulate an appropriate but stronger emotional response from the performer. In using arbitrary or opposite attitudes, however, the purpose of the exercise is to combine and blend them with those suggested by the text. If, for example, the song is sorrowful and the arbitrary attitude is joyful, the singer-actor might integrate the two by remembering the joy, the loss of which creates the present sorrow.

We say "I never would have imagined that!" and often fail to follow through on the implications of what we have just said, namely, that we *did* imagine it because we gave ourselves the challenge to do so. Our imaginative faculties often lie dormant because we have not challenged them. The same is true of our coordinating skills: properly challenged, they will give us results we wouldn't have dreamed of. Many of the exercises in coordinating demonstrate our limited imaginative scope about the complex act of singing-acting, and the necessity for exercising this vital singer-power factor.

Of the exercises that diagnose ratio-misconceptions, one is particularly effective and can be practiced quite early in the program. Two performers begin a *naturalistic* gibberish[7] conversation giving equal weight to physical, emotional, and vocal aspects (P-1/E-1/V-1); on a signal from the group leader, they move into a conversation that is physically and vocally more formalized (P-5/E-1/V-5). At another signal they change to a *sung* gibberish duet-conversation that is physically more naturalistic (P-2/E-1/V-6); then change back to a naturalistic gibberish conversation. The first move, from the naturalistic to the formalistic mode, is a key one, particularly if specific emotional attitudes are also assigned, making the ratio in the first step, say, (P-1/E-4/V-1), and in the next (P-5/E-4/V-5). If there is a tension connection between the emotional energy and the physical and vocal energy, it will be heard immediately when the performer tries to retain the same ratio, thus forcing the emotional level up to an impossible point: (P-5/E-20/V-5). Once the performer realizes the impossibility of doing such a thing, and makes the necessary mental adjustments (which are too complicated to describe more specifically – they must be experienced), she or he gains the freedom to release strong emotions while singing.

3. Analyzing the Unanalyzable: The Path to Awareness

Although the exercises in coordinating may seem so complicated as to be restrictive, they are largely diagnostic and analytic, and are aimed at achieving greater freedom through the overload principle. In each of the skill areas, we make extra demands upon the skill in question even as we exercise it so that it will become stronger and more flexible in actual performance. We isolate the skills, strengthen them through overload, then reintegrate them. The greater the overload, the more is revealed about the singer-actor's individual weaknesses. This in turn leads to new exercises designed to strengthen those weaknesses, and those exercises in turn will act diagnostically as well as therapeutically, revealing further areas to be strengthened. This process of isolate-exercise-analyze can continue indefinitely, or it can return at any point to reintegration with the total act. While analysis of this kind may seem overly intellectual in dealing with such an emotionally volatile form as music-theater, a restatement of Robert Pirsig's view may clarify the issue: the more romantically expressive the form, the greater the necessity for classic analysis if it is to make its greatest impact. This was put in concrete terms by a performer during a Minnesota Opera Institute: "the staff has an amazing and unfailing ability to analyze the seemingly intangible." By not avoiding the difficulties of such delicate and complex analysis, we have been able to release energies that might otherwise have remained locked in the grip of emotional sensitivity. Because the music-theater form is so complicated, there is a tendency to shrink from a careful analysis of its emotional workings, and one hears variations of the "dissection kills" argument. While we do not want to analyze emotion to death, we must be concerned with raising our awareness of how this passionate form works and thus increase our capacity to deal with it. If we expect singer-actor athleticism from our performers, then we must heighten our awareness of every possible factor having to do with that athleticism, whether it be physical or emotional or vocal or all three, in any of the many styles in which they can work. If we wish to increase the coordinating powers of our performers, we must increase our awareness of the factors affecting those powers.

4. Overload and Mystery

Another important aspect of exercising for performing is the overload principle. All the exercises are based upon that principle, but its strongest application is found in the coordinating exercises. Singer-actors should be able to sing higher, faster, louder, and more flexibly in the practice studio than they will ever be required to do in performance. There are several reasons for this, the most obvious of which is the safety factor: so many things can go wrong in a performance that one should always have a reserve; one should never risk damaging a performance by daring one's limits (unless this is the point of the performance, as it is for many rock singers, the late Janis Joplin among them). The other reason, equally valid, has to do with the mind and imagination of the audience. An audience can recognize the limitations of a performance, but when not confronted by an obvious limit, the audience is allowed to imagine whatever limits they please. They may assume the perform-er has superhuman abilities, as long as the performer does not deny that possibility by approaching his or her limits too closely (or by becoming tense, which is virtually the same thing). There is a wonderful mystery about what performers *might do* if they chose,[8] and it is in that mystery—what might be done—that one finds some of the impact of a superb vocal performance. If limits are felt, however, the imagination is squelched, the mystery vanishes, and the performer is seen for the ordinary, albeit talented, human being that she or he actually is. The sense that *infinitely more is possible* is one of the compelling things about such a performance, the feel-ing that infinity itself, and the secrets thereof, are within our grasp; as far as the performer has gone, there has been no diminution of power, and we have been there too. If she or he continues and performs the *perfect* spatial-tonal sequence, the sequence which overcomes all the spiritual and physical challenges of its seeming impossibility, time and the limits of life might be transcended. This is all very mystic, but music *is* mystical in its alteration of time, in its effect upon our emotions and sensibilities. Nowhere, as we have previously pointed out, is this effect more pronounced than in the relationship of the outstanding singer to the audience.

Let us take the argument one step further. If the measure of excitement produced by musical performance is integrally related to the performer's ability to master the score and still seem to have potential to spare—to give a performance which transcends the score—then perhaps the same is true of music-theater. In such a music-theater performance there is no question about the mastery of the score, the staging, the acting, and the singing; any accident, any unforeseen problem could easily be handled. When such accidents do occur, and are handled well, validating that sense of extra potential, they are invariably a gratifying experience for the audience. The excitement of a performance, then, is correlated to the limits of the skills which are imagined by the audience but which are never actually reached. A performance in which all the individual vocal, physical, emotional skills are, to the audience, limitless, is the truly transcendent performance.

The overload principle, then, is important in a number of ways. Not only does it prepare performers to deal with the accidents of performance and allow them to relax with the knowledge that what they will perform is well within their capabilities, but it also offers the bonus of enlivening the imagination of the audience. The performance that transcends may be the direct result of the performer's use of the overload principle in exercising the separate skills of the music-theater form.

Whatever the values of overload work – tangible and intangible – they can only be achieved by actual practice. Whether it involves additional high notes, a heightened degree of concentration or energizing, a greater feeling of spontaneity, better preparedness, a better sense of style, or structuring, one must finally put all elements together in a coordinated whole. That act produces total music-theater.

5. We Have Nothing to Fear But Success: Growth through Failure

In all the skills, but especially in coordination, the performers should be aware that the only good exercise is one that cannot at first be performed successfully, one that pushes them to their limit in performing it. An exercise that you cannot master immediately allows you to encounter and extend your limits. This is not failure in the usual sense, nor should it be felt as such either by the instructor or the performers. Instead it should be regarded as a game with one's self, a game that can only be won by confronting one's limits. Since this confrontation, by its very nature, means temporary defeat, winning and improvement demand the willingness to dare that momentary sense of loss, endure it, and grow from it.

By the time students reach the coordinating exercises, much of the terror engendered by the exercises will have been eased, and the performers will be better able to regard them as creative play. Nonetheless, we must never forget to reinforce positively the play attitude, and to maintain the attack on the authoritarian thinking of our academic backgrounds. To sing a song is to have a composer, a librettist, an accompanist, a coach, and hours of practice working on your side. But to sing an improvised aria in an improvised language to an accompaniment you have never heard before, while trying to concentrate, energize, structure, imagine, stylize, and coordinate at the same time, to have the total creative-performance burden on your own shoulders (aided only by your improvising accompanist) is overload in the extreme. Unless the success-failure syndrome graven on our psyche since kindergarten is rendered partially inoperative, the total improvisatory experience can be a traumatic one. But it can also be marvelously exhilarating, and given the proper mental approach, can open up all sorts of new paths for the performer.

The psychological barrier is great; enormous good humor coupled with a continuous avoidance of the right-wrong trap is of prime importance. In this kind of work-play, *all* the material created is useful in some way in developing the singer-actor. It may be built upon or it may be discarded, but it serves a useful purpose. Whether dealing with the complex mental aesthetic of the ratio-shifting or with the straightforward overload exercises, the feeling of uncriticized free play is essential. It is essential to all of our skills, and it is especially important to the subject of our next chapter— improvisation.

Chapter

7

The Uses of Improvisation

A. The Act of Improvisation

1. Imitation without Safeguards

Improvisation is one of those theatrical events that demand consummate skill and risks failure at every moment. An improvised act can fall flat on its face or it can rise to incredible heights, and those two opposites can follow one another in either order at any moment. It places the moment-to-moment coping of ordinary life in the intense focus of theatrical performance; every decision becomes a literal life-and-death situation: a wrong decision, a momentary sagging of energy means a potential theatrical death; a right decision, a renewed energy commitment means rebirth, a new life. While that may be melodramatic, it explains the uncommon exhilaration that genuinely accomplished improvisation provides for its audience. It is one thing to be fascinated, as most of us are, by the act of acting. To be convinced that a performer has tapped the impulses that feed the life of an imagined person is fundamentally appealing and undoubtedly related to Aristotle's discussion of the imitation of an action. When the performer creates that moment of conviction on the spot and improvises convincingly, it is both fascinating and astonishing.

Watching the Second City troupe on its first visit to New York was just such an experience for me. I was not prepared for what I saw and heard. It did not seem possible to do what they did. Now, having experienced hundreds of even more amazing improvisational moments than that first experience revealed, I find it easy to adopt a blasé attitude about the subject. But I think of that first exposure often, and wonder how we are trained into thinking that only prepared scripts and prepared scores can yield anything of artistic value. When we finally confront the fact that someone *has* created a performance of artistic value (although it will never be repeated) with neither script nor score, but with highly flexible and creative human beings coping with the energies of time and its passage, we wonder how we could have been so lacking in a sense of the possible. (If we have uncommonly good sense, we may wonder what else we are excluding from the realm of the artistically possible even as we rejoice in our new level of awareness.)

Despite the rewards of the improvisational act, it is easy to understand the other side of the argument: if the rewards aren't forthcoming, a sense of bleak unfulfillment awaits the audience and the performer. An audience is needed to develop improvisatory performance skills, but the risk-taking, the indifference to the fear of failure, and the creative energies demanded from the performers are all so extreme that it is no wonder there are so few outstanding theatrical improvisers, and more particularly, *music*-theater improvisers, where the stakes are even higher. The audience demands life and will not suffer the little deaths of improvisation gracefully: "go home and practice," is the unspoken thought if an improvisation does not go well, in spite of the fact that one may be well aware that it *is* an improvisation and therefore subject to stumbles.

2. Exercise vs. Performance

This brings us to an important point: the differentiation between the kind of *performance* improvisation we have been discussing, and the *exercise* improvisations which are the basis for much of the training. The performance situation creates marvelously exciting risks precisely because it is right-wrong, product oriented. The performer has dared to take *process* into the *product* arena and let process *be* the product. That takes a flexible, skilled, concentrated, imaginative, creative, and energized performer, and such performances have rightly been called "the most involving and rewarding entertainment experiences one can encounter."[1] But such is the capability of those for whom many of the exercises in this book would be no more than a modest challenge.[2] Our purpose is to use improvisation for the diagnosis of problems and strengthening of skills outside the judgmental arena of public performance. We will deal with both personal and performance problems as we do so, but the emphasis must be on free exploration, and process must not yet be allowed to identify itself as product, although that is the eventual goal. The performers will develop music-theater skills even as they explore themselves through the process of improvisation; these skills will be useful in both traditional and improvised performances, but it is important to maintain the process-product distinction for an extended period of time.

The distinction between improvised performance and improvised exercise is also helpful in understanding attitudes about improvisation. Audience and performer attitudes toward the subject are largely conditioned by the fact that improvisational performance is associated with a low-life, naturalistic, satiric, easy-joke-but-eminently-alive aesthetic. And this rubs against the grain of the highbrow-ritualized, respectful, deadly serious, disciplined-to-the-point-of-death aesthetic which characterizes grand grand opera. Critics and musicians who have spent their lives extolling the virtues of strict adherence to disciplines of the musical score (à la Toscanini) are unlikely to admire the seemingly undisciplined flow of human energies molded and sculpted as they occur.[3] But they fail to realize that what made Toscanini's adherence to the demands of the score so powerful was his ability to infuse those external composer demands with his own highly volatile personal emotions—a perfect example of the blending of opposites. This basic misunderstanding of the subjective-objective relationship in interpretation must not get in the way of our use of improvisational exercises as a means of promoting personal and performance growth.

3. Risk and Reward

For directors and teachers of singing-acting there is also a difficulty to be faced, for improvisation poses high risks to them as well as to the performers. Teachers must make all aesthetic and diagnostic decisions in an improvisational exercise without the aid of script, ground plan, specified characterizations, or guidelines of any kind. Moreover, improvisatory exercises are a greater problem in this respect than are improvised performances. In the former directors must guide things with constant suggestions and decisions, whereas the latter are completely out of their hands. I can still remember my own trepidations when beginning improvisational exercises. But there was no way to avoid working with such an important method, and I soon found that the only way to learn to work with improvisation was to jump in and do it. Directors must say to themselves precisely what they say to their performers: give your energies to an ongoing, creative interplay, trusting that you will make useful and necessary decisions, keeping your awarenesses as open as possible, avoiding judgmental panic, living in the now as completely as possible. The catch is that beginning directors must have material with which to work — that is, improvising performers — in order to develop their skills. If performers are not willing to give and forgive or are hostile toward the idea of improvisation (in which they may be totally justified by previous experiences) the whole process can be quickly scuttled. But this is a part of the director's problem: to create an initial exercise atmosphere of freedom and trust so that the energies can begin flowing. From there it depends on the director's sensitivities and awareness of the process, for they will determine both her or his growth and the growth of the singer-actor. The singer-actor in turn will grow in proportion to the energy given to the training situation.

4. The Performer as Explorer

Improvisation is a wonderful *opportunity* to take risks, and precisely because of these risks and the intense commitment required it is a superb exercise tool. In overcoming the inhibitions blocking improvisatory skills, it is often useful to find metaphors for the process. For example, one might compare the act of improvisation to the making of new maps. Each role is like a new character-map to be explored as thoroughly and passionately as possible. Our own map is created by the decisions we make as we move through life. We turn left to avoid a confrontation, we slow down and stop as we approach a decision, we backtrack when we see an accident, we twist and turn our way through difficult times, and so forth.

Each choice we make changes our route slightly, and creates a different path from that anyone else would take under the same circumstances.

Every performer knows that he has far more routes on his character-map than are ever exhibited in public. Those of us who feel the need to explore these other possibilities are often drawn into theater, either as performer-explorers, observer-explorers, or as assistants to the explorers. To play a dramatic character is to explore another route on the character-map, and the depth of the exploration is dependent upon the explorer. The playwright gives us a rough guide to the terrain. Sometimes it seems to be an inconsistent, incomplete map, sometimes the terrain seems arid, uninteresting, sometimes it is frightening, haunted. But the point is that the performer *also* creates the map and the terrain; however uninteresting the playwright's map may seem, it is within the performer's power to make it vivid, to fill the vacant areas with beauty.

This process of exploring a new character-map does not necessarily require a playwright. We all make our own maps as we live. Although it is said that the basic routing of our map is established by the time we are six, one can make new routes running parallel to the main route that explore different personal territories. This is improvisation. Using the image of a personal life path, we can see that the playwright's path and our own path—the route *we* would follow under the circumstances set up by the playwright— will coincide in some places and diverge in others. But we must do whatever is necessary to clear new personal paths which follow that of the playwright. It is important that we recognize a simple truth as we do this: all routes are possible and we are limited in the new routes we choose only by our lack of willingness, courage, or new capabilities. Our own route may be a comfortable, concrete thruway, and the jungles on either side may be so thick and terrify-ing that we simply cannot find the strength to leave the main route. But cutting a single tree as we leave our well-traveled thruway may reveal a path we did not know was there. The greatest difficulty is in taking the first step off that basic route, but once taken we learn that it is not only less terrifying than we had imagined, it is usually exhilarating.

Improvisation says, "Make your own new maps, create new paths. You may come to some peculiar and unsettling territory, but you will have experiences that you could have in no other way. Do not insist that the paths you create be as paved and easygoing as either the one you left or those created by librettists and composers. You may blaze only a few modest footpaths at first, but this does not make your efforts any less valid or meaningful."

5. Improvisation: The Ultimate Integrator of Opposites

It is important that we find a new relationship between human experience on the one hand, and plays, operas, and improvisation on the other. Anyone, properly prepared and properly challenged, is capable of a more integrated, creative, and wide-ranging performance than might be imagined. The exercises in this book include a series of challenges to the singer-actor that are steps on the path to a demanding but supremely rewarding goal: the fusion of the person and the performer, the integration of the creative and the re-creative energies of the singer-actor. The answer to the question "Why improvisation?" is that it is the best possible means for unifying several key music-theater opposites: the self and the character, the creator and the re-creator, the memorized and the spontaneous. Improvisation also gets at a problem created by the nature of singer training. The subjugation of singers to the demands of authority has been one of our themes from the beginning. Singers are told what to do, precisely how to do it, and are drilled by taskmasters of every variety from the beginning. In the course of this perhaps necessarily authoritarian training young singers seem to lose touch with their *own* impulses. The best of them regain the connection instinctively, but they are rare and even they should not be forced to struggle for the very freedom of personal expression which makes them exceptional. The others, the vast majority, do *not* break free, because they have been so eager to please their teachers and have been so reinforced in this by the educational system of threats and psychological punishment for not making the "correct" response that their own feelings and responses are repressed.[4] The solution is not to omit part of the necessary musical training, but to supplement and coordinate it with appropriate music-theater training (including work with improvisation) aimed at developing the singer's unused personal resources. In this way the musical techniques and external discipline can be augmented by a flexible set of human responses and interactions. In dealing with music-theater, we must always keep in mind the total instrument: the voice, the mind, and the body. Although we may isolate one element for special exercise, the final goal is always better coordination between words/action/music and voice/body/mind.

Since discipline and technique are already emphasized strongly in singer training, we use their opposites — freedom and emotion — as the focal point of many of the exercises, asking the singer-actor to draw upon personal resources to fulfill them. Each successfully negotiated exercise will be a miniature act of music-theater, maximizing the stretch of opposites inherent in the form.

Almost every music-theater goal can best be obtained by routes that get to their destination by seeming to go elsewhere. Using such indirect routes, we avoid the interference of overly conscious self-scrutinization. For example, there are no exercises devised specifically for achieving freedom from inhibition. Instead, many of the exercises are based on improvisation, which demands freedom from inhibition by its very nature, and thus works toward the goal indirectly. Instead of saying, "let's be free" (which, like asking an actor to be funny, is sure to be counterproductive), we say, "let's make up this or that action;" concentration on that process automatically bestows freedom.

This can be stated as a general rule in dealing with music-theater problems: to tap personal energies, avoid the direct route, because self-consciousness about goals will tend to interfere with progression toward those goals. One does not feel an emotion by trying to feel it — one concentrates on the sensory elements connected with a potential feeling (whether the sensory elements are remembered experiences or the immediate use of physical or vocal techniques) and the feeling comes of its own accord. One doesn't concentrate by trying to concentrate — one thinks about a given image or idea as specifically as possible, and concentration is the by-product. One doesn't achieve style by stylizing — one executes specific vocal and physical tasks, and a specific style is the result. Focusing on results will almost always interfere with the result; result-thinking scuttles itself. The primary challenge in exercising the skills of music-theater is to find tasks that are specific and that allow us to concentrate on process rather than product, to find tasks that exercise the skills *inadvertently*, to find *ways of approaching* our goals that allow their achievement without thinking about those goals. Improvisation is a prime means of achieving that kind of here-and-now thinking, and for that reason alone is a useful base for our exercising for music-theater, along with its more traditional opposite, the memorized score.

PART THREE
Exercising the Skills

*If our educational institutions and private teachers
cannot begin to integrate the acting and singing
abilities of their talented students, if the opera
theaters will not create special seminars of a studio
type with properly qualified instructors, then the
present level of interpretation will probably not be
raised within the forseeable future. The reason is
that a major portion of the time available for the
preparation of a production must be used for
elementary instruction, and only a small part can
be given to creative rehearsals.*

Walter Felsenstein

Chapter

8

The Basic Tools

A. Understanding, Commitment, and Growth

The exercises that follow cover the six areas of skill in order: energizing, concentrating, structuring, stylizing, imagining, and coordinating. In addition there are exercises in the four music-theater quadrants: spoken improvised, spoken memorized, sung improvised, and sung memorized. Groups will want to concentrate upon different quadrants, according to the interests and goals of the participants.

Whatever the plan, it is important that all participants understand clearly the structure and logic of the program. Many of the exercises are based upon improvisation and require unusual sensitivity and awareness. An understanding of the training rationale allows participants to give themselves more freely to what might otherwise seem to be a series of interesting but arbitrary exercises. Training that has an experimental flavor often encounters resistance: "This is all very fascinating, and I'm getting nice and sweaty, but what's the point of it?" Any member of the group, including the leader, should be able to give a straightforward answer to such questions. Each person involved should know where the exercises lead, beyond simply becoming a "better person," and should understand how every exercise in this book relates to an improved traditional performance. If this cannot be done, the exercise should be set aside, and new exercises found.

An understanding of the training rationale, furthermore, not only frees the psychological energies of the participants and allows them to commit themselves fully to the training, but it also gives them a good framework upon which to create new exercises of their own. Any exercise that involves one of the six areas of skill is related to the problems of music-theater performance, and it is important to discuss that relationship frequently. Making such connections between themselves and their performances, between their lives and their performances, between their exercises and their performances is a vital process for singer-actors.

This raises the issue of personal growth and the commitment required to attain that goal. Unless one has a firm dedication to personal growth as a performer, the whole training process can be impeded. The fact that the growth is personal suggests part of the problem: it is easy to take analysis and criticism as a personal attack rather than as a gift that helps one grow. Emphasizing the idea of description rather than criticism is helpful in such a situation. It is not unlike the problem of style. Personal growth can be described as the acquisition of a greater stylistic range in personal and performance behavior. To do this one must first find out what one's present style *is*, then decide what one wants it to *become*, and finally take the steps necessary to get from one state to the other. Each performer should constantly engage in self-analysis with the descriptive assistance of the rest of the group. Descriptive feedback about how and what one *is* leads in turn to the recognition that aspects of one's personal approach to performance need to change, whether by elimination of inhibitions or by mastery of more complex physical and emotional interrelations. But it requires time to develop such freedom and openness in the face of criticism.

A judicious blend of positive reinforcement and specific description is needed from the very beginning. For example, if one says, "she made a choice of keeping the volume low," rather than "she was too soft," or "she has an exciting voice—I would like to feel and see even more physical involvement with the emotion I hear," rather than "she looks rather wooden as she sings," the criticism is made on a more objective level and the potential pain is avoided. Eventually the group will be able to isolate and discuss the smallest details of one another's habits and mannerisms without traumatizing the person under discussion. To reach this state requires a period of careful positive reinforcement. But as one performer said after what he felt was an overly protective discussion, "If a person has difficulty accepting criticism, prolonged positive reinforcement only postpones and renders more difficult the inevitable confrontation with the truth, thus delaying growth." On the other hand, there is absolutely no substitute for a dash of confidence when it comes to performance growth. So, like everything else we have discussed, this topic boils down to the balancing of opposites: encouragement vs. criticism, or positive reinforcement vs. negative evaluation, or you're OK vs. you need to change.

Once one has realized the necessity for change, one is confronted with the problem of making the change happen, of *growing*. Realizations can be very exciting, and they are relatively easy to come by, but the stimulation of a realization can often be mistaken for growth itself. Unless there is the difficult, sustained work necessary to change habits and mannerisms, months may pass, and growth *in actual performance* (as opposed to class exercise) will not have been achieved. It is well to remind ourselves frequently that while realization is a good thing, it is not actual growth; that our minds and bodies must practice daily the new habits and ideas we wish to acquire, just as we practice daily to acquire new vocal habits and ways of being.

In beginning this self and group analysis, it is often useful for performers to evaluate themselves. The following questions may be useful.

1. What aspects of your performance ability would you like to improve? Are there things you would like to change?

2. How do you see yourself as a performer? Strengths, weaknesses?

3. How would you describe your future career if it went exactly as you would wish?

4. What do you need to do in order for your description in #3 to happen?

5. Are you more comfortable as a singer or as an actor? Do you know why? Would you like to change this?

6. Do you enjoy acting while you sing, or would you rather give recitals and concerts? Why? Would you like to change this?

7. Do you feel good about your physical way of being on stage? Explain.

8. Do you feel good (free) about your emotional self on stage? Explain.

9. Do you feel that your singing technique is moving in the right direction? Does it relate well to #7 and #8?

10. Are you able to take risks in rehearsal situations, i.e., are you able to attempt potentially exciting things which might make you look bad if unsuccessful? If not, would you like to be able to do so?

11. How do you feel you take criticism? How much positive reinforcement is necessary for you to feel OK about yourself?

12. If you could play any operatic character you wished, who would it be? Why?

13. Are you able to keep working at things which do not show immediate results, but which you know are necessary?

14. How would you describe the qualities and attitudes of a teacher who would do you, personally, the most good? Be specific about the demands, the ways of work that you think would help you most.

15. You are a critic: describe yourself as a performer as objectively and in as much detail as possible.
(Add appropriate questions as you see fit.)

Since much of what will be accomplished depends upon the feedback process, it is useful for each performer to observe two other performers *carefully* and *minutely*, in and out of class, at performances, during rehearsals, on the street, in order to get a clear picture of the style of those performers, how they function physically and emotionally, and what habits, mannerisms, and tensions stand in the way of either stylistic growth or better performance. Each member of the group should keep a dossier on the observees so that their observations can be passed on to the individuals to aid stylistic and personal growth.

B. Gibberish: Communication through Music Alone

The two exercise tools that should be acquired at the first training session are sound and motion, and gibberish. Because both tools are based on free improvisation, they can be used to exercise any skill involved in music-theater without the use of memorized material. Both of them can involve singing, both can be used to create scenes, and both can be adapted for exercise in all six areas of skill.

Gibberish is communication with sound that has no familiar verbal content. It is made-up language that communicates in the *way* it is said, that is, with its *music*. A person using gibberish to communicate is doing so solely with music, with the *sounds* of his "words" rather than with their denotative content. Recognizable words may occasionally be used (any possible sound is probably a "word" in someone's language) but the communication is a syntax of music rather than a syntax of verbal logic. Gibberish should always *sound* as if it makes sense, and if it does, of course it will. It is a kind of oral Rorschach test: those exercising with gibberish reveal a great deal about themselves and their relationship to the word-making, correct-answer demands of education and the world. This is a crucial area for young singers, and a source of some striking hangups. Some performers, in fact, cannot at first utter a "word" of gibberish; they are so afraid of being "wrong" that having to make a choice where there is no right or wrong is petrifying. Eventually, of course, they make the step (all it takes is a few examples from their fellow students) and the first attack begins on twelve to sixteen years of schooling in verbal "correctness." The experience is invariably both strange and liberating. There is nothing for singer-actors to fall back upon. They have been told what to do all their lives, but now there are no stock phrases, no correct responses, nor any route that "should" be followed. In short, gibberish is a kind of musical improvisation in which the medium and the message merge completely.

Gibberish is easily introduced. With the group standing in a circle, a conversation of non-verbal sound is passed from person to person. It goes without saying that the group leader should be able to initiate any of the exercises, and that one of his or her tasks is to overcome the inhibitory "Will I succeed? Will I look good or bad?" questions, which must be discarded by everyone concerned. The first plunge is the most difficult, and once the right/wrong syndrome is stilled, the free play concept is both stimulating and gratifying. The group should be encouraged to use a wide range of sounds (the gibberish "vocabulary") rather than remaining with one basic sound. For example, "fa la na va ga na" is not as interesting a language as "fesh nyrk oshg gilxmen sochtis frauv fastoli." It should be continually emphasized, however, that *there is no right or wrong in any of the exercises; there are only descriptions.* There is more or less complexity, simplicity, loudness, quietness, control, diffusion, speed, quantity, variety, etc. etc. All combinations are worth examining, and the point should be to expand our personal resources, our ability to draw upon a greater vocal, physical, and emotional vocabulary for communication purposes.

C. Communication Play: The Sound and Motion

To play with sound and motion (the basic materials of communication), to approach the state of Homo Ludens—man the player—is to touch the origin of all artistic effort. It is the source to which artists must constantly return for the refreshment and the remembrance of what it is they are engaged in: creative play. The world works its will upon us all by discipline, regimentation, and rules, and nowhere in the arts more effectively than in the training of singers. Although they have learned to play music, they should also have learned to play *with* music. As they begin to explore the possibilities of playing with language, they also begin to learn about the relationship of music to language, and about music itself as a means of wordless communication. In the second exercise, sound and motion, the students begin to explore the possibility of physical play in combination with sound play.

The sound and motion exercise works as follows.[1] All participants stand in a circle facing in. One person moves into the center of the circle making a repeating abstract sound accompanied by a repeating abstract physical movement, and from there moves to one of the other participants. The second person mirrors both the action and the sound of the first person several times and moves past the first person into the center of the circle. She or he then transforms both the action and the sound into a new repeating pattern, and moves to a third person who mirrors it in turn, moves into the circle, transforms the action, and passes it on to a fourth person. This process continues until everyone in the circle has participated.

When the final participant has completed the transformation, everyone moves to that person and contributes a complementary sound and motion pattern so that the group forms an organic whole. This group organism crescendos or decrescendos to a conclusion. It is possible, of course, to go around the group several times before the conclusion.

Another way of leading into sound and motion is to begin with a call and echo game. One person makes a sound, the rest of the group echoes it. The next person makes a different sound, and again everyone else echoes it. This continues around the circle. The second time around, each person adds a physical action to his or her sound which everyone duplicates while echoing the sound. From that point the step to an actual sound and motion is a simple one.

Sound and motion is an excellent warmup, an inhibition breaker, and an ensemble promoting exercise, in addition to its use in exercising the specific skills of music-theater. Most importantly, however, it promotes the idea of free creative play with the body and the voice, which is essential to our work. Freeing the performer from rigid ideas about what performance can be and making new acceptance boundaries for physical and vocal action is an integral part of the training process. The human mind is limited only by what it conceives as possible or acceptable. Music-theater form encompasses varieties of experience we have only begun to explore. But the form can only expand to fulfill its possibilities when the performer is prepared to do likewise.

The first group session can deal with more than just the tools of gibberish and sound and motion. Since both exercises deal with the concepts of ensemble work and solo work, these concepts can also be introduced as part of the basic structure of the program.

D. Altering Time: Individually and Together

Opera, as we have observed, has as a basic convention the fluctuation of time flow, which creates the greatest difficulties for the singer-actor at the stop-time, lyric expansion end of the continuum. It is for this reason that the following organizational plan is suggested, based on opposites we will call solo and ensemble. It is rare in the theater to find an actor alone on the stage for more than a minute or two at a time; the total solo time in an evening of theater would be five to ten minutes at most, and only then in a highly stylized play. It is even more unusual to find a situation in theater where two or more people speak simultaneously for any length of time. Both of these events, of course, are not only commonplace in opera, they are the very backbone of the form. It is from these opposites that a structure for each training session can be evolved. A general plan would look like this:

Each day, both ensemble and solo exercises may be performed in the skill area being covered. As the group moves through the six skill areas, there is a constant interplay between solo and ensemble exercises. We will elaborate on the overall structure of the training further along, but for now let us suggest a plan for the first few sessions.

E. Introductions and Precipitations

The following outline suggests a series of exercises that may be used as a sequence for the first several sessions. Some exercises can be skipped, of course, and some may not be reached for several months. The sequence merely indicates order of precedence and the group should adapt the exercises and the overall plan to their own needs and create their own variations to serve the situation. Often, for example, one can use an advanced exercise out of sequence if a group shows special capabilities.

ECHO GAME—SOUND ONLY: Go around the circle several times, increasing the length of the sounds each time.
ECHO GAME—SOUND AND MOTION: Each person adds a physical action to the sound. Go around several times, increasing the length of the statement.
MIRROR EXERCISE: One person mirrors the physical action of

another. Concentrate on the relationship, not on fooling the other person. The instructor should signal a shift in initiators every so often, but the mirroring action should not be interrupted.

GIBBERISH PASSING: Go around the circle several times, encourage scene development and continuing participation: a person who has already passed the gibberish idea on might make another comment, join the conversation as it continues up ahead.

MIRROR AND GIBBERISH CONVERSATIONS: Two people engage in a gibberish conversation while doing the mirror exercise, and the instructor should signal a shift in the initiators every so often.

RITUAL DUETS: Two people face each other, *look* at each other. (Stress is placed on the looking because of the common occurrence on operatic stages of "unseeing eyes:" the glaze that passes over a singer's eyes, and results in lack of contact with the other singers. Mention this to any group of opera singers and there will invariably be the laughter of recognition.) Together these two begin moving and making abstract sounds in any way they wish. The purpose is for the two of them to create a structure of sound and motion, to "play" with the materials of sound and motion, and to interrelate in so doing. This exercise can be used as a basis for future exercise and is a wonderful substitute for social dancing. Again, there are no rules, rights or wrongs, except that the two people should be creating the sound/motion structure together.

PRETEND MIRROR OR MIRROR-MINUS-ONE: Individuals *pretend* they have been given a mirror, and proceed through the mirroring of the action they imagine they are being given. They add a gibberish conversation with the same imaginary person, so that they are mirroring an imaginary image and conversing with that same imaginary image.

RITUAL SOLOS: "Pretend that you are doing a ritual duet with an imaginary partner." This is similar to the pretend mirror, except that the actions are a bit freer, and the sounds should be more abstract than the imitation of a naturalistic conversation that is usually implied by a gibberish conversation.

SPONTANEOUS DIALOGUE: Two people begin talking about a topic assigned by someone else in the circle. For example, another person in the group will say "pollution" and the two conversationalists begin talking about that subject until the instructor signals a halt. The only rule is to keep going until told to stop.

SPONTANEOUS MONOLOGUE: One person is given a topic by the person opposite in the circle, and talks about it until signaled to stop. Again, the only rule is to keep going.

GIBBERISH IMPROVISED SINGING: Using gibberish, each person begins singing, just a phrase at first, then passing it on. Go around twice (or more) increasing the length of the phrase or singing two phrases. This is a difficult breakthrough for some singers, but again, there is no right or wrong. Any melody is OK, particularly in light of contemporary views about music.

SPONTANEOUS TOPIC SINGING: One person is given a topic by someone else in the circle and begins immediately singing about it, improvising the music. The instructor should signal when the singer may cease. The only rule, as always, is to do it and keep going until signaled to stop.

Some general notes about these exercises might be useful. One should *avoid planning ahead* in the sound and motion exercise and in all of the improvisatory exercises. Anxiety will tend to drive the performer into preplanning unless it is consciously avoided. We have all been planning in advance for upward of 15 years, and that habit is not easy to break. We should encourage ourselves to think *as* we do something, not before we do it. We can encourage ourselves, for example, to eliminate pauses when we are given a topic or a task on which to improvise, and to keep the energy moving in the call and echo exercises. We should try to think *with* our voice and body, not separately from them; we should mold the structure *as* we proceed, in the process of doing it; we should live and think on our feet, in action. There is nothing right or wrong except hesitation-for-thought as we work on these exercises. If we think and then do, we automatically criticize what we are doing in the light of what we previously thought and intended. But if we think *as* we do, there is no space for the little critical demon to inhibit the action or remove it one step from reality.

F. The Overall Plan

Following the introductory sessions, ensemble and solo exercises can be practiced in each of the six areas of skill. The suggested plan is to go through the skill sequence three times, each time on an increased level of music-theater integration.

ROUND ONE: The first round will be improvised, concentrating on exercises not requiring scored music. The singer-actor will learn the nature of improvisation and personal freedom while exercising the skills and disciplines of music-theater. This will probably be the shortest of the three rounds. Because there is no framework whatsoever beyond the exercises themselves, and because what is done depends upon the creativity of the person, this level is particularly difficult for those who need the security of planning—who are fearful of their own impulses. It is here that people will have "bad days" when they feel "private" and endangered by sharing. Some may hide behind various masks and tensions for weeks or months. But the purpose of the training on level one is to ferret out these very masks and tensions and allow the participants to function on and with their own impulses, to use themselves as freely and naturally as possible. Until one is able to deal with that level, to "be there" totally as oneself, the final combination of oneself and the character can never be achieved.

ROUND TWO: The second round applies the exercise techniques learned in Round One to scored and memorized material, both arias and ensembles. The performer is returned to the security of a planned structure. Exercises that demand total creative participation are also suggested, but there is always memorized material sustaining it. This level exercises the techniques of music-theater more strenuously than will ever be the case in actual performance.

ROUND THREE: The third round will combine the exercises of the first two rounds, interweaving the improvised and the memorized in as complex a way as possible. Here, part of the security is removed, and the singers are placed on the continuum between improvisation and memorization. At times the scored material will sustain them, at times they will be on their own; but as they return to the memorized material, the personal creativity of improvisation will continue to relate to their performance. Here is the reconciliation of the two levels. The self is fully available and the character is fully available; each grows with and through the other. The human energies become free and available for use by the composer-created character and situation energies, and these in turn expand and enlarge the human energies.

Thus the structure of the training period involves the gradual synthesis of opposites we have been urging from the beginning: free improvisation, memorized score work, and finally, the combination of the two in a unified act of music-theater, in which the sense of spontaneity and discipline, of self and musician/character, of words/action and music, of music and theater, become one.

The group is urged to sample the exercises freely, to move at whatever pace or in whatever sequence seems desirable. The preceding plan is only one possibility among many.

At this point, the group may proceed directly to the exercises on page 138, returning to Chapter 9 whenever desired. In that chapter, lists of physical, emotional, and vocal categories are included to help increase the singer-actor's awareness, and to stimulate the creative thinking process. Arousing one's creative energies is a function of question asking; question asking is a function of description; and each list contains descriptions of different ways of using the body, the feelings, and the voice. The lists include use of space, physical masks, centers of energy, gestural characteristics, facial masks, and attitudes, moving from the largest external manifestations of energy to the subtlest internal impulses.

Chapter

9

Energizing Primers

A. Uses of Space and Movement Catalysts

The suggestions in this chapter should be used to help the student think and communicate *with* the body, the gestures, the face, the emotions, and the voice. But as one student executes the assignments, the group should concentrate on what *actually* happens (as opposed to what is *supposed* to have happened). Each new technical challenge to the performer will reveal a different set of limitations and tensions to be overcome. It is particularly important that the tensions—which are inevitably associated with the use of new techniques and the release of new energies—be pinpointed immediately and eliminated. As in singing, one of the most difficult distinctions to make in movement is between intensity and tension. All the techniques suggested in the energizing categories will release greater energy; the unfamiliarity of this energy will often bring on tension either as a means of seeming to motivate the energy or as a means of repressing it. To allow the additional energy to flow freely, the tensions, however small or hidden, must be diagnosed and eliminated.

Use of Space Categories

big	or	small
rounded	or	angular
fast	or	slow

123

smooth-continuous	or	jerky-discontinuous
flowing	or	staccato
relaxed	or	intense

Movement Catalysts

ambling	drooping	lifting	secluding	swaying
ascending	dwelling	loosening	shimmering	swerving
awakening	dying	lunging	shrinking	swishing
balancing	embracing	lurching	shuffling	tapping
bouncing	flexing	opening	skating	tipping
bounding	flopping	painting	skipping	tossing
bowing	freezing	perching	slamming	tracking
careening	galloping	plodding	sliding	trembling
cavorting	gamboling	plunging	slinking	tumbling
circling	gliding	pouncing	slipping	turning
clapping	grooving	preening	slithering	twisting
closing	groping	primping	slouching	uprearing
clumping	grunting	reeling	slumming	walking
conducting	heaving	rescuing	smashing	washing
contorting	hobbling	resolving	spinning	wasting
crawling	hopping	retreating	sprawling	watching
creeping	hovering	rolling	spreading	waving
crouching	hustling	rubbing	springing	whirling
darting	jiggling	sashaying	staggering	wiggling
daubing	jiving	sauntering	stalking	wrenching
descending	jogging	scampering	standing	writhing
destroying	jumping	schlumping	streaking	yawning
dipping	kissing	sculpting	stretching	
diving	leaping	searching	surveying	

B. Centers of Energy: Physical Masks

One's center of energy is largely a matter of mental focus. It can range from a point just above one's head through any part of the body—head, chin, shoulders, sternum, pelvis, stomach, knees, ankles, toes—to a point in the earth below one's feet. Locating each other's center of energy is a good observational exercise for the whole group. It is important, however, that when performers attempt to shift their centers of energy, they let it be a mental process, a mental focus, and not a physical adjustment. The mind, not the muscles, must do the job. If the center of energy is to be in the knees, the performer will be tempted to *show* this, to prove it by exaggerating knee movements. This is not dissimilar to what we call indicating in acting. As we discussed above, indicating is caused by a fear that what is happening will not be communicated, and so the suspicious performer does more than is necessary, usually by displaying tension in the facial or bodily muscles or the vocal mechanism. Wherever the tension manifests itself, the group must point it out.

The corollary to eliminating tensions is encouraging trust of the mind's power. It often seems as if most of the acting and/or vocal problems one encounters come directly from either trying to do something the way you think someone else wants it done, or from trying to make a pleasant or appropriate sound, or from trying to look like something in someone else's judgmental head. We should be encouraging maximum trust in *our own* processes, in *our own* minds. We must persuade ourselves of this truth: that thought process, unimpeded by physical, vocal, or mental tension, will do everything that is needed. Our task as performers is to make the body, the emotions, and the voice the flexible, unguarded, free-flowing tools of the mind. The article of faith is: what the mind can conceive will be created so long as tension does not interfere with the process.

The following list of physical masks to play with is by no means complete. The group is encouraged to come up with its own set of masks.

raised shoulders	nervous hands	wobbling hips
splayed fingers	sagging buttocks	knock knees
asymmetrical body	flabby thighs	anxious elbows
ramrod spine	thrust pelvis	tired stomach
angled head	tilted shoulders	exploding armpits

In working with any masks, there are two important points to keep in mind. All masks should be worn with as little tension as possible, using only the energy necessary to let the mask flow. A sense of movement within the mask is also useful, no matter how slight or slow-moving that movement may be. In addition, the masks should be related to either a character or a situation. Because most of the masks will be used in the context of a specific scene and character, this is an automatic requirement. Nonetheless, the process must be stressed if the use of any of these techniques is to become something more than technique. The feedback process between mask and meaning is as important as that between technique and feeling.

C. Gestural Concepts

The use of gesture is one of the singer-actor's greatest challenges. Because of the extension-of-time problem—which the focus concept solves for the face and eyes—the use of gestural space is much more difficult than in straight theater. The use of gesture must relate to the musical extension of time as specifically as does focus. But focus can be achieved and maintained with the eyes alone (omitting for the moment the necessity of total physical and emotional commitment to that focus); the arms, however, are larger, more conspicuous, and much more difficult to deal with than the eyes. "What do I do with my hands?" is the question most commonly heard from singer-actors in training situations.

We get at this problem in the same way we approach other technical problems: by asking questions. *What* does a gesture do? *How* does it do what it does? How *long* does a gesture last?

The first question can be answered in several ways. A gesture can say, "Here I am," or, relating to one's focus-image, "There it is," or, relating to the ideal audience or to another person, "There you are." One might classify these as *indicating* gestures, or gestures that relate to the object of focus, whether that object is one's self, one's focus-image, the ideal audience, or another character. Palms open and out, arms held out from the sides say, "Here I am." Palms up and reaching toward one's focus-image say, "There it is." Palms up or down, reaching toward the audience or another person say, "There you are."

A gesture can also show a *reaction* to the object of focus. It can say, "how awful," "how wonderful," "stay away," "come to me," and variations of both positive and negative reactions. The melodramatic, back-of-the-hand-to-the-head gesture, which says something like, "God, how terrible!" is an obvious reacting gesture. Those who are worried about formal Delsartean posing should remember that the second question — *how* a gesture is executed — determines the validity of any gesture. There is no conceivable gesture that cannot be made into a vital, believable statement, given the proper execution. Our task at the moment, however, is to find out *what* a gesture can say, not how well it can say it. There is clearly an infinite variety of reacting gestures, from the simple arms-at-the-sides-making-of-a-fist-in-anger, to an exultant, whirling, reaching-for-the-heavens. Our purpose is not to define the many possibilities, but to raise the singer-actor's awareness of the potential gestural functions available. Finally, a gesture can say something about the *character* of the person making the gesture. A hand on the hip, a finger stroking the cheek or scratching the head, hands caressing the thighs, or arms folded across the chest all help *describe* the character and situation of the person making the gesture. Self-descriptive gestures can involve the whole body, the shoulders, the head, the hips, or the legs individually or together. Shoulders slanting to one side, pelvis tilted, total weight on one leg, a foot with toes pointed up, and other uses of the body can be part of the self-descriptive gesture.

Thus we have three basic functions a gesture can fulfill: indicating, reacting, and describing. These three functions can combine in various ways. An indicative gesture can also describe what is being indicated; for example, while singing about one's beloved (a fairly common aria idea), one can make a caressing motion which describes the image as well as indicating its presence. A reactive gesture can describe one's character in addition to showing one's reaction: clutching the head with great energy in response to bad news makes a different statement about the character than does a quick, controlled touching of the forehead. Similarly, one can indicate an idea, or someone else, or the audience as a part of the gesture: pointing a finger with great energy at any of those objects of focus not only indicates them, but defines the quality of our reaction to them as well; an energized, pointing finger, for example, may convey a touch of hostility.

With regard to our second question, *how* does a gesture work, the following list may suggest some possible answers.

gestures can be

smooth	or	staccato		rounded	or	angular
large	or	small		fast	or	slow
expansive	or	tentative		open	or	closed
flowing	or	jerky				

above the midsection	or	below the midsection
full arm oriented	or	hand-wrist oriented

and they can be described in any number of ways:

dabbing	twisting	flicking	squeezing
wrenching	caressing	chopping	punching
flitting	floating	flailing	nudging
skipping	pressing	jabbing	etc.

Both lists are incomplete, and the group as well as the leader should search for additional verbal stimulants to the gestural process. Any gesture can be made using any of the preceding descriptions. Each description contains many different possible meanings, but here as elsewhere the rule holds: any external techniques can be connected to any internal feeling; it all depends upon the imagination and flexibility of the performer.

The third question, how *long* should a gesture last?, is crucial to the problem of music-theater. As a general rule, it should relate to the musical and verbal phrasing. One should not ordinarily drop a gesture in the middle of a musical phrase; but there are times when a distinctly naturalistic throwaway gesture can be used to depart from the musical letter of the law. These, however, are exceptions to one of the basic principles of music-theater: when in doubt, always use the music to help make physical and emotional choices.

A common problem in the use of gesture is our old enemy, tension. Instinctively, many singers sense the necessity of sustaining the gestural energy in response to the music. At the same time, they do not have the freedom to commit themselves to a full gestural statement. So they end up with a sustained half-gesture which defeats both purposes and neither makes a statement nor structures it. Moments for gestural *release* must be found to avoid this sustained tension. The condition of gestural release might be defined as a relaxed but ready state of the arms—no tension in fingers or wrists or elbows or shoulders, but a readiness to respond to and flow with the gestural impulse. The gestural release point will vary with the style, of course, with an eighteenth-century release point differing from a twentieth-century naturalistic release point. It will also vary with individual style, but it must not involve a sense of held tension or an inability to flow.

Gestural freedom is difficult to achieve. Many singers, having been told that the only good gesture is no gesture, allow the hands to hang freely at the sides. Singer-actors should certainly be able to sing as long as desired from the gestural release position. But just as certainly singer-actors should also be able to use gesture maximally if they or the director so desire. And the capacity to *not*-gesture with vitality depends upon the capacity to gesture with freedom. Conversely, one can only gesture well if one is free to *not*-gesture. Vital repose is a function of one's capacity to move; vital movement is a function of one's capacity to be still. Out of the gestural release flows the gesture; out of the gesture flows the gestural release.

D. Facial Releasing

We have discussed the difference between facial mask-making and indicating (mugging). There are two functions of the facial mask-exercises: the exercises make singer-actors aware of and able to relax those tensions which have come to be associated with the act of singing. In addition, they make singer-actors aware of and able to relax habitual facial tensions that are used to repress the open expression of feeling, a repression that is often encouraged by the highly disciplined nature of their vocal and musical training.

To put it simply: there are no facial tensions necessary to the act of singing. I have known numerous instances of singers who were not hired for a role precisely because they had excessive facial tensions that had become for them part of the act of singing. The rule can not be repeated too often: there is no such thing as useful tension: intensity, yes, flowing muscular effort, yes, but not sustained tension which stops process or is disconnected from process.

Every singer-actor has moments on stage when she or he becomes aware of facial tension from smiling or frowning in a way that is unnatural or that has been held without release or flow. Every teacher or director is familiar with the deadpan singer-actor who conceals emotion. Both are evidence of the problems of using the face, the greatest single communicator the singer-actor possesses besides the voice.

We will approach habitual tension problems from two angles: we will attempt to release the tension and let the process flow, and we will extend the tension in an extreme manner. The most difficult thing about habitual tension is that it resides just below the threshold of awareness; it is a habit, and a habit must be recognized before it can be discarded. Sometimes an acute observer can spot a low-grade tension habit and call it to the performer's attention in a way that allows its release. At other times, however, the tension has become so much a part of the performer's way of being that it is not detected until an extension of energy is called for. Then, under the increased pressure, tensions pop out and can be analyzed and released. The energizing provided by music-theater exercises is an excellent way to diagnose and release such tensions.

It is important to watch the performer as a person as well as a performer, for it is in the movement between the two roles that one can spot the adjustments that lead to performance tensions. Not that there should not be a difference between the two modes —between everyday life and music-theater performance—and not that we are disinterested in extensions of energy and expression beyond their everyday levels. That is precisely what we *are* interested in, but the low-grade tensions and performance tics that one picks up in moving from life to performance will stifle a genuinely energized performance. If a low-grade tension is associated in any way with performance expression, any attempt to increase expressive power will automatically be connected with and cut off by increasing tensions. As mentioned previously, one must be able to isolate the facial musculature from the act of singing. If there is any connection between a facial tension, such as raised eyebrows, and the act of singing, the muscles involved in that tension will be incapable of accompanying the movement of the voice through say, a coloratura passage. At the same time the singer will find it difficult to release the tension, because adopting it in the first place created the sense that it is necessary to the act of singing. The face must be responsive to the emotional event and not to any tensions connected with the singing process, *except* as the heightened energies of relaxed singing vitalize the emotional demands of the event. The use of mask mirror exercises helps develop this ability to isolate the face and the vocal process. Once this capability is acquired, we can proceed to the more difficult task of playing the emotions of the scene which can now flow freely, rather than connecting automatically with the discarded vocal-facial tension hookup.

Some suggested facial masks:

facial screams	face masks: gargoyles
facial widening	animals
asymmetrical faces	primitive masks
facial compression	caricatures of real people

E. Attitudes

The following list of attitudes is intended to stimulate the imagination of the singer-actor. The attitudes are not blanks to be filled correctly or to be "graded." Whatever they release by way of stimulus is useful. If one thing has become evident in working with singer-actors, it is that *any* kind of energy is better than no energy; the more specific that energy is, the better. In demonstrating the use of arbitrary attitudes for opera educators from all over the country, several singers drew random attitudes to play while singing arias. They carried out the assignments with convincing skill, even though most of the attitudes were contrary to the standard interpretation of the arias. Although these attitudes were given sense by the performers, an educator in the audience asked the singer-actors if they didn't think that playing the "wrong" attitude was harmful to them. With no coaching a performer replied, "When you are sad, you often think of how happy you used to be, which makes the feelings of the actual situation even more powerful by contrast. And if you think a bit, you find that almost any attitude can be made to work. So rather than being harmful, it makes you think more clearly about the meaning of what you are doing and makes you more flexible." We should not train singer-actors to do it "right" or "wrong;" the directors and conductors for whom they will work can be trusted to make these decisions. Our aim must be to develop flexibility and energy in playing whatever is called for, as well as the ability to give themselves to any choice and make sense out of it. In most instances, we are not aware of the many emotional possibilities inherent in a dramatic moment, and by testing arbitrary choices we not only stretch our mental awareness of the additional possibilities, but exercise the imaginative flexibility necessary to incorporate such choices.

I have found it useful to write attitudes on separate cards so that they can be drawn arbitrarily. One can also give a singer-actor two cards and ask her or him to *blend* the two attitudes, or one card and blend the attitude with the attitude implied by the aria (which is what one does in playing arbitrarily chosen attitudes anyway).

The feedback relationship between these attitudes and one's personal experiences is obvious, and that feedback process should be exercised as often as possible. For example, to draw three attitudes and then consciously search for situations in which one has experienced the attitudes can be a useful exercise. On a more instinctive level, this is precisely what happens whenever one looks at an assigned attitude, say, "exultant," "melancholy," or "feverish," and then plays it. One immediately relates to how it felt at some time in the past. This process should be nurtured.

A Vocabulary of Attitudes

Attitudes chiefly rational: Explanatory, instructive, didactic, admonitory, condemnatory, indignant, puzzled, curious, wistful, pensive, thoughtful, preoccupied, deliberate, studied, candid, guileless, thoughtless, innocent, frank, sincere, questioning, uncertain, doubting, incredulous, critical, cynical, insinuating, persuading, coaxing, pleading, persuasive, argumentative, oracular.

Attitudes of pleasure: Peaceful, satisfied, contented, happy, cheerful, pleasant, bright, sprightly, joyful, playful, jubilant, elated, enraptured.

Attitudes of pain: Worried, uneasy, troubled, disappointed, regretful, vexed, annoyed, bored, disgusted, miserable, cheerless, mournful, sorrowful, sad, dismal, melancholy, plaintive, fretful, querulous, irritable, sore, sour, sulky, sullen, bitter, crushed, pathetic, tragical.

Attitudes of passion: Nervous, hysterical, impulsive, impetuous, reckless, desperate, frantic, wild, fierce, furious, savage, enraged, angry, hungry, greedy, jealous, insane.

Attitudes of self-control: Calm, quiet, solemn, serious, serene, simple, mild, gentle, temperate, imperturbable, nonchalant, cool, wary, cautious.

Attitudes of friendliness: Cordial, sociable, gracious, kindly, sympathetic, compassionate, forgiving, pitying, indulgent, tolerant, comforting, soothing, tender, loving, caressing, solicitous, accommodating, approving, helpful, obliging, courteous, polite, confiding, trusting.

Attitudes of unfriendliness: Sharp, severe, cutting, hateful, unsocial, spiteful, harsh, boorish, pitiless, disparaging, derisive, scornful, satiric, sarcastic, insolent, insulting, impudent, belittling, contemptuous, accusing, reproving, scolding, suspicious.

Attitudes of comedy: Facetious, comic, ironic, satiric, amused, mocking, playful, humorous, hilarious, uproarious.

Attitudes of animation: Lively, eager, excited, earnest, energetic, vigorous, hearty, ardent, passionate, rapturous, ecstatic, feverish, inspired, exalted, breathless, hasty, brisk, crisp, hopeful.

Attitudes of apathy: Inert, sluggish, languid, dispassionate, dull, colorless, indifferent, stoical, resigned, defeated, helpless, hopeless, dry, monotonous, vacant, feeble, dreaming, bored, blasé, sophisticated.

Attitudes of self-importance: Impressive, profound, proud, dignified, lofty, imperious, confident, egotistical, peremptory, bombastic, sententious, arrogant, pompous, stiff, boastful, exultant, insolent, domineering, flippant, saucy, positive, resolute, haughty, condescending, challenging, bold, defiant, contemptuous, assured, knowing, cocksure.

Attitudes of submission and timidity: Meek, shy, humble, docile, ashamed, modest, timid, unpretentious, respectful, apologetic, devout, reverent, servile, obsequious, groveling, contrite, obedient, willing, sycophantic, fawning, ingratiating, deprecatory, submissive, frightened, surprised, horrified, aghast, astonished, alarmed, fearful, terrified, trembling, wondering, awed, astounded, shocked, uncomprehending.

F. Spoken Energies

Although our work is aimed primarily at the *singing* actor, we must not forget that all actors make music, whether in the conventional sense of singing or in the use of spoken language. Every singer-actor must occasionally speak a line, and involvement with the music of language is an excellent way to heighten one's sensitivity to the expressive power of musical language. It can also lead to a greater understanding of the use of nuance in singing. One of Stanislavski's injunctions to singer-actors deals directly with words and music: "You must love words and know how to interweave them with the music. An actor is creative only when he uses sound to paint an image he visualizes. Make it a rule not to sing a single word without a purpose. Unless there is an organic relationship which binds the words to the music there is no art in opera."[1]

Actors dealing with language must be equally careful to find the naturalness in the techniques they use. When actors are first assigned the descriptive techniques listed below, they invariably get stuck in them. If they are told to use "high (pitch) and staccato" as a means of characterizing a speech, they will inevitably grab on to those two descriptions and not let go until the speech is done. I have a sort of Zen koan which I use continually in the first few weeks of training students in technique. If the assignment is "fast and high," the koan is "fast is not fast, high is not high," which means that no simplistic description is sufficient unto the meaning; within the context of fast and high one must find the lows and slows, the ebb and flow of life which makes it sound natural. We must hear that fast and high are predominant characteristics, but there must be sufficient variation to lend them life.

It is the same with every technique—"technique is not technique" —for one must always find the way of dealing with technique so that it sounds (or looks or feels) natural. Technique that feels like technique is flawed technique; if the technique is perfectly integrated with the meaning it will sound natural. If it does not sound natural, we should be able to diagnose it, analyze it, and describe the flaw in objective terms. This is much harder to do than it is to say, "feel it more," or "I didn't believe it," or "you've got to give us a sense of distrust." All these statements may or may not be helpful, but they avoid more difficult and more useful descriptions such as "you paused so often that it seemed to deny the energy of a person in that state of mind," or "you changed pitch process so often, without seeming to connect with the changes in the meaning of the words, that it was hard to follow," or "you stayed in one rhythm so long that it became monotonous and hard to understand."

The assignment of specific technique categories for spoken language is largely a diagnostic exercise: it tells the listener precisely which techniques give the speaker difficulties (assuming that the listener's ears have become sufficiently discriminating). One can then give the performers specific assignments to increase their flexibility and technical range. For this reason it is important that the performers carry out two steps in any technique assignment. They should execute the assignment — that is, that they do what is called for no matter how strange or unnatural it may feel — and they should make sense of the assignment, make it seem natural. The second step, of course, cannot be accomplished unless the first is executed. Our aim is to equip performers with the ability to *make sense of* or to make natural the use of any technique or combination of techniques they (or the director) desire. Only then are they artistically free — until then they are in partial bondage to their own limitations.

The list below includes a number of ways of describing the use of language. It can be used for exercise and diagnosis, or simply studied for heightened awareness of how language is used. We must become aware of how we use the language before we can expand our usage of it.

Language Categories

high	and	low	fast	and	slow
relaxed	and	intense	legato	and	staccato
continuous	and	discontinuous	loud	and	soft

Language can be colored in various ways; its *tone color* can change: nasal, hollow, pinched, booming, fluting, steely, reedy, breathy, phlegmy, guttural, bubbling, buzzing, etc.

Language can involve:

Significant pauses: Pauses that are consciously used for special emphasis, and not the unconscious dragging variety.

Sensual words: Words that are colored in special ways to make a point. If they are very low, at the bottom of one's range, we might call them "bumps;" if at the very top, with an upward, disappearing inflection we might call them "pops." All sensual words will use color devices in ways that help make the meaning of the word clear: a low, sensual, breathy sound for seductive purposes; a high, steely, ping for hostility, etc.

Nonverbal sounds: These are sounds that are not words, but that help to make the meaning of a statement clear. As an initial means of freeing the performer, it is useful to assign an arbitrary nonverbal sound made by another member of the group, and have the performer use it in a speech.

Language *must* involve:

Operative word choices: Operative words are simply those words that carry dominant meanings. We use them naturally in everyday life, but when performers first attempt to use them, they will treat such words all the same, use too many of them, or use them unnaturally. The listeners must be aware of the gap between technique and meaning when operative word exercises are performed, and help the performer find the way to a natural use of the technique. The operative words are a way of making the meaning clear, and the performer can only find them by understanding the *spoken* meaning (as opposed to the intellectual meaning) perfectly. The search for the operative words is really a search for the meaning of the speech.

Phrasing exercises: When dealing with the language of Shakespeare, we are forced to solve the problem of phrases that are longer than we are used to in everyday life. Any playwright who uses language in an extended, rhetorical way sets up many of the same time expansion problems we have encountered in music-theater. An experience that might take ten seconds becomes sixty seconds in the language of Shakespeare. As a result, much more variety and control of language is required, especially in the phrasing, which deals directly with the expansion of time. Naturalistic speaking will tend to cadence (a downward inflection that signifies the end of a thought) more often than can be permitted with a rhetorically oriented soliloquy. If the thought goes on for six lines, the actor cannot allow a full cadence until the end of that time. If he or she does (and it is one of the most common problems for the naturalistically oriented actor) the meaning will be betrayed. Making the phrasing *sound* as long as it *means* is our problem here.

Chapter
10

Round One — Improvised

Energizing

1. Warmups

Warmups for music-theater exercise have three basic functions which correspond to the word-action-music trilogy. The vocal, the physical, and the psychological processes each need a bit of stretching before they can move from the everyday, real-time oriented world to the world of music-theater where the ordinary rules of life, time, and behavior do not apply, and where vulnerability and commitment to unusual modes of behavior is a necessity. The purpose of warmups beyond "warming up" is to help the singer-actor make that transition.

To accomplish this, and to prepare the singer in each skill, variations on the gibberish and the sound and motion exercises are suggested, along with other pertinent games. Any of the gibberish exercises may be sung as well as spoken; this depends on the instructor's wishes and the skills of the group.

   a. Gibberish passed around the circle (see p. 114). Once the skill is established, attitudes may be added to the exercise (see p. 132 for suggestions).
   b. Gibberish conversations across the circle. The instructor signals the participants to start and stop, allowing ten to twenty seconds for each dialogue. Again, attitudes may be added to the basic exercise.
   c. Echo game (see p. 117). Once the basic echo game is established, attitudes can be added to the sound and motion combination. The rest of the group then mirrors the attitude as well. The imitators should mirror what they actually got from the initiator, and not expand upon the

138

suggestion, because the projective power is as important as the thing projected, and the initiator should be made aware of her or his projective power.

d. Sound and motion (see p. 116). Once the basic exercise is understood, attitudes may be added. The initiator focuses strongly upon the person to whom she or he will pass the attitude, sound, and motion; that person, of course, mirrors the attitude as well as the sound and motion, and transforms the attitude as well as the sound and motion before passing it on.

e. Forward and back. Physical readiness is of prime importance in solo work. It means assuming a relaxed but ready physical position, equally balanced on both feet, one foot slightly advanced, because the movement potential is greater in that position than when the feet are at attention. The Army places a soldier at attention with heels together, toes on a line, because it is the most unready, unavailable, defenseless physical position there is. The athlete, on the other hand, adopts a foot position that allows maximum readiness, and so should the singer. The nineteenth century melodramatic performer who goes into balletic foot position is not our model, but the general idea is correct, for there is mobility in the third and the fourth positions.

This exercise tests the performer's ability to move in *any* direction without adjustment of the pelvis or the body weight. The performers should be relaxed—no tension can be permitted—but should also be ready to move, even if it is not necessary. The instructor signals forward or back or side to side with a hand as the group stands facing her or him, each in readiness. Watch for tension. Hold the position for an extended period of time. The performers should find release from tension within their state of readiness. Attitudes may be added and changed with each move.

f. Gibberish with gestures. As each person speaks or sings a gibberish sequence, he or she gestures continually. This is a diagnostic exercise to find out how the performer feels about gesturing, and to locate the inhibitions or technical difficulties of gesturing. Once this initial exercise in the use of gesture has been tried, the basic gestural categories (see pp. 126 ff.) can be introduced.

g. Facial masks. As the instructor gives the signal, everyone in the group makes a mask with the face and holds it. On a second signal everyone transforms it instantly to another mask. This is another diagnostic tool which makes clear very rapidly the mobility of the performer's face and its projective freedom. It is important to stress the idea of making masks, and not of indicating emotions in a naturalistic way. Indicating or mugging is one of the most common acting faults, and simply involves doing too much, too often for the demands of the situation. The facial muscles are moving constantly, the eyes rove about, and there is general diffusion of energy. This is the opposite of what we mean by facial mask making, which is holding exaggerated but relatively motionless (with as little tension as possible) expressions for extended periods of time.

The main point about all physical energizing exercises is that tension must be spotted and eliminated. The moment performers equate energizing and physical tension, they are in long-range trouble unless the instructor sees it, points it out, and helps correct it.

h. The personal experience. The members of the group lie on the floor and close their eyes. As they lie there, they try to visualize an event from their lives that has some emotional impact. They try to see it, smell it, describe it to themselves, hear it, touch it: in short, remember as much of the sensory detail of the experience as possible. They should *not* try to *feel* the way it was, but should let that happen as a result of thinking about the sensory details of the event. The instructor may talk to them during the process, encouraging them to remember the feeling of the air, the colors of the surroundings, the smells, the atmosphere, the sunniness or cloudiness, the appearance of the people. He or she may also ask them to reach out for the experience, to hum into it, to vocalize into it. The piano may play some mood music *after* the class is well embarked on the exercise. The problem is to maintain remembrance of the sensory elements regardless of the music, while letting the music and the experience come together, even if they are in a different vein. Once the personal experience base is established it can be used to energize any scenes.

i. Centers of energy. After discussing briefly the fact that everyone has a slightly different center of energy, some carrying their energy in the chest, some in the pelvis, some in the head, the instructor pairs the group off. One person stands behind the other; the person in front tries to imagine her or his center of energy as a ball of white light overhead. The person in back holds a hand over the other person's head, and then begins moving down very slowly, touching the other person's head, neck, shoulders, etc. The person in front imagines the center of energy moving to wherever the other person touches. The piano may provide a mood accompaniment for this exercise. The person behind reaches the floor, pauses for a moment, and then moves back up the body, ending over the head again. Then partners reverse.

j. Mirror exercises. These are very useful for relating warmups, but because there are so many variations of the basic exercise, I suggest that the instructor devise her or his own. Among the possibilities, beyond the standard version in which two people face each other and one mirrors the actions of the other, are the following:

(1) Mirrors involving sounds (much like the game children play of try-ing to echo what one says as rapidly as possible), or with gibberish conversations carried on with the mirroring partner.

(2) Mirrors in which a physical movement evokes a sound from the other person, or the sound of one person evokes a physical move-ment from the other.

(3) Double or triple mirrors in which two people mirror the actions of two other people who are relating to each other.

It is useful in the mirror exercises for the instructor to call for a shift of initiators and reflectors every few moments. The action should not stop, but the mirror impulse should shift without any noticeable change. Ideally, it should be impossible to tell who is the initiator and who is the reflector at any point. The aim is not to trick the other person, or move so quickly that the action cannot possibly be mirrored, but to create a relationship in which the two move as one.

k. Attitude mirrors. Add attitudes to the usual mirror exercise. Variation: the initiator gives a physical image to the mirror, but the reflector gives back an attitude which the physical initiator must reflect.

l. Mask responses to music. As the pianist plays, the performers create mask responses to the mood of the music. Here, again, there can be no right or wrong, but the mask chosen must be projected with as much clarity and power as possible.

m. Physical responses to music: Perform the exercise above, but use the whole body to react and project.

n. Music that elicits a personal experience: This exercise reverses the per-sonal experience exercise. In this instance, the pianist (or a recording) plays, and the performers, lying on their backs, let it arouse a specific emotional experience from their past. If the pianist changes mood, the performers should let it affect their experience, even letting it move into imaginary areas.

2. Spoken

a. Ensemble exercises (A general rule: let the task involved *give* you energy, *let* it operate, derive your energy *from* it).

(1) Gibberish conversations with a facial mirror;[1] with a physical mirror; with an attitude mirror. The attitude mirror can be com-plementary rather than imitative. The mirror might give an "angry" image, the reflector might present a "placating" image in return.

(2) Gibberish energy matching: One person begins a gibberish conversation at a specific energy level. The other person matches the level of energy in response.

(3) Ritual duets with attitudes: Two people create a sound and motion sequence as a duet. It is not a mirror exercise, but a true duet in which each person contributes something to complement or supplement the other. It is important to keep the physical and vocal relationship in a formal style even while taking specific emotional attitudes.

(4) Gibberish scene that matches mood of accompanying music. As the pianist provides musical accompaniment (which may shift in mood and style as often as desired) the scene follows the emotional energy thereby provided.

(5) One person speaks about a personal experience in gibberish. Another performer enters and begins a conversation with the first person, picking up the mood and attitude conveyed.

(6) Gibberish scene with manipulation and incorporation. While two performers create a gibberish scene, two other members of the group manipulate them physically. The performers attempt to *incorporate* the physicalizations into the scene. For example, if the manipulators hold the performer's hand up, the performer can convert it into a shaken fist, a waving hand, a Papal greeting, or a Hitler salute.

(7) Gibberish scene with assigned attitude: Each performer is assigned an attitude unknown to the other. They integrate the two as the scene is played. (See p. 132 for suggested attitudes.)

b. Solo exercises

(1) Gibberish conversation-minus-one, with facial masks, physical masks, or attitudes, or any two or all three together. Each person pretends to carry on a conversation with an imaginary partner. There should be no long pauses in waiting for the person to reply; the performer is carrying most of the conversational burden, telling a fascinating story, trying to sell the person something, etc.

(2) Gibberish description of an imagined event with an attitude about that event. As in the conversation-minus-one, the performer pretends to see an event and describe it.

(3) Mirror and gibberish-minus-one with attitude pickup. The performer pretends to do a mirror exercise with an imaginary partner and carries on a conversation with that imaginary person with attitude pickup as well as physical and vocal pickup.

(4) Ritual duet-minus-one (ritual solo) with attitude pickup. Imagine

a partner for a ritual duet, and respond to the partner's sound, motion, and attitude.

(5) Gibberish soliloquy with shifting centers of energy. One person stands behind the performer, and touches various places on the body. The performer shifts her or his center of energy according to the touch.

(6) Gibberish soliloquy with an attitude. (In general, the students should select their own attitudes for this sequence. But if blocks occur, attitudes can be assigned arbitrarily, and the blocks will usually disappear.)

(7) Gibberish soliloquy with personal experience. The performer concentrates on the sensory memories of an experience—not on the feelings, which appear of their own volition—and talks in gibberish at the same time.

(8) Gibberish soliloquy with gestures. Gestures must be continual; however, it is important to begin in a total release position. Then follow the impulse to completion, release completely, and begin a new gesture. Either make a complete gesture, or do nothing—no halfway maneuvers. The instructor may assign a specific sequence of gestures from the indicative-descriptive-reactive list, or call out the gestures desired as the soliloquy proceeds.

(9) Gibberish soliloquy with facial masks. Each mask should be held until the instructor signals for a change.

(10) Gibberish soliloquy with readiness. As the performer delivers a gibberish soliloquy, the instructor signals forward, backward, or sideways movements. The performer should be able to execute them without any physical adjustment before the movement.

(11) Gibberish soliloquy with assigned language-music tasks:

high	or	low
fast	or	slow
jerky	or	smooth (or staccato or legato)
loud	or	soft
relaxed	or	intense

Here comments such as "high is not high" or "slow is not slow" will be useful. When a student is first assigned any technique, she or he will invariably use that technique to the exclusion of everything else. But any technique assigned must be surrounded by a full range of support from the performer's natural techniques. How would *you* say it in a higher register? In using a higher tessitura, one can still draw upon the lows in one's voice. A useful exercise to make sure vocal highs and lows are being used freely is *popping* and *bumping*. To *pop*, in our terminology, means to emote a rising inflection, allowing it to squeak upward as far as the free voice will permit without increasing the volume. The sound must be free; it must literally disappear, and if it does, a great deal of vocal flexibility and freedom will result.

To *bump*, in contrast, is to hit the lowest possible note on one word, letting it growl freely without being forced. The point of both *popping* and *bumping* is to keep the vocal energy free and open and still touch the extremes of one's range.

(12) Gibberish improvised poems with specific attitudes, or gibberish poems created in response to music played by the pianist.

3. Sung

a. Ensemble exercises

(1) Mirror exercises with sung gibberish, or English dialogue and attitudes. The standard mirror exercises discussed previously can be used, along with the more complicated varieties; but the exercises should not be so complicated that they break the connection between the performer and the partner. It is probably best to remain with gibberish at this point rather than moving into English, but that can be left to the discretion of the instructor. Once the basic exercise is mastered, the attitudes reflected may be complementary, or extensions of the mirror.

(2) In the ritual duet format explained above (see p. 142, exercise 3) use sung gibberish or English as the vocal mode but keep the physical communication in a formal, stylized vein. One performer is assigned an attitude which is either picked up, complemented, or extended by the partner.

(3) Ritual trios, quartets, and larger groups, with sung gibberish or English and a formal physical style. One person in the group is assigned an attitude which the others pick up, complement, or extend.

(4) Two members of the class begin a sung dialogue in gibberish or English. They pick up each other's energy level; whatever the energy level at which one person concludes a statement, the other person tries to pick it up.

(5) The piano provides an improvised accompaniment to which two singers create an improvised sung dialogue in gibberish or English, with attitudes drawn from the mood of the music. They may also create a gibberish poem together, taking alternate lines.

(6) Sung gibberish scene with attitude pickup. One performer is

assigned a secret attitude by the instructor. The other performer attempts to pick it up and extend it or complement it.

(7) Sung gibberish scene with pickup of physical center of energy. One performer is assigned a physical center of energy, and the other performer picks it up and uses it.

(8) Sung gibberish with conductor. One person, using her or his whole body, "conducts" the sung gibberish of another person. Once a relationship is clearly established, its reverse can be practiced: that is, the sung gibberish can evoke a physical response.

(9) Sung gibberish scene with personal experience basis. One performer begins a scene using a personal experience as an emotional base. The partner responds appropriately and gradually relates the scene to a personal experience of hers or his. The first performer responds appropriately.

b. Solo exercises

(1) The performer, with an imaginary mirror (a mirror-minus-one), sings a monologue in gibberish or English with an assigned or chosen attitude.

(2) The singer carries on a sung conversation-minus-one in either gibberish or English with an assigned or chosen attitude. This exercise may be added to the mirror-minus-one exercise if desired, the monologue becoming a conversation-minus-one.

(3) The performer describes an imagined event in sung gibberish or English with an assigned or chosen attitude. "Seeing" the partner or the event should be a primary goal.

(4) Ritual solos (ritual duet-minus-one). The performer sings in gibberish or English while maintaining the formal style of the physical action, with an assigned or chosen attitude.

(5) The singer imagines a person, event, or experience, with an assigned or chosen attitude, and sings in gibberish or English. Different physical centers of energy or different facial masks may be used in addition.

(6) Improvised songs in gibberish based on a personal experience. The singer should not try to feel what happened, but remember the sensory elements of the situation; the emotion takes care of itself.

(7) Improvised gibberish singing with attitude, and readiness to move forward, back, and sideways. The instructor signals for movements. The group may watch for the physical adjustments before each move that reveal lack of readiness.

(8) Improvised gibberish singing with attitude and gesture. The instructor signals for specific gestures (indicative-descriptive-reactive) as the song proceeds.

Concentrating

1. Warmups

a. Gibberish passing with attitudes around and across the circle. The performers concentrate on one another and on focusing emotional energy.

b. Echo game with attitudes and points of focus that are mirrored by the rest of the class.

c. Sound and motion exercise with attitudes and focus on the person to whom the event is being passed. As the event is passed from one performer to the next they create a mirror relationship that is sustained for several repetitions before continuing.

d. Sound and motion exercise with attitudes and with focus just above the head of the person to whom the action is being passed. The person passing the action should imagine she or he sees someone behind and above the person receiving the action.

e. Forward and back with attitudes and changing focus. Each time the instructor signals a change, the performers' focus and attitudes should shift as well.

f. The add-on game. This is an exercise in concentration that can be played with actions, words, music, any two, or all three together. The group divides into two equal parts. One person in the first group performs a physical action or speaks a gibberish word, or sings a short melody. The rest of the first group mirrors that action. The second person performs the same action, but adds another to it. The rest of the group mirrors that sequence. The third person performs the first two actions and adds still another. The group repeats that sequence, and the process continues until the memory of a single person or of the group fails. The second group begins the process and attempts to match or surpass the number of add-ons achieved by the first group. The performers should strive for accuracy of observation and duplication in addition to memory and concentration. The instructor-judge-referee of this game may give extra credit for difficulty of execution so that complexity of action is encouraged.

g. The add-on game with attitude masks. The first person makes a facial mask that the others mirror. The second person makes that mask, then adds another. The group mirrors both. The third person makes the first two masks and adds a third, and the group continues until the concentration slips. The second group tries to outdo the first. Sound, motion, and attitude masks can also be used.

h. The gibberish add-on game can use any language, sung or spoken, and can include a physical action. In this instance the inflection, phrasing, melody, rhythm—in short, the *music* of the verbal statement must be duplicated as well as the words or sounds themselves. If desired, the sound can be restricted to an "ah", thus emphasizing the melodic and rhythmic elements. Each person should add three notes to the continuing melody.

i. Exercises with music using records or an accompanist. Any number of responses to music exercises can be used as warmups. One can hardly stress too often the need for the singer to become *physically aware* of the accompanying music. And this can be encouraged by doing response exercises to any music whatsoever. A particularly good concentration exercise uses chamber ensemble or symphonic music with clearly differentiated voice groups; each member of the group warms up physically by responding to one specific instrument or group of instruments.

The accompanist is vital to the exercises in this book, and should begin improvising and providing musical accompaniments to which the singer can also improvise as soon as possible. Any of the exercises above can involve the accompanist. The accompanist can provide the impetus for sound and motion, changing music just before each transformation. It is the singers' responsibility to *relate* not only to their physical partners, but to their musical partner as well. Once this process is begun, the singers and the accompanist will be able to improvise gibberish arias and scenes readily.

j. As the accompanist improvises or plays a passage from a score, each performer focuses on an idea, a person, or an event, and maintains that focus, *keeping it alive* until the instructor signals a shift. The performers should do this exercise one by one, so that the group may validate one another's ability to keep the focus alive.

2. Spoken

a. Ensemble exercises

(1) Mirror exercises with simultaneous gibberish or improvised English conversations.

(2) Ritual duets. Two people create a sound and motion sequence as a duet with attitudes (either complementary or supplementary). Once they have begun, the instructor sends in two more people to "attack" them, to try to disturb their concentration. The disrupters may lift the performers, massage them, cover their eyes, tickle them, or do anything that is not actually hurtful in an attempt to break their concentration. The observers should note whether the connection between the speakers is maintained despite the efforts of the attackers.

(3) Ritual trios, quartets, or quintets. The same principle as the ritual duet, using any sound and motion relationship. All the individuals try to relate to the group creation in a complementary or supplementary fashion. The concentration problem increases with the number of participants.

(4) Two people begin improvised conversation in gibberish or English, with attitudes. Disrupters "attack" them, as described in exercise 2.

(5) Two people describe an event, a thing, or a person, or improvise a free-form poem in gibberish or English. One person begins, and the second person attempts to relate in idea and attitude to what the first person has initiated. The second person progresses with the attitude or idea, and the first person must then relate to that statement in continuing.

(6) An accompanist plays mood music. Using that music, two people make a poem in gibberish with attitudes, each taking alternate lines. The speakers should attempt to relate to the mood and music of the piano and to the statements of each other as well. The "attack" may be added.

(7) One person in the circle carries on improvised conversations in gibberish or English with two or more people in the circle, shifting from one to the other and back on the instructor's signal. The problem is to remember each conversation and be able to return to it. The observers should watch for the return to the attitude and mood as well as the subject matter of each conversation.

b. Solo exercises

(1) Gibberish or English conversations-minus-one with attitudes. The performer pretends to carry on a conversation with an imaginary person, not pausing for the person to reply, but carrying most of the conversational burden, telling a fascinating story, trying to sell the person something, etc. Two other members of the group "attack" the person speaking, attempting to break the concentration by touching, lifting, speaking, and so on. The performer's task is to maintain the focus-concentration despite the interference. In solo exercises we exercise the concentration of exclusion, i.e., we maintain the focus without acknowledging the interference. In ensemble exercises, the concentration of incorporation is exercised.

(2) Gibberish or English descriptions of an imaginary event. As in the conversation-minus-one, the performer pretends to see an event and describes it. The performer may move back and forth between two events once the basic exercise has been mastered.

(3) Mirror-minus-one and gibberish. The performer pretends to do a

mirror exercise with an imaginary person, and carries on a conversation with attitudes at the same time. Once the exercise has been mastered, other performers "attack."

(4) Ritual duets-minus-one (ritual solos). The performer imagines a partner for a ritual duet, and responds to that person's sound and motion. Once the exercise has been mastered, other performers "attack."

(5) Gibberish or English conversation-minus-one with attitudes as above.

(6) Multiple focus conversations with imaginary partners. The soloist selects two or more points of focus and carries on separate conversations with attitudes with each of them in gibberish or English, shifting from one conversation and attitude to another on the signal of the instructor.

(7) The accompanist plays an improvisation in any mood or style. The performer senses the mood of the music and creates a gibberish poem with attitudes that relate to the music as organically as possible. The performer should display at least three separate points of focus.

Note: in many of these exercises the students will try to think of the "right" thing to do, or intellectualize in advance, or plan, or inhibit themselves in some way. Whenever the instructor senses this, she or he should encourage them to quit thinking and *do*. Think *with* the voice and the music (or *with* the body, if the exercise involves the body), not with the intellect. Jump in and swim instead of thinking so hard about the process of swimming that you never get wet. There is no right or wrong, there is only the giving of energy or the non-giving of energy. Another method of avoiding right-wrong thinking is to think of all actions and decisions in terms of usefulness. Any commitment of energy is useful — it is simply a question of *how* useful. It is important to avoid the hang-up of success-failure, right-wrong thinking in exercising with improvisation.

3. Sung

a. Ensemble exercises

(1) Sung gibberish aria with mirror and attitude. The singer mirrors the movements and attitude of the reflector. Once the exercise is under control, other performers "attack."

(2) Sung gibberish aria with mirror, facial and physical masks, and attitude. Other performers "attack" the singer who, concentrating

on incorporation, makes use and sense of the motions without acknowledging the attackers.

(3) Ritual duets with sung gibberish and attitudes. Keep the physical style formal. Other performers "attack" the singers when the exercise is secure, and the singers incorporate the motions without acknowledging the attackers.

(4) Sung gibberish conversation with the performers picking up an energy level from each other. When the relationship is firmly established other performers "attack," and the performers incorporate the motions presented. The observers should be especially aware of whether the connection is maintained and the energy levels are actually picked up as the "attack" proceeds.

(5) Sung gibberish scene with attitude pickup. One performer is assigned a secret attitude by the instructor. The other performer picks it up, complements it, or extends it. Other performers "attack" the singers, who incorporate the motions.

(6) Sung gibberish scene with physical centers of energy picked up (see Energizing, Sung Ensemble). Other performers "attack" the singers, who incorporate the motions. Make certain the basic center of energy is not given up as the motions are incorporated.

(7) Sung gibberish with conductor. One person "conducts" another person's sung gibberish. Other performers "attack" the singer, who should incorporate the motion. Observers note whether the incorporation interferes with the singer's attention to the conductor.

(8) Sung gibberish scene with personal experience base. See p. 143, exercise 7. Other performers "attack" the singers, who incorporate the manipulation.

b. Solo exercises

(1) Mirror-minus-one with sung gibberish and attitude. Other performers "attack" the singer. The performer may either exclude or incorporate the attack.[2]

(2) Duet-minus-one with sung gibberish and attitude. Other performers "attack" the singer. The performer may either exclude or incorporate the attack.

(3) Soliloquy describing (seeing) an event in sung gibberish with attitude. Other performers "attack" the singer, who may either exclude or incorporate the attack.

(4) Ritual duet-minus-one (ritual solo) using sung gibberish and attitude, keeping the physical mode abstract or formal. Other performers "attack" the singer, who may exclude or incorporate the motions.

(5) Sung gibberish. The performer carries on either a dialogue with an imagined person or a monologue about an imagined event or an imagined experience, including different attitudes, or different physical centers of energy, or different facial masks. Other performers "attack" the singer, who may exclude or incorporate the motions.

(6) Improvised gibberish singing with focus, attitude, and forward and back exercise. The instructor signals for the forward and back movement.

(7) Improvised gibberish singing with focus, attitude, and gesture. The instructor signals for specific gestures (indicative-descriptive-reactive) as the song proceeds.

Structuring

1. Warmups

a. Echo game. Each sound and motion exercise is to have two distinct sections, A and B. Movement from one section to the other can be instant or gradual or somewhere between. As we work on the problem of structure and the idea of progression that is implicit in it, we must be as aware of the *kind* of progression as of the progression itself.

b. Gibberish around the circle. Each person picks up the specific style and energy from her or his neighbor, makes a progression, transforms it, and passes it to the next person.

c. Sound and motion. Each performer transforms the action before passing it to the next performer. That transformation can be either instant or gradual.

d. Phrasing exercise. As the pianist plays a musical sequence, the group members outline the phrasing of the music either with the arms or with the whole body.

e. Mirror exercises in three-part, ABA form. The initiator uses a pattern for A which can be returned to, and a contrasting pattern for the B section.

f. Rondo facial masks. A basic facial mask is created; as the instructor signals, the performers adopt variations and hold them until the next signal; then they resume the first mask. At a signal, they make a new variation, followed by a return to the basic mask: ABACADAEAF.

g. Open and closed physical phrasing to music or counting. Each member of the group moves from the most closed physical position (fetal, on the floor, or crouched), to the most open position in 10 counts (or a musical phrase or two) and back in 10 counts. The counting may be speeded or slowed.

2. Spoken

a. Ensemble exercises

(1) Three-part, ABA, gibberish scenes with mirrors. The structure is defined by the kind of "music" the gibberish makes. For example a low, slow legato conversation becomes higher, faster, and more staccato, and returns to the low, slow, legato. The transitions can be either gradual or. sudden as assigned by the instructor. For the purposes of music-theater the gradual transition is more difficult but more generally useful in its relationship to the problem of time extension. The sudden transition is highly theatrical, more immediately telling, and is very useful for training mental flexibility. Stress incorporation, i.e. making sense of all external stimuli. Watch for tension.

(2) Gibberish scenes with three attitudes assigned privately to one performer. The other performer must follow the lead of the first person, who shifts from attitude to attitude: the second person may be assigned one of the attitudes and pass it on to the first person after picking up the first attitude. The transitions may be sudden or gradual as assigned by the instructor.

(3) Ritual duets in three-part ABA form. The sound and motion may change either suddenly or gradually as the instructor indicates.

(4) Ritual duets in three-part ABA form. The first person is assigned one attitude, the second assigned another. The first person's attitude is picked up by the second person and played by both performers in the A section. In the B section the second person's is picked up by the first and both play it, taking care that they blend with each other. Each plays her or his own attitude in returning to the A section. Transitions may be gradual or sudden as the instructor wishes.

Note: the structure in all of the preceding exercises may also be defined by changes in physical centers of energy, gestures, physical or facial masks, use of space, or fantasy environments. Heighten awareness and avoidance of tension, and stress sense-making incorporation.

b. Solo exercises

(1) Gibberish or English conversation-minus-one (or description of an imagined event) with three different facial masks, to be changed at a signal from the instructor. The transition from one to the next may be sudden or gradual as desired.

(2) Gibberish and mirror-minus-one with three changes in either

attitude, facial or physical masks, or energy centers. Transitions may be sudden or gradual as desired by the instructor.

(3) Ritual duet-minus-one, A B A, in assigned attitude, as well as sound and motion. Sudden or gradual transitions.

(4) Gibberish or improvised English soliloquy with three assigned attitude changes, or A B A attitudes. Sudden or gradual transitions.

(5) Gibberish or improvised English soliloquy with a personal experience basis, transition from that basis to an opposing or contrasting attitude, and return to the original personal experience, A B A. Gradual or sudden transitions.

(6) Gibberish or improvised English soliloquy with gestural A B A form: for the A section any two of the categories (indicative-descriptive-reactive), for the B section any other two. Sudden or gradual transitions.

(7) Gibberish or improvised English soliloquy with the following progressions, A B A form, or the reverse.
High to low
Fast to slow
Discontinuous to continuous
Staccato to legato
Loud to soft (soft should be audible)
Relaxed to intense

(8) Gibberish poems in A B C form with sections contrasted by language techniques (speed, rhythm, pitch, volume, intensity), attitudes, or physical or facial masks. (The language should be affected by the physical changes.)

(9) Gibberish poems in a form dictated by the pianist, who plays mood music, shifting as often as desired. The performer should follow the changes in mood and energy with matching language mood changes.

(10) Gibberish or improvised English soliloquy with three different focus points, using any or all of the following transitions as assigned:
(a) Sudden shift
(b) Searching shift (eyes search for the new focus)
(c) Eyes shut (opening to the new focus)
(d) Strong rejection of one focus that drives one to a new focus.

3. Sung

a. Ensemble exercises
(1) Sung gibberish scene in A B A form, with mirror. The A B A form may be determined by music, physical and facial movement, or

attitude combinations. Transitions may be gradual or sudden as specified by the instructor.

(2) Sung gibberish scene in three-part ABC form, with the structure created by attitudes. Each person is assigned an attitude. Section A: the first performer's is picked up by the second performer. Section B: the second performer's attitude is picked up by the first performer. Section C: the performers blend the two attitudes. Alternatively, the form may be determined by:

(a) Use of space assigned alternately.

(b) Physical masks or centers of energy.

(c) Gestural characteristics.

In all of these exercises, the transitions may be sudden or gradual.

(3) Ritual sung duets, ABA, the form determined by assigned attitudes. Each person may be assigned two attitudes, which are played in sequence by each of them, each performer modifying the attitude so it relates to the partner's musical, physical, and facial action. Transitions may be sudden or gradual.

(4) Ritual sung duets in ABC form with assigned attitudes and music. One person begins, the other person picks up or complements the music and attitude; on a signal from the instructor, the second person plays her or his attitude and music combination and the first person picks up or complements them in turn. In the third section each performer uses the attitude and music originally assigned and relates them to those of the partner. Sudden or gradual transitions.

b. Solo exercises

(1) Sung gibberish or improvised English conversation-minus-one (or description of an imagined event or experience) with three facial masks, or three assigned attitudes, or three physical masks or energy centers. The performer moves among the three on signal from the instructor. Sudden or gradual transitions.

(2) Sung gibberish mirror-minus-one with three changes in attitude, physical mask, or facial mask on signal from the instructor. Sudden or gradual transitions.

(3) Ritual sung duet-minus-one, ABA, form determined by assigned attitudes, as well as sound and motion. Sudden or gradual transitions.

(4) Gibberish sung aria with a personal experience changing to a contrasting personal experience, and then returning to the original. Sudden or gradual transition.

(5) Gibberish sung aria with gestural characteristics creating ABA form: for section A, select two from the categories of gesture

(indicative-descriptive-reactive); in the B section, use the remaining category and one other. Sudden or gradual transitions.

(6) Gibberish sung aria with assigned music progressions or their opposites:

Legato to staccato

High to low

Loud to soft

Relaxed to intense

Fast to slow

Special musical effects, such as trills, cadenzas, coloratura, fermati, etc. can also be made a part of the exercise.

(7) Gibberish arias to piano accompaniment. Structure determined by pianist, singer, or both.

(8) Gibberish aria with three different focus points, using any or all of the following kinds of transitions:

(a) Sudden shift—light bulb effect.

(b) Searching shift (eyes search for the new focus).

(c) Eyes shut (opening to the new focus).

(d) Strong rejection of one focus that drives one to a new focus.

(e) Panoramic focus which grows larger and larger.

(f) Environmental focus with at least four different items.

Imagining

1. Warmups

a. Echo game with abstract sound and motion in the manner of an operatic character (how would Susanna do a sound and motion?), an imagined character, a fantasy character, or in the manner of some abstraction like a color, an object, a machine, etc. (what sort of sound and motion is suggested by the color blue, a serving knife, a rock, a sports car?) Performers should avoid literal imitation but try for imagined abstractions based on the real object or idea.

b. Sound and motion in the manner of an operatic character, an imagined character, a fantasy character, a color, an object, a plant, or a food.

c. Prop creation and transformation: The first person makes up an imaginary prop, uses it, and passes it along to the next person, who transforms it into something else, uses it, and passes it on to the next person. (This can be performed to musical accompaniment.)

d. Each person speaks in stream-of-consciousness style in English. The instructor signals and, using the last word spoken before interruption, the performer improvises a song, exploring all its implications in cadenza style. Use only the single word.

e. Imagined characters or fantasy environments based on the music played by the accompanist. The performers move like the imaginary characters in the environments imagined.

f. Magic garments: Each person pretends to put on an article of clothing— a hat, a shoe, a glove, a bra—and is transformed by the item, extending the part of the body involved. This exercise is best done to music that begins when the performer has donned the magic garment. The performer should move, using both the implications of the magic garment and of the music.

g. Mirror with improvised aria. Adapt the mirror actions to fit the aria.

2. Spoken

a. Solo exercises

(1) Imaginary prop transformations with a gibberish commentary and explanation. This exercise may be accompanied by music that modifies and shapes the commentary and action.

(2) Story telling by one person. The person may be given a theme but should begin the story immediately without stopping to plan. If the performer encounters a block, she or he should speak in gibberish until a new idea is found. Alternatively, the instructor may signal for moves into gibberish.

(3) Everyday magic. A performer tells a personal experience but extends all the ideas within it: for example, "the person who yelled at me" could become "the wicked magician who yelled at me." Embroider on attitudes, give them to the characters of your experience, even where they may not have existed: "he asked me" could become, "he asked me with an evil grin."

(4) Gibberish soliloquy in a fantasy environment. The performer describes the environment and characterizes it by the music of the language.

(5) Gibberish soliloquy with three magic garments. The performer puts them on one by one, each magic garment influencing the music of the language. The specific magic garments can be assigned. Music can accompany the exercise, thus affecting the use of the magic garment.

(6) Gibberish soliloquy with physical center of energy extensions—for example, a fifty-pound big toe, an enormous neck, a superstrong arm, floating shoulders—any kind of extension that can be imag-

ined. The performers choose three of these and shift from one to the other as signaled by the instructor.

(7) Gibberish soliloquy in the manner of an imagined extension of another person. The performer isolates several aspects of another person and blows them up, extending them.

(8) Three persons say three words of any kind simultaneously so that the selection is arbitrary and the speakers do not influence each other's choices. These three words are to be used at the beginning, middle, and end of the performer's improvised soliloquy, and the structure of the soliloquy built around the them.

b. Ensemble exercises

(1) Duet story telling. One person recites a story. He or she may stop at any point; a partner picks up the story without pausing and continues it. The second person stops at any point and the story returns to the first person. There are no limits — any fantasy at all is permissable and desirable. The story may be mimed or demonstrated as it is told.

(2) Group pass-along story telling. Use the exercise above, but include the whole group. The story may be acted out as it proceeds. The acting should be nonliteral: that is, if a tree character is described, it is not necessary to imitate a tree literally, with arms for branches, etc., for we already have that information. What we want to know is the attitude of the tree, its emotional style, its idiosyncrasies.

(3) Environment description. One person moves into the center of the circle and describes a fantasy environment: "I'm looking at a purple sky, the stars are shining a bright red, and they drip. . . ." Those around the edge should ask questions to promote the process. The person in the center should focus upon the vision of the strange environment.

(4) Character description and assumption. As the rest of the group describes a character to a person in the center, that person takes on the characteristics and attitudes and physical attributes described.

(5) Gibberish scene in fantasy environment. Scene between two people only one of whom knows what the environment is; the other person must pick it up and play it. When the instructor signals, the second person changes the environment, plays it, and the first person must pick it up. The kind of environment may be assigned.

(6) Character from a prop. One person creates an imaginary prop, uses it in a gibberish scene, and gives it to a partner who then adapts her or his character to the prop. The partner transforms the prop,

hands it back, and the first person adapts her or his character to the new prop.

(7) Gibberish or English scene built around props assigned on the spot.

(8) Gibberish scene; each person performs in the manner of an imagined extension of another person. For example, picture the style of a person in the class, then imagine an expansion or extension of that style.

(9) Three persons from the group say words of any kind simultaneously so that the selection is arbitrary. These three words are to be used at the beginning, middle, and end of the scene by the performers (not the three who select the words).

3. Sung

a. Solo exercises

(1) The performer does a series of imaginary prop transformations, making a sung gibberish commentary on each one. The instructor signals the move from prop to prop, the pianist provides an improvised accompaniment.

(2) Sung stream-of-consciousness commentary about a character from an opera. The performer says the name of the character, and lets thoughts flow, using repetition whenever necessary, and lyric expansion whenever possible.

(3) The performer tells a story in song, with improvised piano accompaniment. The performer may use gibberish or a vocalization whenever stuck in the story.

(4) Everyday magic. The performer sings about an everyday experience, but extends all the ideas in fantastic or magical ways (see p. 156, exercise 3).

(5) Gibberish aria. The performer imagines a fantastic environment and sings a gibberish aria about it. Attitude and music provide the sense of place.

(6) Gibberish aria with three magic garments which are put on one by one. The music becomes the extension of the garment.

(7) Gibberish aria with physical center of energy extensions: a giant little finger, a swelling head, a string neck, plastic fingers, or any other kind of extension that can be imagined. The performer should use three centers and shift from one to the other on signal.

(8) A gibberish aria based on a personal experience that is converted into a magical fantasy experience by letting it change itself. If it does not change itself, the performer should give it an assist—the

car begins to fly, the freeway blows up 400 yards ahead, the rain begins to change color, etc.

(9) A gibberish aria in the manner of the imagined extension of another person. The performer isolates the physical manners of another person and extends them.

(10) Three people say three words of any kind simultaneously. These three words are to be used at the beginning, middle, and end of an improvised aria.

b. Ensemble exercises

(1) Sung story telling. Two or more people pass a story back and forth, making it up as they go. The accompanist provides piano music, which may lead the story as well as follow it.

(2) A performer sings about or describes a character; a partner becomes that character, adopting characteristics as they are described. The "character" sings in response, also describing a character, but in the manner of the character he or she is impersonating. When both characters are established, they sing a duet. The piano improvisation may lead or follow the story.

(3) Group pass-along story. The entire group participates in exercise 1, above.

(4) One person goes to the center of the circle. The others sing, describing an environment that is fantastic: "the trees are swaying, and changing color—now they begin to sing." The person at the center reflects what they are saying, reading to it, singing with it, etc.

Alternatively, the person at the center sings about an environment: "I am at the foot of a glass mountain." The group around the outside promotes the process by asking questions the person in the center must answer.

(5) With one performer at the center, the group around the outside describes, one by one, the attributes of a character. The character should be unusual, with fantastic characteristics. The person at the center sings in reaction, assumes the characteristics, and relates to the singing of the group.

(6) Sung gibberish scene in a fantasy environment. Only one person in the scene knows the environment, but the other has to sense it, pick it up and play it: When the signal is given by the instructor, the second person plays a new environment, which the first person must then pick up and play.

(7) Sung gibberish scene. Each person has on a magic garment. As the scene proceeds, they exchange the garments, and the extensions which follow from them.

(8) Sung gibberish scene. Each person performs in the manner of an *imagined extension* of another person, taking the style of another person and extending it or blowing it up in some way.

(9) Three persons say three words of any kind simultaneously. These three words are to be used at the beginning, middle, and end of the improvised duet.

Stylizing

1. Warmups (Sung or Spoken)

a. Echo game in the manner of another member of the group. The group performs a sound and motion in a way characteristic of one member. This exercise will stimulate the process of observation described on p. 114.

b. Sound and motion in the manner of another member of the group. How does the person use the body and voice under the pressure of sound and motion improvisation?

Note: These two exercises should raise the question of style: how do other people act under differing external circumstances? What do they do to make sense of themselves and their role? How we do something is our style; the dramatic problem is to find out how someone else would do something, then practice that something until it is as natural to us as our own pattern of behavior. The stylistic challenge is to make total sense out of actions that are foreign to our way of being. By beginning with the "style" of fellow classmates, the whole question of style becomes a very real and tangible problem rather than a vague generalization about fashion in the eighteenth or nineteenth century. Once an understanding of the idea of style is clear, it is easy to move into more removed areas. It is never easy to *make sense* out of a particular style, but once the problem is defined, it can be practiced.

c. Character walks and physicalizations in the manner of a group member or someone observed outside the class. The performers should become aware of the physical masks used by other people and the location of their centers of energy.

d. Gibberish in the manner of someone else in the group. This may be done in two ways, either as that person does gibberish, or as gibberish in the manner that she or he speaks English.

e. Gibberish in an abstract, formal style or in a naturalistic style.

f. Mirror exercises. (1) The performer creates a facial mask *mirror* to be reflected, or creates an appropriate full body mask to complement the facial mirror. (2) The performer directs a gibberish reading—sung or spoken—at another person, who answers it with an appropriate physical and facial mask. The instructor (3) gives a performer a physical and facial mask and the performer responds with appropriate sung or spoken gibberish.

2. Spoken

a. Ensemble exercies
   (1) Ritual duet in ABA form. Both the sound and the actions move from a formal style to a naturalistic style and back again. The sound should range from abstract to naturalistic gibberish. Alternatively, the performers may begin with an abstract physical action and naturalistic gibberish in the A section, followed by a more natural physical pattern and improvised English dialogues in the B section.

   Note: One of the sets of opposites we have discussed deals with the formal-natural continuum. It is often difficult to clarify the idea of this continuum, and this ritual duet exercise helps make it clear. Various comparisons can be drawn to demonstrate the idea, e.g., a "Candid Camera" conversation at one end of the continuum, a Baroque oratorio at the other.

   (2) Several variations of the ritual duet in ABA form are possible: Sound constant, either naturalistic or formal, with the physical style moving between naturalistic and formal. Sound moving from naturalistic to formal and back, with the physical moving from formal to naturalistic and back. Other variations can be created including ABC or ABACAD forms.

   (3) Attitudes and attitude changes can be added to any of the above exercises. When this is done, watch very carefully for tensions connected with the emotions. The floating cooperative isolation of the vocal, the physical, and the emotional is tested and exercised here.

   (4) Gibberish or improvised English conversations with language assignments (see p. 143). Special attention should be given to the idea of style: *how* the language is used determines the style as much as *what* is said. The use of different language characteristics demands a search for the sense *behind* the characteristics, that is, for the *why* of the style. This, of course, is what we mean by incorporation.

   (5) A gibberish or improvised English scene. One person is assigned language characteristics or physical masks which the other person must identify and complement or supplement in some way. The first performer establishes a specific way of being, a style, which the second identifies and relates to without actually mirroring.

Constant stress on the idea of style as *how* something is done is important if style is to be removed from generalized artificiality. Certain styles may seem artificial, but they were as natural to their creators as our style is to us. Our problem is to make these styles as natural to us as they were to their creators.

(6) A gibberish scene in which both performers play in the manner of someone else in the group or of someone outside the group.

(7) Manipulation and incorporation. Two members of the group manipulate two performers in a gibberish scene. The performers must attempt to incorporate completely the manipulations as style statements. Alternatively, they are given mirror images by two other people before the scene begins and must use the style suggested by the mirrors in the scene.

  b. Solo exercises

(1) Gibberish to English to gibberish. The exercise may be in the form of a conversation-minus-one, a soliloquy, or a description of an imagined event. Language characteristics may also be assigned which affect either gibberish or English.

(2) Ritual solos in ABA form with changes and combinations of changes. The physical style may be formal or natural, and the sound may be formal or natural for the A section; the B section reverses whatever is chosen for the A section; the return to the A section may involve some variation as an ABC form.

(3) Gibberish or improvised English soliloquies with physical masks or centers of energy. The performer should make sense of (incorporate) the masks and centers.

(4) Gibberish or improvised English soliloquies in the manner of someone else either in the group or outside the group.

(5) Gibberish or improvised English soliloquies with facial masks ranging from natural to formal.

(6) Gibberish or improvised English soliloquies with gesture assignments alternating between formal and natural styles, or as signaled by the instructor.

3. Sung

  a. Ensemble exercises

(1) Ritual duets in sung gibberish, ABA form. The physical style should move from formal to natural or natural to formal, and back. The musical style should change as well, with either styles assigned by the instructor (folk, romantic, classic, baroque, musical comedy, etc.) or created by the performer.

(2) Sung gibberish scene in ABC form with assignments to be passed from one person to another. Each partner is given one of the following assignments: in the A section, the first performer plays her or his task, which the second person picks up. In the B section, the second person plays her or his assigned task, and the first performer picks it up and plays it. Moving to the C section, each plays her or his own task, but blends it with that of the other performer.

   (a) Physical masks or centers of energy.

   (b) Musical styles or musical characteristics.

   (c) Gestural characteristics with formal or natural styles.

   (d) Manipulation by two other people and incorporation of the manipulation, interrelating it with the partner's style.

   (e) Facial characteristics.

   (f) Attitudes in the manner of someone else in the group or outside the group.

b. Solo exercises

(1) Improvised singing in ABA form moving from gibberish to English to gibberish or the reverse. The performer may treat the solo as a conversation-minus-one, a description of an imagined event, or a soliloquy.

(2) Ritual solos moving between improvised traditional singing styles and abstract sounds. The performer should execute one of the following problems in ABA form:

   (a) Move from a formal physical style to a naturalistic physical style and back again.

   (b) Create facial masks ranging from formal to naturalistic characteristics.

   (c) Display gestural characteristics in formal and naturalistic styles.

   (d) Incorporate manipulation by another member of the class.

   (e) Sing in the manner of two people from in or outside the group in succession.

(3) Gibberish improvised aria in ABA form with the following additional problems:

   (a) Create physical masks moving between formal and natural characteristics.

   (b) Create facial masks moving between formal and natural characteristics.

   (c) Incorporate manipulation that is structured by the manipulator in ABA form.

   (d) Perform a mirror exercise in which the initiator uses ABA form. Incorporate the movements.

(e) Display formal or natural gestural characteristics.

(f) Sing in the manner of someone else in or outside of the group.

(g) Sing with assigned attitudes in the manner of someone else.

Coordinating

1. Warmups

a. Echo game. The participants act in the manner of an observed character, with a two-part progression in sound, action, and attitude.

b. Sound and motion. The first person begins in the manner of an observed character, with an attitude and a physical center of energy. When she or he moves to the center, the physical pattern is continued, but the performer speaks or sings on an assigned topic in English, then continues with the abstract sound and motion, passing the attitude, physical center, and manner to a mirroring performer. As soon as the mirror has picked up the image, that performer is given a topic for the English improvisation. The second performer takes the abstract package to the center, speaks on the assigned topic, and transforms it into a new style, physical center, sound, and attitude, and passes it on, assigning a new topic.

c. Gibberish passing sung or spoken. The performers act in the manner of an observed person, with a gestural idiosyncrasy and progression in music or language focused on and relating to a fantasy environment.

d. Mirror game. The initiator displays a physical characteristic and an attitude and allows them to progress. The second person adopts a complementary attitude and makes an extension of the physical image. The initiator makes a sound phrase which is answered, not mirrored, by the mirror.

2. Spoken

a. Ensemble exercises. Although it is easy to devise exercises that are impossibly difficult to accomplish, we will begin with an exercise that has already been established and add elements to it until the student encounters limits that must be extended. The first exercise to be treated in this way is the ritual duet. Two people create a sound and motion duet which can be of any length and in any style. To complicate this basic exercise, two or more of the following problems should be assigned or chosen and used according to the overall ABA or ABC pattern as indicated. Progressions between sections may be fast or slow. The "attack" may be added and continued throughout the three sections.

RITUAL DUETS

	A	B	A or C
LANGUAGE	Formal gibberish.	Naturalistic gibberish.	Formal gibberish or a mixture of formal and natural.
PHYSICAL	Two physical themes are used by each performer.	The performers exchange themes used in A.	They repeat the first two or combine them in different ways.
ENERGY CENTERS	Each person chooses a center of energy.	Each person uses the center of energy he or she observed in the other.	Each person uses his or her first center, or combines the two.
ATTITUDES	The first person plays an assigned attitude. The second person relates to it, either imitating or complementing.	The second person plays an assigned attitude to which the first person relates.	Each person blends the two attitudes.
STYLE	Each person adopts the style of a person he or she has observed.	The performers exchange styles.	They blend the two styles.
GESTURAL CHARACTER-ISTICS	Each person uses an assigned set of characteristics.	The performers exchange characteristics.	They combine the two sets used.
PROPS	Each performer is given a prop to incorporate into the scene in normal ways.	The performers exchange props.	They return to their original props, but this time they use them in atypical ways.

Another basic exercise that can be treated in this way is a gibberish scene for two people. To that exercise, two or more of the following problems can be added, using an ABA or ABC structure as indicated. The "attack" may be added and continued through the three sections.

GIBBERISH SCENE

	A	*B*	*A or C*
ATTITUDES	The first person plays an assigned attitude. The second person relates to it, either imitating or complementing.	The second person plays an assigned attitude to which the first person relates.	Each person blends the two attitudes or evolves a new attitude from the events in A and B.
PHYSICAL	Each performer uses an assigned center or magic garment.	The performers exchange centers or magic garments.	They return to the original centers or garments, or evolve new ones.
GESTURAL CHARACTER- ISTICS	Each performer uses assigned gestural characteristics.	The performers exchange gestural characteristics.	Each performer combines both sets of characteristics.
STYLE	Each person plays in the manner of someone observed.	The performers exchange styles with each other.	They return to the first styles or combine the two.
SPACE	The two performers relate to one part of the ground plan, either to a piece of furniture or to a specific space.	They relate to another part of the ground plan.	They use both parts or as much of the ground plan as possible.
PROPS	Each performer uses a prop in normal ways.	The performers exchange props and use them in normal ways.	They return to their original props but use them in atypical ways.
BACKGROUND MUSIC	The first performer *uses* the music (plays *with* its energies), the second performer plays *against* it.	They reverse these usages.	Both performers use the music.
LANGUAGE	Naturalistic gibberish to	Stylized gibberish to	English or naturalistic gibberish.

b. Solo exercises. We have established two kinds of solo improvised exercises: the ritual solo, which relates to the formalistic end of the sound and motion spectrum (and also, by means of gibberish, to the naturalistic end), and the gibberish soliloquy, which, when English is included, can encompass the rest of the stylistic continuum. In utilizing these two basic exercises, the procedure will be the same as for the ensemble exercises: under the two categories (ritual solo and gibberish soliloquy) we will simply list the possible tasks, leaving it up to the instructor to assign combinations according to the students' needs. It is often useful to have the performers draw the assignments from a hat and take as many as they wish; usually they take more than the instructor would have assigned. Progressions between sections may be fast or slow. The "attack" may be used through the three sections or dropped and resumed at the instructor's signal.

| | *RITUAL SOLO*   or   *GIBBERISH SOLILOQUY* | | |
	A	*B*	*C*
LANGUAGE STYLE	Ritual — formal abstract to	Naturalistic gibberish to	Abstract extensions of natural gibberish.
	Gibberish — naturalistic gibberish to	English to	Stylized gibberish.
PHYSICAL	Assigned centers of energy or magic garments.	Performer's choice of new centers or garments.	Combine the two centers or garments.
ATTITUDES	With two assigned attitudes in sequence.	Play the opposites of each of those attitudes in sequence.	Play the first two attitudes in reverse order.
GESTURE	Assigned characteristics.	Performer's choice of different characteristics.	Combine the two sets.
STYLE	In the manner of a person the performer has observed.	In the manner of another person.	The two styles are combined.
SPACE	Within a ground plan, use one part of the space or object within it.	Use another part of the space or another object.	Use as much of the ground plan as possible.

PROPS	Use a prop in typical ways.	Use another prop in atypical ways.	Use both props in either typical or atypical ways.
BACKGROUND MUSIC	Use the music.	Play against the music.	Alternate using the music and playing against it.

3. Sung

a. Ensemble exercises. These exercises follow the same general pattern used for spoken improvised coordinating but may combine spoken with sung sounds. The pianist should be involved in all these exercises, although it is possible to practice them without accompaniment. The progressions between sections may be fast or slow. The "attack" may be continued through the three sections.

SUNG RITUAL DUETS   or   SUNG GIBBERISH DUETS

	A	B	A or C
ATTITUDES	The first performer plays an assigned attitude; the second person relates to it, either imitating or complementing.	The second person plays an assigned attitude to which the first person relates.	Each person blends the two attitudes.
PHYSICAL	Two physical themes are used by each performer.	They exchange the themes used in A.	They repeat the first themes used or combine them in different ways.
ENERGY CENTERS	Each person chooses a center of energy.	The performers exchange the centers of energy used in A.	They combine the two centers.
GESTURAL CHARACTER-ISTICS	Each person uses an assigned set of characteristics.	The performers exchange characteristics.	They combine the two sets.
STYLE	Each person adopts the style of a person he or she has observed.	The performers exchange styles.	They blend the two styles.

SPACE	The two performers relate to a ground plan, using one part of the space or object within it.	Both relate to another part of the ground plan.	Both use as much of the ground plan as possible.
PROPS	Each performer is given a prop to incorporate into the scene in normal ways.	They exchange props.	They re-exchange props, but this time they use them in atypical ways.
LANGUAGE STYLE	Ritual—formalistic abstract to Gibberish— naturalistic gibberish to	Naturalistic gibberish to Stylized gibberish to	Stylized gibberish or formal abstract. English or naturalistic gibberish.
MUSIC	Change of style and/or mood from section to section.		

b. Solo exercises. Here again the two basic exercises—the sung ritual solo and the gibberish aria—provide the fundamental problem. From the list of tasks below, the instructor may assign two or more to be accomplished during the exercise. The performers may also draw the assignments from a hat.

RITUAL SOLO   or   *GIBBERISH ARIA*

	A	B	A or C
PROGRESSIONS	Fast or slow in moving to	Fast or slow in moving to	
LANGUAGE STYLE	Ritual—formal abstract to	Naturalistic gibberish to	Abstract extensions of naturalistic gibberish.
	Gibberish— naturalistic gibberish to	English to	Stylized gibberish.
PHYSICAL	Assigned centers of energy or magic garments.	Performer's choice of new centers or garments.	Combine the two centers or garments.
ATTITUDES	With two assigned attitudes in sequence.	Play the opposites of each of those attitudes in sequence.	Play the first two attitudes in reverse order.

GESTURE	Assigned characteristics.	Performer's choice of different characteristics.	Combine the two sets.
STYLE	In the manner of a person the performer has observed.	In the manner of another person.	Combine the two styles.
SPACE	Within a ground plan, use one part of the space or an object within it.	Use another part of the space or another object.	Use as much of the plan and the objects within it as possible.
PROPS	Use a prop in typical ways.	Use another prop in atypical ways.	Use both props in either typical or atypical ways.
ATTACK	Attack game continues through all three sections, but is alternately excluded or incorporated as signaled by the instructor.		

Chapter

11

Round Two — Memorized

Energizing

1. **Warmups**

    a. Echo game using phrases of actual arias with

        (1) Attitudes

        (2) Gestures (Indicative, Reactive, Descriptive)

        (3) Facial masks

        (4) Physical masks

    b. Sound and motion using aria or soliloquy phrases as the repeated sound with formal physicalizations and with attitudes.

    c. With the group standing in a circle, aria or soliloquy phrases from person to person (each person using his or her own phrase, not repeating what is passed to him or her) using:

        (1) Attitudes or

        (2) Gestures or

        (3) Facial masks or

        (4) Physical masks or

        (5) Centers of energy or

        (6) Personal experiences

    d. Mood response exercise: The pianist plays accompaniments of arias for the entire group. But instead of anyone singing, the group relates to the mood of the music and projects it by one of the following means:

        (1) Facial masks

        (2) Gestures

    (3) Physical masks

    (4) Attitudes

    (5) Personal experience

  e. Mirror games: The reflector sings or speaks the aria or soliloquy with the initiator providing:

    (1) Facial masks

    (2) Physical masks

    (3) Attitudes

    (4) Gestures

  (Reflector to *incorporate*, make sense of, all of the above.)

  f. Add-on game with actual aria or soliloquy phrases plus actions or attitudes or facial masks or combinations.

2. Spoken

  a. Ensemble exercises. All of the following exercises require memorization of a short dialogue which can be drawn from any source desired. It is more demanding, and perhaps more useful and appropriate, if a scene with genuinely musical language is used, the best examples being those of Shakespeare, but a better introduction to some of the concepts may be provided by more realistic material. Although we do not deal with the problems of acting the scene in traditional, accepted style, it is well for the performers to play the scenes several times in a relatively "normal" fashion before beginning the exercises. Surprisingly, actors often perform better doing the exercises than when they are striving for a known, "correct" style of acting. All of the exercises have in mind some purpose other than a straightforward performance of the scene. The instructor, however, should be capable of dealing with any of the straightforward acting problems that the young performer encounters. And it is of the greatest importance that neither the instructor nor the performers lose sight of what the scene is *about*, for success depends upon the ability of the performer to use the exercises *in terms* of the scene and not simply as technical calisthenics. The successful execution of the technique of each exercise deserves praise, of course, but if the technique has not been incorporated or been made sense of in terms of the scene, the instructor should point this out even while praising the execution. Unless the assigned technique is actually executed, however, it is impossible to make sense of it, so that is the necessary first step.

    (1) Memorized dialogue scene in which one person is assigned a physical mask or center of energy; the other person identifies and uses it. Both performers incorporate the assignment into the scene.

    (2) Memorized dialogue scene in which one person is assigned gestural

characteristics (e.g., small, rapid, large, smooth, jerky, curved, floating, etc.). The other person identifies the characteristics, uses them, and amplifies them.

(3) Memorized dialogue scene in which one person is assigned a way of using space (quickly, nervously, with large steps, small twists, or huge circular motions, etc). The other person identifies it, uses it, and amplifies it.

(4) Memorized dialogue scene in which one person is assigned a facial mask; the other person identifies it and uses it; both performers incorporate it in terms of the scene.

(5) Memorized dialogue scene in which each person is assigned an attitude. One person begins playing an attitude; the other person takes on that attitude. On signal, the second person switches to her or his own attitude, and the first person picks it up. Both performers incorporate both attitudes into the scene.

(6) Memorized dialogue scene in which the pianist plays mood music as a background; the performers use the mood and energy of the music and incorporate it into the scene.

(7) The first performer chooses a personal experience on which to base the scene; the second person responds to that personal experience and plays in harmony with it. When the instructor signals, the second person uses her or his personal experience to which the first person responds.

(8) Memorized dialogue scene in which each person is assigned one of the following language tasks:

High or low

Fast or slow

Continuous or discontinuous

Staccato or legato

Intense or relaxed (relaxed does not mean low energy)

Loud or soft (soft means audible from anywhere in the house)

Significant pauses (pauses that occur at unconventional times, i.e., not when a sentence ends, but rather when it gives special and unusual emphasis to the word that follows).

Sensual words (words that are given a nuance, snarl, curl, caress, growl, gasp, grind, bump, or onomatopoeic sound to make a special point).

Nonverbals (sounds that are not words, but help communicate some special meaning about the line. They can range from the most common of them — the laugh — to various kinds of wheezes, groans, gasps, grunts, sighs, hoots, gurgles, bubbles, etc.).

A typical assignment for one person might be: high and staccato as the prevailing characteristics; one significant pause, one sensual word, and two nonverbals. As always, everything should be incorporated.

(9) Memorized dialogue scene with manipulation and incorporation. The performers amplify the energy suggested by the manipulation.

b. Solo exercises. Like the ensemble exercises, these require memorization of a short soliloquy, which may be drawn from any source desired by the instructor. It is perhaps best if the playwright chosen uses truly musical language like that of Shakespeare, Sheridan, or Goldsmith. The same rule applies here as in the ensemble scenes; the point of the soliloquy should not be lost as the exercise—which may have nothing to do with the sense of the scene—is executed. Good execution should always be acknowledged, but if that execution is not incorporated into the scene itself, the failure should be pointed out.

(1) Memorized soliloquy scene with physical masks or centers of energy chosen by the performer or assigned by the instructor.

(2) Memorized soliloquy scene with an assigned way of using space (see p. 123, exercise 3), chosen by the performer or assigned by the instructor.

(3) Memorized soliloquy scene with specific gestural assignments (Indicative, Reactive, Descriptive) chosen by the performer or assigned by the instructor.

(4) Memorized soliloquy scene with facial masks chosen by the performer or assigned by the instructor.

(5) Memorized soliloquy scene with attitudes, assigned, chosen, or drawn at random from cards.

(6) Memorized soliloquy scene with a personal experience as a base.

(7) Memorized soliloquy scene with assigned language tasks (pitch, speed, rhythm, intensity, dynamics, significant pauses, sensual words, nonverbals). Here it is important that the *task* give the performer energy; the performer should not try to indicate the energy before the task is done.

(8) Memorized soliloquy scene with a musical accompaniment which should be matched in terms of mood, energy, and style.

(9) Memorized soliloquy scene with manipulation by others and incorporation of their motions; the performer should derive energy from the manipulators without acknowledging their presence and should amplify the suggestions received from them.

(10) Mirror exercise: The performer expands and extends the reflection of the initiator, i.e., incorporates and amplifies it.

(11) Memorized soliloquy scene with a readiness exercise. The group leader signals when the performer should move and in which direction. It is useful to have two judges watching from the sides to see if any major alignment adjustments are made before each move.

3. Sung

a. Ensemble exercises. The following exercises require the preparation of an ensemble which can be sung from memory, and which the students understand sufficiently to perform in a traditional manner. It is probably best to use duets at this point, but larger ensembles are possible, depending upon the needs of the class. The same admonition applies here as in the spoken scenes: perform the exercise, but make sense of it. Make certain the technique is exercised, but always find a reason for the technique: incorporate it. The observers' awareness of this twofold distinction should be heightened. The execution or the incorporation deserve praise, but the highest praise should be reserved for the unification of the two.

(1) Duet in which one person is assigned an attitude; the other person identifies and plays that attitude, then amplifies it—gives it more energy. The first person responds to the increased energy level.

(2) Duet in which one performer is assigned a physical mask or center of energy; the other performer identifies it and plays it, extending the energies of the statement. The first performer matches the amplification.

(3) Duet in which one person is assigned a use of space; the other person identifies it, plays it, and expands upon it; the first person responds to the amplification.

(4) Duet in which one person is assigned a sequence of gestures (Indicative, Reactive, Descriptive); the other person picks them up as they occur, amplifying them.

(5) Duet in which one performer is assigned a facial mask; the other identifies it, uses it, and extends it; the first performer then responds to the increased energy level.

(6) Duet in which one person uses a personal experience as a basis for performance; the other picks it up and amplifies it. The first person responds to the increased energy level.

(7) Duet in which two other people manipulate those playing the scene. The performers incorporate and expand the energy suggested by the manipulators.

(8) Duet in which two other people provide a mirror for the scene. The

performers then incorporate and amplify the energies suggested by the initiators.

(9) Duet with manipulation of language for expression. Without unduly distorting the music, the performers find ways of nuancing key words, giving them a special, sensual meaning, using nonverbals between the phrases. They should explore all the possible non-scored ways of inflecting the music and giving it expression. Since this is merely an exercise, do not be afraid to violate the music; "violations" may turn out to be potentially useful elements of expression.

b. Solo exercises. These exercises require the memorization of an aria which the singer understands sufficiently to perform in a traditional manner. It is helpful for each performer in the class to give a formal audition with an aria before beginning the exercises, and to repeat such auditions at intervals throughout the training period. These "auditions" should be treated as formally as possible in order to create a situation which places the performer under the stress of an actual audition. Training exercises and performance (and an audition may be the most difficult performance a singer-actor ever gives) are another set of opposites that need to partake of each other: the exercises need the concentration and desire of performance, and the performance needs the sense of freedom, exploration, and risk of exercises. The audition-performance situation serves to diagnose those weaknesses that need strengthening through exercise, and the exercises make one aware of new strengths that can be used in performance. The relaxation of free-to-fail exercising is too seldom a part of performance; similarly, the intensity and significance of performance are necessary elements of exercise.

(1) Memorized solo with a physical mask or a physical center of energy. Whatever the assignment, the performer should incorporate it into the fabric of the scene itself.

(2) Memorized solo with assigned use of space.

(3) Memorized solo with assigned gestures. These may be given to the performer on a slip of paper before the performance, called out during the scene, or indicated on signs held up during the performance. The gestures should be drawn from the descriptive, reactive, indicative categories.

(4) Memorized solo with assigned facial masks.

(5) Memorized solo with assigned attitudes.

(6) Memorized solo with a personal experience base.

(7) Memorized solo with language manipulation for expressive purposes. The performer should use nuanced words, sensual words,

or nonverbals to explore all possible ways of inflecting the music expressively.

(8) Memorized solo with the readiness exercise. The instructor signals the performer to move forward, backward, or from side to side.

(9) Memorized solo with mirror. The performer incorporates and amplifies whatever is indicated by the initiator.

(10) Memorized solo with attack, incorporation, and amplification of the energy incorporated.

Concentrating

1. Warmups

a. Echo game using phrases of arias or speeches combined with abstract, formal physicalizations. One person combines an aria or speech phrase with a physical action to make a sound and motion. The rest of the circle echoes it and mirrors it in unison. The next person does a sound and motion in a similar fashion, the rest of the group echoes it and the game continues around the circle.

b. The sound and motion sequence using phrases of arias or speeches and formal physical gestures.

c. The participants pass phrases of arias or speeches around the circle, each person using a phrase from his or her aria or speech and making them *seem* to connect by the way in which the energies interrelate.

d. Mirror game. The initiator provides the physical image which the reflector mirrors while singing an aria. The instructor signals for reversal of roles.

e. The add-on game with aria phrases and formal actions.

2. Spoken

a. Ensemble exercises. The following exercises require the performance of a two-person scene. It is important that the performers be comfortable enough with the scenes to perform them in a standard staging.

(1) Scene in which other members of the group "attack" the performers and try to disturb their concentration.

(2) Scene in which other members of the group "attack" the performers, and the performers incorporate the attack into the scene without acknowledging it.

(3) Scene in which the performers try to "penetrate" each other with their focus, with their words, and with their thoughts. Any helpful image can be used to illuminate the idea of penetration: imagined

ESP transference, energy rays, a physical line between the two performers, etc.

(4) Scene in which two people provide a mirror for the performers. The performers must relate to each other and pick up the mirror image as well. They should try always to incorporate and make sense of the images they are mirroring.

(5) Scene in which one performer is given a "secret" (which may be a physical mannerism, a vocal mannerism, an attitude, a way of using space, etc.) which she or he must use, but conceal from a partner. The partner must try to discover the mannerism and use it even more broadly. The performers should make sense of the mannerism in terms of the scene.

(6) The performers play the scene without looking at each other — with a screen between them, or with eyes shut, or back to back — and concentrate on "penetrating" each other. If the communication is not well established, one of the performers or the group leader can say "What?"

(7) As the performers play the scene, the group leader holds up instruction cards: "writhe," "twitch," "grow taller." The performers must incorporate the action into the scene without giving any indication that they are reading instructions and obeying them.

(8) Before the scene, each performer is assigned a task that has nothing to do with the scene. The task should be verifiable (for example, adding a long column of numbers). The idea is to add an additional burden of concentration to the scene. The group should watch carefully to see that the execution of the new task does not detract in any way from the playing of the scene. The task should be incorporated as completely as possible into the sense and mood of the scene.

b. Solo exercises. All the exercises below require the memorization of a soliloquy or monologue, which the student should know well enough to perform in a traditional manner.

(1) Soliloquy with attack. As the performer delivers the speech, other members of the group attempt to disturb her or his concentration.

(2) Soliloquy with "attack" and incorporation. As the performer plays the scene, other participants "attack," and the performer attempts to incorporate the attack without acknowledging it.

(3) Soliloquy with verifiable tasks. The performer is given a task which must be executed during the scene. The soliloquy must not be thrown away in order to perform the assigned tasks. Tasks might include writing a paragraph on a subject other than that of the

soliloquy, adding a list of numbers, drawing a picture, counting a pile of money, or anything requiring concentration.

(4) Soliloquy with mirror. Physical and facial masks are provided by an initiator as the soliloquy proceeds. The performer should incorporate and make sense of the initiator's actions.

(5) As the performer delivers a speech, the instructor calls out commands or holds up large cards with actions written on them. The performer must execute and incorporate the indicated actions. The commands may refer to gestural, vocal, or physical actions. For example: "use the right hand," "higher or faster," "move rapidly downstage," etc.

3. Sung

a. Ensemble exercises. Each of the exercises requires memorization of a duet well enough to be performed in a standard staging.

(1) Other students "attack" the performers during the duet and try to disturb their concentration and their connection to each other.

(2) The other students "attack" the performers during the duet, but this time the singers must incorporate the attack without acknowledging the attackers.

(3) One of the singers is given a specific attitude that is not logical for the scene. The other singer must then see the attitude, understand it, and respond to it, either supplementing it or complementing it. For example, if Susanna were told to play spitefully and nastily in the opening duet of *Figaro*, Figaro would have the choice, assuming he picked up the attitude, of playing it back or adopting an attitude which would help her get over her mood. If he chose the latter course, Susanna would have the choice of giving in to his attempt or increasing her anger until Figaro was forced to get angry in turn. The important things are clarity of observation and clarity of response.

(4) One of the singers is given a physical center of energy or a specific gestural problem which the other singer must observe and use in a similar or contrasting manner in the scene. For example, a very low center of energy, perhaps in the ankles, might call forth a similarly low center from the other singer, or a very high center in contrast. In either instance, both singers should try to use the problem for the purpose of the scene.

(5) One of the singers is given a way of using space: sweeping through space, moving timidly, lightly, delicately, coarsely, smearing it,

dabbing it, or punching it. The partner must identify the use of space, and either imitate it or oppose it.

(6) The singers perform the scene trying to "penetrate'" each other with their focus (see page 177, exercise 3).

(7) Two other members of the class provide mirrors for the performers for playing the scene.

b. Solo exercises. All the exercises below are to be practiced while singing an aria that can be performed easily under normal conditions.

(1) Aria with "attack." The performer is "attacked" by other members of the group and attempts to maintain concentration.

(2) Aria with "attack" and incorporation. The performer is "attacked" by other members of the group and incorporates the attack without acknowledging it.

(3) Aria with verifiable tasks. The singer is given a task to execute while playing the aria-scene. The meaning of the aria must be maintained, and the task should be incorporated into its meaning.

(4) Aria with mirror. Another member of the class gives the singer a mirror, physical, facial, and attitudinal, which the singer must reflect and incorporate.

Structuring

1. Warmups

a. Echo game using a phrase of an aria with sudden or gradual progressions assigned by the instructor in the following areas:

(1) Attitudes

(2) Physical centers of energy moving from one area of the body to another

(3) Two facial masks

(4) Two physical masks

b. Sound and motion using a phrase or part of a phrase from an aria as the repeated sound, but making it progress in one of the following areas before passing it on:

(1) Attitude

(2) Speed, pitch, volume, rhythm, or intensity of the sound

(3) Facial masks

(4) Size, speed, rhythm, intensity, or shape of motion

c. The group passes aria phrases from person to person in a circle, connecting them by pickup of energy, but adding a progression in one of the following as the phrase is sung:

      (1) Attitude

      (2) Gesture

      (3) Facial masks

      (4) Physical centers or masks

      (5) Personal experience

d. Mood pickup and progression. The pianist plays music from an aria and the performer, instead of singing, takes on the mood of the music and projects it, making a progression in ABA form in one of the following:

      (1) Attitudes

      (2) Facial masks

      (3) Physical masks

      (4) Personal experience and free association

e. Mirror with progressions. The nonsinging initiator provides progressions in ABA form in one of the following areas for the performer:

      (1) Attitudes

      (2) Physical masks

      (3) Facial masks

      (4) Gestures

f. Physical phrasing of arias. Instead of singing the arias, the group indicates by physical phrasing the energy flow of the aria as it would be sung. Make certain the energy of the gesture-phrase does not cease until the vocal phrase has concluded. Note also with the physical phrasing the distinction between a phrase that ends and a phrase that continues over a rest to the next phrase.

2. Spoken

a. Ensemble exercises: The following exercises require performance of a memorized two-person scene with ABA, ABC, or ABAB progressions in the areas suggested. Transitions may be either gradual or sudden as assigned by the instructor.

      (1) Physical masks or centers of energy. A—first person assigned, second person picks up the assignment; B—second person assigned, first person picks up and plays the assignment; A—return, or C— evolve a new relationship out of the first two.

      (2) Facial masks. Same pattern as (1)

      (3) Assigned attitudes. Same pattern as (1)

      (4) Personal experience base. Same pattern as (1) but based on personal choice

      (5) Physical use of space. Same pattern as (1)

      (6) Gestural characteristics. Same pattern as (1)

(7) Language techniques. Progressions are assigned to both partners in pitch, speed, rhythm, intensity, or volume. For example, the first person may have a progression in pitch which the second person will pick up and play; the second person, assigned a progression in speed, begins that progression which is picked up and played by the first person. They both return to the A section, or evolve a new relationship, each using a separate progression for the C section. Incorporation should always be encouraged.

(8) The accompanist provides music for the scene; as the music changes, the mood and energy of the scene should change in corresponding ways.

b. Solo exercises. The following exercises require performance of a memorized soliloquy. The performer should display progression in ABA, ABC, ABAC form in the suggested areas. The transitions may be sudden or gradual.

(1) Soliloquy with two or three physical masks or centers of energy assigned by the instructor.

(2) Soliloquy with two or three uses of space assigned by the instructor.

(3) Soliloquy with gesture sequences. For example: A—Indicative; B—Descriptive, Reactive; C—Indicative, Reactive.

(4) Soliloquy with two or three facial masks assigned by the instructor.

(5) Soliloquy with two or three assigned attitudes.

(6) Soliloquy with two or three personal experience attitudes.

(7) Soliloquy with vocal progressions in pitch, volume, speed, intensity, or rhythm.

(8) Soliloquy with a changing musical accompaniment which the performer should match in mood and energy.

(9) Soliloquy with a mirror: the speaker-reflector creates a progression in attitude or language while reflecting a progression given by the initiator in physical masks, facial masks, or gesture.

3. Sung

a. Ensemble exercises. The following exercises require performance of a memorized two-person scene with ABA, ABC, or ABAC progression. The transitions may be gradual or sudden as assigned by the instructor.

(1) Physical masks or centers of energy. A—first person assigned, second person picks up the assignment and plays it; B—second person assigned, first person picks up the assignment and plays it; A—return or, C—evolve a new relationship out of the first two.

(2) Use of space. Same pattern as (1)

(3) Gestural characteristics. Same pattern as (1)

(4) Facial masks. Same pattern as (1)

(5) Assigned attitudes. Same pattern as (1)

(6) Personal experience base. Same pattern as (1) but based on personal choice

(7) Language used expressively for the purposes of communication, within terms of the score. (Example: A—fast, staccato; B—high, intense)

b. Solo exercises. The following exercises require memorization of an aria or a song to be performed with a progression in ABA, ABC, or ABAC form. The progressions may be gradual or sudden as assigned by the instructor.

(1) Aria with two or three physical masks or centers of energy.

(2) Aria with two or three uses of space.

(3) Aria with two or three gestural characteristics.

(4) Aria with two or three facial masks.

(5) Aria with two or three assigned attitudes.

(6) Personal experience based attitudes.

Note: It is possible to mix (5) and (6) so that the performer deals with two more opposites: what I have felt, and what I must feel. The interrelationship between them is vital, for whatever attitude is assigned must inevitably find its source in the performer's personal experience, and one's past always provides the initiating energy for new attitudes in the present.

4. Consolidating the First Three Skills

Having completed the three basic skills of Round Two, the performer is ready to bring them all to bear on the problem of the aria—the solo situation—and to find a means of dealing with this basic problem in both music-theater performance and music-theater auditioning. The skills have been exercised and are available for use; now the singer-actor must make specific choices in the use of these skills in individual arias. The following list of questions, based for the most part on the first three skills, will help give the singer-actor a sense of power, which proceeds directly from the choices one can and should make as a total performer.

What has happened just before the aria?

What is my emotional state as the aria begins?

What is my physical state as the aria begins? Readiness? To do what?

Is there an introduction to the aria? If so, what happens during that introduction to allow the first phrase to grow directly out of it?

How do I progress into my initial focus? Suddenly? Gradually? Searchingly?

When does the focus shift?

Where does it shift?

How often does it shift?

How do I make the transitions between my points of focus? Suddenly? By going inward and then out? By searching?

What is my specific feeling or attitude about each point of focus?

Is there a change of process in each attitude? Is it sudden or gradual?

What is the progression of attitude during the aria?

What kinds of gestures or gesture combinations best communicates each focus-attitude? Indicative, reactive, descriptive, or combinations of the three?

How do I deal with interludes? Do interludes follow from what I have just sung, do they lead into what I will sing next, or do they do both?

Have I identified all my habitual tensions and eliminated them from performance? Do I launch the aria experience from my own natural, available source of energy?

Am I aware that in audition or performance, I must allow whatever skills and techniques I have acquired through exercise to flow freely and uncritically, and that neither situation is an appropriate one for critical self-monitoring? That in performance or audition, the only thing I can be concerned with is communicating the experience of the aria?

What happens in the aria? Can I state clearly what event the aria discusses? For example, in Mozart's "Dove Sono," the Countess moves from a condition of psychological fearfulness and timidity to hopefulness and confidence, which allows her to take charge of the outcome of the opera.

Am I aware that *I* frame the aria, that the experience begins *before* the accompaniment begins and concludes *after* the accompaniment has concluded? Is my accompanist aware of this, and have I worked it out with her or him?

If I am singing in a foreign language, do I know the meaning and implication of every word and phrase both literally and figuratively?

Do I know how the aria relates to the rest of the opera?

Imagining

Before beginning these exercises for imagining, it might be useful to ponder some questions that stimulate this faculty. Answering the questions is not as important as thinking about them, allowing them to put the fantasizing process in gear, and letting it go where it will.

a. In what ways might the character fantasize about his or her situation?

b. Where would an extension of the dominant impulses in the character lead? (For example, what if she or he were to follow through completely on impulses?)

c. If I were in the situation of the character, how would I fantasize about it?

d. Am I able to imagine strange environments or character fantasies while singing the role as written? (For example, could I sing "Porgi Amor" while imagining I was up to my neck in molasses without feeling as though I were desecrating either Mozart or opera? Do I understand that what I use as an imaginative stimulus will not be apprehended as such by the audience but will simply add personal energy to the actual meaning, and that that is the most useful thing one can do, even though the audience might reject the stimulus if they knew what it was?)

e. Can I free myself from my own critical monitoring? Can I let my imagination work in front of other people without worrying about being "right" or "wrong?" Can I take large imaginative risks? Am I aware that the greater the imaginative risk, the safer I actually am as a performer?

f. Have I found ways to practice heightening my imaginative thought processes?

g. Is it fun for me to imagine? If not, why not?

h. Am I critical of other performers' imaginative efforts—or am I supportive?

i. Do I always ask myself when given a strange direction, "What can I make up, what ideas or energies can I give to that action to make it work?" rather than resisting it or proving myself right by making the action look wrong?

j. If I were in a fantasy environment, how would I answer these questions:
How does the air smell?
How dry or humid is the air?
How thick or thin is the air?
What color is the air?
What effect does breathing it have on me?
What is the ground or floor like?
How hard or soft, rough or smooth, slippery or uneven is it?
What color is the ground or floor?
What is around me? Oceans, forests, buildings, mountains, plains?

k. How are these different from ordinary experience? Are the forests made of hair, or sausages, or spaghetti? Are the mountains made of glass, metal, jello, ground beef, or plastic? How are the colors and shapes of the things around me different from ordinary experience? Are the oceans, forests, buildings, mountains, plains made up of living entities or many separate parts: a sea of skulls, a mountain of eggs?

l. What unusual beings inhabit the environment?
   How do these beings relate to me?
   How does the environment relate to me? Does it move physically?
   Does it change color in response to my mood? Does it change shape, transform itself?

m. The body or parts of the body—head, neck, shoulders, arms, wrists, hands, fingers, chest, upper back, lower back, stomach, hips, pelvis, thighs, knees, calves, ankles, feet, toes—can be imagined as being composed of any of the following materials or combinations thereof:

   Balloons, razor blades, needles, marshmallows, worms, grass, cotton, lead, gossamer, liquid (thick or thin, sweet or sour, lumpy or smooth), wood, glass, gravel, leaves, machinery, pudding—the list can go on indefinitely; use your favorite materials.

1. Warmups

a. Echo game in the manner of the character of the person singing an aria or duet being used for class work. An abstract sound should be followed by a short phrase of the aria or duet, both accompanied by an abstract motion.

b. Echo game as though in an imaginary and strange environment.

c. Sound and motion in the manner of the character being worked on in an aria or duet. The performers should incorporate a snatch of the aria or duet into the middle of the abstract sound and motion, keeping the action abstract all the way.

d. Double prop transformations: the performers create an imaginary prop, use it, and transform it into another prop, then pass it on. Add a gibberish commentary.

e. Stream of consciousness passing in the manner of the character in the aria or duet.

f. The performers create a character based on unrelated aria music using physical movement in space; or they create an environment based on the music and move in that environment.

g. The performers select an appropriate magic garment for the character in the aria or duet. How would it affect the character? Use unrelated aria music.

h. Echo theme and variations: one person makes a short sound pattern; the next person develops and varies it.

i. Physical variations: one person performs a physical action; the next person develops and varies it.

2. Spoken

a. Ensemble exercises. The following exercises require memorization of a two-person scene. The problems below should be incorporated into the meaning of the scene.

(1) Scene in your own style, and then in as dissimilar a style as you can imagine. Each person starts with the opposite point of view — one like herself or himself, the other unlike — and then shifts as the instructor signals. (This is a particularly good exercise for self-analysis; the class can offer validation or disagreement with the individual's self-depiction.)

(2) Scene as other characters from the work or from other works might play it.

(3) Scene with attitudes and moods at opposite extremes of those implied in the scene. The performers should incorporate them as much as possible, but play them whether they can incorporate them or not.

(4) Scene with a secret in mind that cannot be revealed: your partner will die in two days, you have just failed an important exam, you have just received a million dollars, etc.

(5) Scene as if in a fantasy environment that you accept and ignore, but must nevertheless cope with. This can be done as an exchange: the first person knows, the second person observes and incorporates; when the instructor signals a shift, the second person plays a new environment which is observed and incorporated by the first. The challenge here, as in the previous exercises, is to make the scene play *because* of the environment, not in spite of it.

(6) Play the scene as if a new thought or image hits each performer on every line — a stream of consciousness separate from the scene itself which is actualized in attitude only.

(7) Play the scene as if your words were extensions that actually got into the other person's head, and that you could manipulate as physical objects.

(8) Scene with one or more props, exploring unusual ways to use them.

(9) Scene in a given ground plan and furniture. The performers explore ways to use the space and objects in it.

(10) Scene with spoken stream-of-consciousness sequences that are not acknowledged, and that deal with subject matter unrelated to what the scene is about.

(11) Play the scene as though expecting something from your partner, something that your partner does not know.

b. Solo exercises. The following exercises require performance of a soliloquy or monologue exercising with one of the following problems:

(1) Play it as much like yourself as you can imagine, and then as much unlike yourself as you can imagine. Class observation and validation or disagreement with the performer's self-depiction is important here. Incorporate the opposite.

(2) Play it as you imagine other characters from the work would play it, or as characters from a different work might play it.

(3) Play it with attitudes and moods opposite from those implied. Incorporate them as much as possible, but play them whether you can incorporate them or not.

(4) Play it as if something incredible has happened to you which you cannot reveal: "I'm going to die," "I've inherited a million dollars," "this building is on fire," etc.

(5) Play it as if in a fantasy environment which you accept and do not comment upon, but with which you must cope. For example, on a shifting floor; in heavy, acid air; with a red haze over everything, with everything changing shape all around, etc.

(6) Play it as if new images and thoughts hit you on every line, or as if a stream of consciousness went on on another level which you actualize in attitude only.

(7) Play it as if the words took you over and did extensions on their own: the words speak to you, and do what they will; or as if the words were spoken through you by someone else.

(8) Play it with several props, using them in as many ways as possible apart from their normal use.

(9) Play it in a ground plan with furniture using the space and the objects integrally in as many ways as possible apart from their logical use, e.g., standing on a chair or lying beneath a chair rather than sitting on a chair.

(10) Play it in the manner of another character or person you have observed.

(11) Play it with a *spoken* stream of consciousness, voicing everything the character is thinking about in addition to the subject of the scene.

3. Sung

a. Ensemble exercises. The following exercises require memorization of a two-person scene with one of the following problems:

(1) Play the scene in the manner of other characters from the same opera or other operas.

(2) Play the scene as much like yourself as you can imagine, and as much unlike yourself as you can imagine. One person may initiate the exercise as the other person picks up the style. When the transition is made, the first person picks up and plays the style changes. Class observation and validation or disagreement with the individual's self-depiction is important.

(3) Play the scene with attitudes and moods opposite from those implied. Incorporate them as much as possible, but play them whether you feel you can incorporate them or not.

(4) Play the scene extending the attitudes and emotions suggested by the scene as far as possible. For example, gentle joy becomes ecstasy, annoyance becomes rage; each emotion is converted into its ultimate extension.

(5) Play the scene as if you knew an extraordinary secret which you cannot reveal: your partner is a UFO occupant in disguise, you are going to die in one day, your partner can win one million dollars, you are pregnant (or your partner is if you are male).

(6) Play the scene as if in a fantasy environment which you must accept but ignore and cope with. The first person imagines the environment, the second person picks up the sense of it; the second person plays another environment, the first person picks up the sense of it. Shift when the instructor signals. The scene should work because of the environment, not in spite of it.

(7) Play the scene as if a new thought or image hits you on every line; a stream of consciousness on another level which you actualize only in attitude.

(8) Play the scene using several props in as many unusual ways as possible.

(9) Play the scene in a ground plan with furniture or objects and use the space and the objects in as many unusual ways as possible.

(10) Play the scene as an imagined extension of another character from the opera or from another opera.

(11) Play the scene as if expecting something from your partner, something your partner does not know.

(12) As the music of the scene is played, each performer speaks in stream of consciousness style, about all the *other* things going through the character's mind besides the actual words of the scene.

b. Solo exercises. The following exercises require performance of an aria or song with one of the following problems:

(1) Play it as much like yourself as you can, and then as unlike yourself as you can imagine. Class observation and validation or disagreement with the performer's self-depiction is important for this exercise. Move back and forth between the styles several times.

(2) Play it in the manner of another character from the same opera or a character from another opera.

(3) Play it with attitudes and moods opposite those implied by the scene. Incorporate these opposites as much as possible, but play them whether you are able to incorporate them or not.

(4) Play it as if you had an amazing secret that you cannot tell, but which is strongly affecting, having to do with love, death, wealth, fame, or catastrophe.

(5) Play it as if in a fantasy environment which you accept and do not comment upon, but with which you must cope.

(6) Play it as if a new image or thought were hitting you every other measure — a stream of consciousness on another level which is actualized in attitude only.

(7) Play it using several props in as many unusual ways as possible.

(8) Play it in a ground plan with furniture and objects, using the space and the objects in it in unusual ways, but in ways which are incorporated into the scene.

(9) Do a spoken stream of consciousness concerning the character's thoughts and impulses underlying what would be sung.

Stylizing

1. Warmups

a. Echo game in the manner of someone you have observed, using fragments of an aria or soliloquy with an abstract physical gesture.

b. Sound and motion in the manner of someone you have observed with parts of an aria or soliloquy phrase as the sound and with an abstract physical motion.

c. Group extensions and compressions. One person sings a short aria phrase, or speaks a soliloquy phrase, adding an abstract motion and repeating it. The group picks it up and repeats it twice, then *extends* the action for two repetitions, but keeps the musical values precisely the same. (The extensions should be individual, each person creating her or his own individual extension.) After the two extended repetitions, the group *compresses* the action, moving from whatever extension they have chosen to a scale smaller than that of the original action, without changing the musical values of the line, and repeat it for two repetitions. Then the group *naturalizes* the action, modifying it so that it becomes stylistically realistic, for two repetitions, again keeping the musical line constant. Finally the group *internalizes* the action, places the original movement inside themselves with no external movement, but with an imagined sense of the original energy. Just as singing must not change simply because the physical style desired by the director might change, so the musical values should be preserved throughout the course of this exercise. Nuance changes, yes; generalized changes in energy level, decrescendos, and ritards, no.

d. Character walks and physicalizations in the manner of someone in the class, or in the manner of someone you have observed. Give special attention to the physical centers of energy, physical use of space and gestural characteristics.

e. Mask and body adjustments. Make a facial mask in the manner of someone you have observed, then pass it to the next person, who adapts her or his body to the mask given. That person sculpts a new facial mask, and passes it to the next person.

Note: The instructor or the group should point it out when the impersonations are less fluid, less flexible, and less real than the reality of what they are drawn from — *we* must be part of our impersonations, and our impersonations must be part of us.

f. Characterizations drawn from the music of arias not known to the performer. Once the style of the music is sensed, move to it, gesture and physicalize to it.

2. Spoken

a. Ensemble exercises. The following exercises require memorization of a two-person scene with attention to the following problems:

(1) Each person plays the scene in the manner of someone in the class, or someone they have observed. Exchange styles on signal of the instructor, then return to original styles.

(2) Each person plays the scene in a very formal, artificial style they have observed, moving to a very natural style on signal of the instructor, and back again. The performers should be able to identify the sources of their styles.

(3) Each person employs the facial characteristics, the gestural characteristics, or the physical posture and mannerisms of a person they have observed. Exchange characteristics on signal of the instructor, and then return to original styles.

(4) Each person concentrates on the language style of another person they have observed. Exchange language characteristics on signal from the instructor and then return to the original styles.

(5) The accompanist provides background music from specific periods which is used to help define the sense of language and movement; the problem is to get into the style-world of the music.

(6) Two other people manipulate the performers, who must incorporate the manipulations and give them meaning.

(7) In styles that the performers have observed or have some knowledge of: Tennessee Williams, Shakespeare, rural American, Deep South, Classical Greek, nineteenth-century melodrama. (Some of these are necessarily generalized, but all are useful for analysis and discussion.)

Note: The preceding exercises can be performed with the ABA, ABC, or ABAC structure described in the structuring exercises.

b. Solo exercises. The following exercises require memorization of a soliloquy or monologue using the style of someone the performer has observed, with attention to the problems below. The performer should be able to specify the qualities observed and utilized so that the intention to project can be checked against the projection itself. Because style in performance necessitates selection and emphasis, the specific characteristics of the people chosen may have to be exaggerated to be stageworthy. But they must also be incorporated.

(1) Physical masks or centers of energy.

(2) Uses of space.

(3) Gestural characteristics. The performer uses the gestural categories in the manner of someone else.

(4) Facial masks and mannerisms.

(5) Language characteristics.

(6) The emotional, attitudinal tone of the person. Everyone has a prevailing emotional weather system; the performer should try to identify that base and incorporate it.

(7) Idiosyncrasies of any kind that help define the person.

(8) The person's style in a very formal situation and then in a very relaxed, natural situation.

(9) Manipulation by someone else in the class. The performer should incorporate those manipulations into the style of the person being played.

(10) Mirror exercise incorporated into the style of the person.

(11) In a series of styles with which the performer is familiar selected

from the following list: classical Renaissance, Baroque, eighteenth-century court, nineteenth-century romantic melodrama, twentieth-century expressionist, nineteenth-century heightened realism, twentieth-century naturalism, Greek Statuesque, nineteenth-century operetta, twentieth-century cabaret.

(12) In the performer's *own* style, then in an opposite style.

3. Sung

a. Ensemble exercises. The following exercises require memorization of a duet to be performed in the style of someone the performers have observed, with attention to the problems below. Again, emphasis and extension may be necessary if the observers are to perceive the performer's intention. Equal attention should be given to incorporation.

(1) Physical masks, centers of energy, postural characteristics.

(2) Use of space: physical rhythms, speeds, size, etc.

(3) Facial masks. These may involve movement of the facial muscles as well as set masks.

(4) Mannerisms, idiosyncrasies.

(5) Emotional tone.

(6) Language or musical nuance characteristic of singers the performers have observed.

(7) With manipulation and incorporation. Here, the manipulation is being imposed on a person who has already adopted an impersonation, a kind of mask upon a mask. The problem is to incorporate the manipulations into the style of the impersonation.

(8) In the performers' *own* style, then in an opposite style.

Note: Because each performer in these duets will have picked a different person for stylistic impersonation, the problem is for each to adjust the styles so that the scene has a stylistic unity. It is not enough to simply "do" the person; the performers are playing a scene together, and everyone's style must be taken into consideration.

b. Solo exercises. The following exercises require memorization of an aria song in the style of someone the performer has observed, with attention to the problems below. Extension and emphasis of the traits involved may be necessary for communication.

(1) Aria with physical masks or armoring, postural statements, centers of energy.

(2) Aria with use of space: rhythms, speeds, size, etc.

(3) Aria with gestural characteristics. The performer uses the gestural categories in the manner of the person observed.

(4) Aria with facial masks and facial movement, tics, etc.

(5) Aria with mannerisms, idiosyncrasies.

(6) Aria with emotional tone.

(7) Aria with language or musical nuance characteristic of a singer the performer has observed.

(8) Aria with manipulation and incorporation. The performer should be singing in the manner of someone else, and the manipulations must be incorporated into that style.

(9) Aria in the manner of someone else the singer has observed. When the instructor signals a change, the performer should use his or her own manner.

4. Focusing the Stylistic Skills

The stylizing skills have now been exercised using memorized material, and it is time to focus these skills by examining a series of questions that deal with specific operas and characterizations. The questions cut through all levels of music-theater experience, from internal emotional events to external technical skills. Although some questions are more important than others, it is essential that the singer-actor give some thought to all of them. Some have to do with one's personal style, others with the style of the given opera and its individual characters, and still others with the ultimate problem — the integration of period style and personal style.

a. What happens in the opera? What is the story? What is the dominant mood of the story?

b. How does your character relate to the events of the story? What is she or he? What does she or he do in life?

c. How does the music interpret the story? How does the story affect the mood of the music?

d. How does the music define your character? How is your character's music different from the rest of the score?

e. Where is the climax or crisis of the story? How is it treated musically?

f. Where is the climax or crisis for your character? How is it treated musically?

g. Is your character sympathetic or unsympathetic? How is this reflected musically?

h. What changes take place in your character? Can you think of possible changes besides those suggested by the story? Does the music suggest the same changes, different changes, or fewer changes than those of the story? Where are the transitions, musically and verbally? Do they agree?

i. What are your character's needs and desires? Likes and dislikes? How important are they to her or him? What will your character do to get what she or he wants? Does she or he get it? Where are these needs and desires most clearly communicated? Which scenes?

j. Who opposes or aids your character? Who likes or dislikes your character? What is your relationship to each of the other characters?

k. How intelligent is your character? How sensitive? What does she or he say in the piece? How does your character express herself or himself? Forthrightly? Vaguely? What are your character's beliefs and convictions?

l. How does your character feel about each of the other characters in the opera? How do they feel about your character? What do they say about him or her? Are they speaking truthfully? Why do they react as they do?

m. What actions are implied in your lines? How are these actions modified or expanded by the music?

n. Drawing only upon the libretto, describe your own character in detail including age, status, personality, physical characteristics, temperament, etc. How does the music describe your character? Do the descriptions agree?

o. Make a similar description of yourself. Then compare your own characteristics and those of your character. What adjustments would you have to make in yourself to become more like your character? Be especially aware of physical rhythms.

Coordinating

1. Warmups.

The warmups for this section require memorization of a scene from a play, a soliloquy from a play, and/or a memorized duet, trio or quartet from an opera, and an aria from an opera.

a. Echo game. The performers use part of a line or part of an aria phrase, and repeat it three times, developing it in speed, rhythm, volume, intensity, or pitch, with a progression in attitude.

b. Sound and motion. The performers begin with an abstract sound and motion in the manner of a character from an opera or a play; while continuing the abstract movement, they add a short line or phrase which is repeated three times and developed, then return to the same abstract sound and motion with a new attitude, and pass it on.

c. Sung or spoken gibberish. The performers sing or speak in the manner of a dramatic or operatic character, with idiosyncratic gestures, focused on an imagined person, with an attitude, with a progression in either the language or the music (i.e., in rhythms, speed, volume, pitch, etc.).

d. Mirror game. The initiator makes a gradual progression in physical action and attitude. The reflector responds with extensions of both physical actions and attitudes, or assumes a complementary attitude. At the same time, the two carry on a dialogue of phrases from two different arias or soliloquies—a snatch of one is answered by a snatch of the other.

2. Spoken

a. Ensemble exercises.

(1) The Shakespeare game (or the Wilde game, the Williams game, or the twentieth-century American Dramatist's game, depending upon the material available to the class). Any two actors who are not partners can play the game. The two exchange lines of dialogue from different scenes. The dialogue will make no sense verbally— except by accident—but can *seem* to make sense if the actors make it sound that way. They can make sense of it by *listening* carefully, by *relating* to what is said to them in mood and attitude and style, by *altering* the delivery of their own lines so that they make as much connection as possible with what they respond to, and by *creating* a new situation out of the combination of two separate strands of dialogue. Thus the exercise tests many of the actors' basic skills: how well they listen, how well they relate, how flexible they are in responding to what is actually happening rather than to what they wish would happen, and how well they are able to create the circumstances of drama through the use of language and creative interplay. Although it seems difficult to imagine, it can be done, and it is a superb exercise of the actor's craft. (Not surprisingly, the best actors I have worked with are also the best at playing the game.) By sending in replacements for each person in turn, the whole class can be involved in a very short time, and the exercise makes an excellent warmup.

(2) Scenes using structure, and two of the following problems. Although the exercises can be performed when the participants know each other's assignment, observation and relating will be more fully exercised if the performers know only their own assignments and must adjust to those of others. There are two basic kinds of pattern that can be used in these exercises: an exchange pattern and a shared pattern. In the exchange pattern, one person is assigned a concept to play and the other person has to identify it and use it; the second person plays a different assigned concept, and the first person must identify it and use it; in the third section they may either return to the first relationship and expand upon it, or be

given a third assignment together. In the shared pattern, each person is given or develops a separate concept; then moves to another set of assigned or developed concepts and integrates them. In the third section the performers either return to the first section and expand on it or create still another disparate but interrelating sequence. The problem here is to relate the two disparate concepts. The pattern or combination to be used is left to the discretion of the instructor.

(a) Structure: ABA, ABC, ABAC, $A_1 A_2 A_3$ (theme and variations)

(b) Attitudes assigned:

A—first person assigned, second person pick up

B—second person assigned, first person pick up

A—return, but with exchanged attitudes

C—logical evolution of preceding attitudes

$A_1 A_2 A_3$—first person initiates, second person does variation, first picks up; first person does variation, second person picks up, etc.

(c) Physical: Masks (physical or facial), centers of energy, or magic garment extensions.

A—each with a separate assignment

B—exchange

A—combination of the two

C—each evolves a new extension from B

$A_1 A_2 A_3$—each evolves variations on the basic style

(d) Style: Each performs in the manner of someone else from the same play

A—each with a separate character

B—exchange

A—each combines the two

C—evolve a new extension based on B

$A_1 A_2 A_3$—each evolves variations on the basic style

(e) Space: Within an arranged ground plan. Use the given space and objects in as many ways as possible, incorporating them into the meaning of the scene.

(f) Gesture:

A—each person with an assigned set of gestures—characters

B—exchange them

A—each combines the two

C—each evolves a new set from the old

$A_1 A_2 A_3$—each evolves variations on the basic set

(g) Props: Use of three assigned props, to be exchanged, one for each section, so that each performer uses one in each section. (This implies the ABC form. Other possibilities include a single prop used in a different way each time.)

(h) Music: To be taken from scored music. The performers adapt the scene to the energy of the music.

(i) Language:

A—first person assigned, second person pick up

B—second person assigned, first person pick up

A—each combines both characteristics

C—each evolves new characteristics from those in B

$A_1 A_2 A_3$—each evolves a set of variations from the basic characteristics

(3) Scene in which performers are assigned tasks having nothing to do with the scene, but the accomplishment of which can be verified. For example, they can be asked to add a column of numbers or count the number of lights in the theater or room, or to build a structure together, or to pick up scraps of paper from the floor. The scene should be made to work despite the task. All performers in the scene should do the task.

(4) Scene including a nonspeaking person who must be incorporated into the action. The mute should also try to relate to the scene.

b. Solo exercises. The following exercises require memorization of a soliloquy or monologue with structure and two or more of the problems below. The instructor should signal for transitions.

Structure: ABA, ABC, ABAC, $A_1 A_2 A_3$ (theme and variations).

Soliloquy with assigned attitudes. If the theme and variations structure is chosen, one attitude should evolve.

Soliloquy with personal experience. The personal experience can be expanded upon, changed, or reversed to form the structure. The manner in which the experience changes should be assigned.

Soliloquy with physical masks, center of energy extensions, or magic garment extensions assigned as a sequence.

Soliloquy with facial masks assigned as a sequence.

Soliloquy with use of space and furniture. Find contrasting ways to use these to outline the structure. Assign the sequence.

Soliloquy with use of gestures. Sequences from the gestural categories on pp. 126-129 should be assigned.

Soliloquy with use of props. In what ways can props be used to clarify the meaning of the soliloquy?

Soliloquy with use of background music. The accompanist provides music from a score; the performers shift with music while maintaining the other structural elements.

Soliloquy with use of language. Select two categories and two specials (see pp. 134-137). For example, high to low, fast to slow, a significant pause, and a nonverbal.

Soliloquy with stylization. In the manner of two people (consecutively) from the play, or from other plays, or imagined extensions of actual people. Tasks having nothing to do with the scene but which can be verified should be assigned. Another person may enter the scene; the performer should integrate the newcomer into the scene, and that person should also use the soliloquy and its performer.

3. Sung

a. Ensemble exercises.

(1) Worlds in collision. This is a musical version of the Shakespeare game. It should be preceded by a group exercise like sound and motion. The pianist lays out the scores of all the ensemble numbers known to the class so that they are accessible. The pianist begins one of the ensembles, the people involved in that ensemble sing it, as the rest of the group finds ways of relating to the ensemble. Everybody is part of every ensemble, singing or not. The pianist may shift at any time (it is sometimes useful to strike a gong to indicate changes; this allows a brief transition). When the pianist moves to another ensemble, new singers begin singing, and a new situation is evolved from the old. There should be no dropping of character or situation, but continuity and creation of new situations. There will at first be bewilderment, arbitrary actions, nonrelating, etc. But the skills called for are primary to singing-acting: *listening* to what is actually happening (not to what one expects to happen), *relating* to the music, words, and actions as they are actually happening (as opposed to knowing what is going to happen), *creating* a situation from this observation by *interacting* with the other performers. Arias can be included, but ensembles are easier at first, because they establish the relating concept immediately, and provide potential polarities around which the rest of the group can organize.

(2) Scene using ABA, ABC, ABAC, or $A_1 A_2 A_3$ structures *against* the structure of the scene if desired. The instructor should signal the transitions of the exercise as opposed to those of the ensemble. The following categories for structural organization should be used.

Exchange pattern with observation and incorporation, or two shared, different, interrelating sequences (see p. 196).

(a) Physical masks, center of energy extensions, or magic garment extensions

(b) Facial masks (exchange or shared)

(c) Assigned attitudes (exchange or shared)

(d) Personal experience ("   "   "   )

(e) Use of space   ("   "   "   )

(f) Use of props

(g) Use of language nuance within the context of the music

(h) Style: In the manner of other characters in the opera, or other operas, or *imagined extensions* of other people (exchange or shared)

(3) Scene with assigned tasks that can be verified but that have nothing to do with the scene.

(4) Scene including a nonspeaking person who must be incorporated (and who must incorporate the scene).

b. Solo exercises. An aria using ABA, ABC, $ABAC$, or $A_1 A_2 A_3$ structure with the problems below. (The structure may be with or against the actual structure of the aria, depending upon the needs of the performer and the desire of the instructor.) The instructor should signal the transitions.

(1) Aria with physical masks, center of energy extensions, or magic garment extensions as assigned.

(2) Aria with facial masks as assigned.

(3) Aria with use of space and furniture as assigned. Find contrasting ways to use both to define the experience.

(4) Aria with use of gesture as assigned from the categories on p. 126.

(5) Aria with use of props. Find *contrasting* ways of using them to outline structure.

(6) Aria with assigned attitudes.

(7) Aria with personal experience which is then altered, expanded, and reversed to create the structure.

(8) Aria with language nuance. No structure is necessary.

(9) Aria with stylization. Consecutively in the manner of two characters from the opera (or other operas), or as *imagined* extensions of actual people.

(10) Aria with assigned tasks that can be verified but have nothing to do with the aria.

(11) Aria with one or more nonspeaking characters. The performer should relate to them and incorporate them.

Chapter

12

Round Three — Improvised and Memorized

Energizing

1. Warmups

The idea of extension and implosion-compression may be reexamined at this point. By extension we mean the increase in scale and energy of a given statement. For example, nodding the head can become a nodding or undulating of the whole body. And the extension need not remain in the same plane: the nodding head can be converted into a side to side "nodding" of the shoulders or hips, or spiraling nodding of the knees. It is not simply a "blowing up" of the movement; extension should involve imagination, as do all aspects of our work. One can even conceive of translating extensions from the physical to the vocal or the reverse; for example, a leg movement could be translated into a vocal sound and then extended, or translated as a vocal extension immediately. The concept of extension is exceptionally congenial to music-theater work because, as previously suggested, one can look at any aria or sung ensemble as an extension of a spoken version of the same text.

The idea of implosion is also useful to the music-theater concept. Physically and emotionally one often needs a tremendous amount of contained energy when singing. So the notion of implosion or compression is the psychological opposite of extension; it means converting the external energy of an action, physical or vocal, into psychological, internal energy. In the example above the nodding of the body could be compressed and *"thought"* by the performer without the use of external action. The *thought* of the movement gives the performer an energy that would not otherwise be available to her or him.

201

Felsenstein often applied this device to the voice in order to get a higher level of emotional energy from a performer. For example, a performer might be asked to think of the rhythm of a passage as tripled or quadrupled to feel the true psychological excitement of the character, which may often be much stronger than the musical rhythms would imply. Or the performer might be asked to think of the actual pitch aimed for in an ascending passage as being a fifth or an octave higher than it is, which accomplishes two things: it makes the note easier to sing, and it gives the performer an image of greater intensity (assuming that this is desirable), psychologically enhancing the performance. Both of these concepts—extension and implosion-compression—are used in the warmups that follow.

    a. Echo game. Aria or soliloquy phrase merging into an abstract phrase (or the reverse), with one of the following problems:

        (1) Specific attitudes

        (2) Gestures (Indicative, Reactive, Descriptive)

        (3) Physical centers or physical masks

        (4) Facial masks or gestures

    b. Sound and motion. The repeated sound should be a mixture of aria or soliloquy phrase and an abstract sound, one merging into the other. The performers add a motion that merges a natural gesture and an abstract gesture. In both instances the abstract extends the natural, the natural implodes the abstract. Include an attitude.

    c. Aria or soliloquy in a circle with abstract extensions. The first person begins with an aria or soliloquy phrase, then extends it into an abstraction and passes it on. The next person answers the abstraction in the same style—that is, abstractly—and makes a transition from the abstraction to her or his own aria or soliloquy phrase. From there, the performer moves into extension-abstraction and passes it on. Add attitudes, gestures, facial masks, physical masks, centers of energy, or personal experiences.

    d. Mood projection. The pianist moves back and forth between improvisation and aria accompaniment. The singers, without making any actual sounds, relate to the mood of the music, extend it, amplify it, and project it by means of facial masks or gestures, physical masks, gestures, attitudes, or personal experiences.

    e. Add-on game. The performers alternate aria or soliloquy phrases with abstract sounds, or gestures (indicative, descriptive, reactive) with abstract motions.

2. Spoken

    a. Ensemble exercises. The following exercises require memorization of a two-person scene. As each scene is performed, the instructor signals one of the performers (previously designated) to begin improvising; the partner joins in. At a second signal, the partner steers the improvisation back to the scene. This sequence can be repeated as often as desired. At the same time the performers should deal with one of the following energy problems:

(1) Scene with physical mask or energy center assigned privately to one person. The other person picks it up, transforms it, and returns it. Keep repeating the sequence until the scene is finished.

(2) Scene with use of space assigned to one person. The other performer picks it up, transforms it, and passes it back. The sequence may be repeated as often as necessary throughout the scene.

(3) Scene with gestural characteristics assigned to one person. The other person picks it up, transforms it, and passes it back, The sequence may be repeated throughout the scene.

(4) One person is assigned a facial mask which the other person picks up, transforms, and passes back. The sequence may be repeated throughout the scene.

(5) Each person is assigned three attitudes. The first performer plays an attitude which the second person picks up and transforms to her or his first assigned attitude. The first performer then picks up that attitude and transforms it to her or his second attitude. The scene continues until all three attitudes have been played on both sides.

(6) Each performer selects three personal experiences to serve as bases for attitudes. The attitudes are passed back and forth as in exercise 5 above.

(7) Each person is assigned language tasks. The first person passes a task on, the second person picks it up, amplifies it, and makes a transition to her or his own assignment which is in turn picked up and amplified, by the first person. The first person then makes a transition back to her or his own assignment which is picked up, and so forth until the scene is completed.

(8) The accompanist plays background music. The mood and the energy of the music (which should change frequently) should be matched and incorporated by both performers, with special attention to those moments when the music changes.

(9) Each performer is manipulated by someone else from the class. Each should incorporate the energies suggested by the manipulation and make them relate to the other performer.

(10) Other members of the class provide mirrors for the performers, who should incorporate, amplify, and relate the suggestions of the mirror initiators.

b. Solo exercises. The following exercises require memorization of a soliloquy, using the principle of the previous ensemble exercises. On a signal from the instructor, the performer moves from the memorized speech to an improvisation or back again. At the same time, the performer deals with one of the energy problems below. The improvised sections can be in stream of consciousness or gibberish form, character and situation oriented, or based on a previously assigned topic.

(1) Soliloquy with assigned physical masks or centers of energy. Several can be assigned and on a signal from the group leader, the performer moves from one to the next.

(2) Soliloquy with two assigned uses of space. Movement from one to the other takes place on signal from the instructor or at the performer's will.

(3) Soliloquy with assigned or signaled gestural tasks (Indicative, Reactive, Descriptive).

(4) Soliloquy with three assigned facial masks. The instructor signals for movement between them. It is important to incorporate these masks so that they are made a part of the scene.

(5) Soliloquy with three assigned attitudes. Movement between them takes place on signal from the instructor or the performer's will.

(6) Soliloquy with a personal experience which is transformed, extended, and returned to. The performer should then move away from the original experience with a different kind of energy and return.

(7) Soliloquy with two assigned language tasks. The instructor signals for movement back and forth between them. Include pauses, nonverbals, sensual words, speed, pitch, rhythm, intensity, volume.

(8) Soliloquy with another person providing a mirror. The image should be incorporated and amplified or extended.

(9) Soliloquy with another person providing a mirror for physical masks, facial masks, or attitudes. The performer should take the image and amplify it in the area given. For example, a shoulder energy image could become giant sized, and incorporated; a jolly attitude image could become exuberant, overjoyed, or some other blowup of the original even as it is incorporated into the scene.

(10) Soliloquy with the readiness game. The instructor should signal for movement.

(11) Soliloquy with manipulation by another member of the class. The performer should incorporate and extend the energy.

(12) Soliloquy with musical accompaniment which changes frequently. The performer must match the mood and energy of the music, shifting in these areas as the music does.

3. Sung

    a. Ensemble exercises. The following exercises require memorization of a duet. The memorized scenes move into improvisation and back as often as desirable, signaled by the group leader, the accompanist, or a performer. The performers should deal with one of the energy problems below.

       (1) Duet with one person assigned a physical mask or center of energy. The other person picks it up, transforms it, and passes it back. The process is repeated throughout the scene.

       (2) Duet with one person assigned a facial mask. The other performer picks it up, transforms it, and passes it back. The process is repeated throughout the scene.

       (3) Duet with one person assigned a use of space. The other picks it up, transforms it, and passes it back. The process is repeated throughout the scene.

       (4) Duet with one person assigned gestural characteristics. The second performer picks them up, transforms them, and passes them back. The process is repeated throughout the scene.

       (5) Duet with one person assigned an attitude. The second performer picks it up, plays it, transforms it, and passes it back. The process is repeated throughout the scene.

       (6) Duet with one person choosing a personal experience base. The other person picks up the attitude, transforms it to a personal experience base of her or his own, and returns it. The process continues throughout the scene.

       (7) Duet with manipulation by two members of the group. The performers incorporate the suggested energy and amplify it.

       (8) Duet with mirrors provided by two members of the group. The performers incorporate and extend the images and energies thus initiated.

       (9) Duet with language manipulation for expressive purposes: nuanced words, sensual words, nonverbals and the like, exploring all the possible ways of inflecting the music expressively.

    b. Solo exercises. The following exercises require memorization of an aria. The memorized material moves into improvisation (or the reverse) either on signal from the instructor or the accompanist, or at the performer's will. The performer deals with one of the following problems at the same time.

       (1) Aria with two assigned physical masks or centers of energy.

       (2) Aria with three assigned facial masks.

       (3) Aria with two assigned uses of space.

(4) Aria with assigned or signaled gestural tasks (Indicative, Reactive, Descriptive).

(5) Aria with three assigned attitudes.

(6) Aria with a personal experience base which the performer transforms and extends, then returns to the original experience base. The performer moves away from the original experience with a different kind of energy and returns again.

(7) Aria with language manipulation for expressive purposes: sensual words, nonverbals, and nuanced words.

(8) Soliloquy with a mirror provided by another member of the class. The performer should incorporate and extend the energies thus initiated.

(9) Soliloquy with manipulation by one or two other members of the class. The performer should incorporate and extend the energies suggested by the manipulation.

(10) Soliloquy with the readiness game. The instructor signals for movement forward and back and side to side.

(11) Soliloquy with mirrors that provide specific physical masks, centers of energy, gestural devices, or facial masks mirrored and then amplified by the performer.

Concentrating

1. Warmups

a. Echo game. Each person repeats a phrase from an aria or speech, gradually turning it into an abstract sound and extending it. The process should be accompanied by a physical action, preferably abstract, which develops and extends along with the vocal line. When each individual has completed an extension, the rest of the group repeats it, duplicating the pattern as closely as possible.

   This exercise can be reversed—that is, the performer can begin with an abstract sound and motion pattern and convert it into an aria or speech phrase. The physical accompaniment to the aria or speech phrase can be in one of the three gestural categories (Indicative, Reactive, Descriptive), and the physical extension can grow from that base.

b. Extension and compression. One person sets up a repeating pattern using an aria phrase (only a bar or two) and a physical action. When the pattern is established, the rest of the group picks it up and repeats both sound and motion along with the performer. When the group pattern is well established (with, say, two repetitions), the instructor says, "extend," and the group extends the physical but not the vocal pattern. Each individual extends it in his or her own way. When the extension has been attained, the instructor says, "implode," and everyone compresses the action to a scale below that of the original sound and motion. When this has been attained, the instructor says, "internalize," and the group displays no visible external action. This is an excellent exercise for isolating and disciplining the tendency to speed up or slow down musically when physical action increases or decreases in speed or scale. The instructor should be ready to point out any change in the vocal line as the physical action changes. The goal should be an undisturbed vocal repetition with a wide variety of accompanying physical actions. (One can, of course, ask that the vocal line be extended, compressed, and internalized along with the physical action. This, in fact, might be a good introduction to the discipline demanded in the exercise described above.) The instructor may vary the exercise as necessary.

c. Sound and motion in which the repeated sound used by each person is an integral mixture of an abstract sound and an aria or speech phrase. The abstract sound can be thought of as an extension of the aria portion and the aria portion can be thought of as an implosion-compression of the abstract energies.

d. Aria or speech phrases passed around the circle using the compression-extension idea discussed above. The first person begins with an aria or speech phrase which becomes an abstract extension; this extension is *answered* by the next person, who responds in the same style; that person then implodes the extended style from which will emerge her or his own aria or speech phrase, which is in turn answered and extended by the next person. (Since each extension is a more generalized form of energy, it can be imploded and converted into any number of aria or speech phrases.)

e. Mirrors in which the reflector implodes the extensions of the initiator or extends the implosions of the initiator. Both processes should be practiced. For example, if the initiator moves the hands up and down while wiggling the legs, the reflector might compress this into a handshake or a gesture of repulsion; if the initiator performs a concrete action such as a "come hither" gesture, the reflector might extend this into a strong flapping of the arms and a body undulation. (Remember that neither extensions nor implosions are simple changes in scale; rather they are both *metaphors*, and both are dependent upon the imagination of the metaphor-maker for their vitality.) The instructor should signal the shift of initiators and reflectors.

f. Focus exercises moving back and forth between English and sung or spoken gibberish. It is important to remember the concepts of extension and implosion-compression as they pertain to verbal meaning and musical generalization, the gibberish being verbally specific and less evocative musically. The task is to reconcile these two opposites as much as possible by making the gibberish as specifically meaningful as possible.

An "attack" can be added to this exercise as well, with the shift from gibberish to English accomplished at the signal of the instructor while the other members of the class attempt to disrupt the focus and concentration of the performer.

2. Spoken

a. Ensemble exercises. The following exercises require memorization of a two-person scene. As the scene is played, the instructor signals one of the performers (previously designated) to begin improvising; the partner joins in. When the instructor signals a second time, the partner steers the improvisation back to the original scene. Add to this exercise one of the following problems:

(1) Scene with "attack." Other members of the class try to disturb the concentration of the two performers.

(2) Scene with two nonspeaking characters who are treated as silent partners entering the scene and who are included in the improvisation section. The two can be asked to speak during the improvisatory action, and to find an exit as the scene returns to memorized material.

(3) Scene with unrelated task. Each performer is given a verifiable task which must be completed during the scene. The tasks can involve adding a row of numbers, rearrranging furniture according to a given ground plan, changing or exchanging of articles of clothing, etc. Accomplishing the task, however, must not detract from the performance of the scene as such; it must be incorporated.

(4) Scene with isolated performers. The performers are not allowed to see each other. A screen may be placed between them, they may keep their eyes shut, or play the scene back to back. They should attempt to "penetrate" each other, to communicate with the sound alone. If the communication is not successful, one of them or the instructor should say "what?"

(5) Scene with unexpected commands. The instructor calls out verbal commands or holds up signs with instructions on them. The instructions can involve vocal, physical, facial, or gestural problems: "speak faster and higher," "move rapidly in large circles," "drop

your mouth open as far as possible while speaking," "caress the air with your left hand as you talk." Once again, the performers must attempt to incorporate the task without breaking from the scene and without any awkwardness or sense that the task does not belong in the scene.

(6) Scene with assigned secrets. Each performer is assigned one or more "secrets:" physical, vocal, facial, or gestural mannerisms, or ways of using space, props, or furniture, which the other person must try to see or hear. Each performer is trying to conceal or incorporate an individual "tic" completely while she or he tries to ferret out those of others. Once the performers learn each others' secrets, they use them openly, thus unmasking them.

(7) Scene with mirrors. Two other members of the group provide mirrors for the performers. The performers must attempt to incorporate the mirrors completely, without letting that task interfere with the scene.

b. Solo exercises. The following exercises require memorization of a soliloquy, to be performed with shifts to improvised material at the signal of the instructor. The performer should deal with one of the following problems:

(1) Soliloquy with "attack." Two or more members of the group try to distract the performer. The performer should not break concentration.

(2) Soliloquy with incorporated "attack." The performer is attacked but this time should incorporate the physical situation without acknowledging the attackers.

(3) Soliloquy with nonspeaking characters. Two or more people enter the scene and are incorporated into it by the performer. They may either remain silent or speak, depending upon the wishes of the instructor, but they should relate to whatever the soliloquizer gives them.

(4) Soliloquy with unrelated task. The performer is assigned tasks which can be verified. The continuity and meaning of the soliloquy should be maintained and played.

(5) Soliloquy with mirror. Another class member provides a physical and facial mirror that the performer must incorporate.

(6) Soliloquy with unexpected commands. The instructor holds up cards with actions written on them which must then be executed and incorporated by the performer. For example: "hop on one foot," "faster and slower," "make a facial mask," etc.

3. Sung

a. Ensemble exercises. One of the ensembles already learned for previous exercises may be used. The instructor signals the pianist to move from memorized to improvised material. The singers must necessarily improvise as well, either in the style of the scene or in a related style. The performers may continue the implications of the scene, or do a stream of consciousness exploration of the character's thoughts. They may either sing or speak, but the accompaniment should continue. Or the singers may improvise verbally on a theme that relates to the characters and their situation. The following problems are added to the scene.

(1) Scene with "attack." The performers must maintain their concentration.

(2) Scene with incorporated "attack." The performers incorporate the attack without acknowledging the attackers.

(3) Scene with unrelated task. The performers are assigned verifiable tasks to accomplish without breaking the mood or meaning of the scene.

(4) Scene with isolated performers. The performers are not allowed to see each other. A screen may be placed between them, they may play it in the dark, but they must attempt to communicate or "penetrate" each other.

(5) Scene with unexpected commands. The performers play the scene, executing commands which the instructor holds up on printed cards.

(6) Scene with assigned secrets. Each performer has a "secret" (physical, facial, or vocal) which she or he conceals, but which the other person tries to detect. When they learn each other's secret, they play it themselves.

(7) Scene with mirrors. Two other performers provide mirrors for the performers that must be incorporated with a minimum of distraction.

b. Solo exercises. The exercises below require memorization of an aria, to be performed with a shift to improvisation on the signal of the instructor or ad libitum by the pianist. The improvisation may be sung or spoken, and may be either a stream of consciousness monologue based on the character, a continuation of the ideas in the aria itself, or a subject suggested by the class, which must then be incorporated into the character's world. When the signal to shift back to the memorized aria is made, the performer may make the transition gradually, but the challenge is to make it as seamless as possible; that is, to disguise the break as completely as possible. At the same time, the following problems are added to the performance.

(1) Aria with "attack." The performer must maintain concentration.

(2) Aria with incorporated "attack." The performer incorporates the attacker's actions without acknowledging them.

(3) Aria with nonspeaking characters. Other members of the class are added to the scene, silent partners, and are incorporated by the performer. They in turn relate to what the performer gives them.

(4) Aria with unrelated task. The performer is assigned a verifiable task which must be completed without breaking the mood or meaning of the scene.

(5) Aria with mirror. Another member of the class provides a mirror which the performer must incorporate as organically as possible.

(6) Aria with unexpected commands which the instructor gives either by means of written signs or spoken commands.

Structuring

1. Warmups: sung or spoken

a. Echo game. Aria or soliloquy phrases should move between abstract sung and spoken sounds with gradual or sudden progressions in the following areas:

(1) Physical masks or centers of energy

(2) Facial masks

(3) Gestures (move from one category to another)

(4) Attitudes

b. Sound and motion. The abstract sound and motion is transformed to an aria or soliloquy phrase with an abstract motion, which is then transformed to a new abstract sound and motion, which is then passed on. The person picking up the sound and motion should not mirror it, but complement it. The first transformation should be gradual, the second sudden (or the reverse).

c. Circle passing, abstract to aria. The first person begins with an abstract sound, moves to an aria or soliloquy phrase, and passes it to the next person. That person, however, makes the connection with an abstract sound, which is then transformed into an aria or soliloquy phrase and passed on. Each abstract to aria-soliloquy solo should have a progression in one of the following areas:

(1) Physical masks or centers of energy

(2) Facial masks

(3) Gestures

(4) Attitudes

2. Spoken

a. Ensemble exercises. The following exercises involve scenes for two persons moving between memorized and improvised material. At the same time a progression in one of the areas below is made in ABA, ABC, or ABAC form. In the A section, the first person picks up the assignment of the second person and passes his or her assignment back in the B section. The first person picks up the assignment on the return to the A section. In the optional C section, both performers evolve a new set of assignments out of the previous two. It is important to incorporate the problem into the terms of the scene.

(1) Physical masks or centers of energy

(2) Gestural characteristics

(3) Facial masks

(4) Use of space

(5) Attitudes

(6) Personal experience base for attitudes

(7) Language assignments—pitch, volume, speed, rhythm, or intensity of language

(8) A changing musical background to which the performers must adapt in terms of mood and energy

b. Solo exercises. The following exercises use a soliloquy or monologue which moves between memorized and improvised material. At the same time a progression is made in ABA, ABC, or ABAC form in one of the following areas. Progressions may be sudden or gradual, depending upon the assignment.

(1) Physical masks or centers of energy

(2) Gestural characteristics

(3) Facial masks

(4) Use of space

(5) Attitudes

(6) Personal experience based attitudes

(7) Pitch, volume, speed, rhythm, or intensity of language

(8) A changing musical background to which the performers must adapt in terms of mood and energy

(9) A mirror. While the initiator gives the speaker-reflector a progression in physical masks, gestures, uses of space, or facial masks, the speaker-reflector does a progression in attitudes or use of language.

3. Sung

    a. Ensemble exercises. The following exercises involve scenes for two people which move between sung memorized and improvised material. At the same time progressions in ABA, ABC, or ABAC form are made in the areas below. The transitions may be gradual or sudden, depending upon the instructions of the group leader. For each progression, one person picks up the assignment from the other in the A section, passes her or his own assignment to the other in the B section, and picks up the other's assignment for the A section. If a C section is used, both performers evolve a new set of assignments out of the previous two.

        (1) Physical masks or centers of energy

        (2) Gestural characteristics

        (3) Facial masks

        (4) Use of space

        (5) Attitudes

        (6) Personal experience based attitudes

        (7) Expressive use of language assignments: pitch, volume, speed, rhythm, or intensity. Each person is assigned three of these, and the performers try to pick up and use each other's devices.

    b. Solo exercises. The following exercises involve an aria or song moving between memorized and improvised material. At the same time a progression in ABA, ABC, or ABAC form is made in one of the following areas with sudden or gradual transitions.

        (1) Physical masks or centers of energy

        (2) Gestural characteristics

        (3) Facial masks

        (4) Use of space

        (5) Attitudes

        (6) Personal experience based attitudes

        (7) Sensual words and nonverbals. Three of each are assigned and used in alternation.

        (8) A mirror. The singer makes a progression in attitude, while the initiator gives an image progression in physical masks, gestures, uses of space, or facial masks.

Imagining

1. Warmups (sung, spoken, or both).

    a. Echo game. Move between aria or soliloquy phrases and abstractions in the manner of someone imagined, i.e., in the manner of a character you have not played, or a character you make up. Or move from an observed character to an extension of that character.

b. Sound and motion. The first performer moves from an observed character to an imaginary character and from an aria phrase to an abstract sound at the same time. The imagined character and abstract sound is passed on to the next person, who then transforms it to a new observed character and aria phrase.

c. Prop transformations with aria phrases. The performers pass the prop from person to person. Each person transforms it and sings a phrase of her or his aria at the same time.

d. Phrase passing around the circle. The first person begins with an aria phrase which is transformed into a stream of consciousness about the character. The next person answers with an aria phrase which is transformed into a stream of consciousness.

e. The pianist plays unfamiliar aria accompaniments and the group uses physical gestures and attitudes to create characters based on music. The pianist moves to improvisation and the characters alter to suit the new music.

f. Around the circle. One person sings an aria phrase and each person in succession creates a variation on that phrase, passing it on rapidly. Another person sings a phrase, and the circle again creates variations. The same can be done with physical variations.

2. Spoken

a. Ensemble exercises. The following exercises involve two-person scenes which move between memorized and improvised material. The following tasks are incorporated at the same time. The improvisation may be in English or gibberish.

(1) The performers play the scene with attitudes and moods opposite to those implied by the scene. Then, in moving to the improvisation, they play the attitudes implied by the memorized scene, returning to opposite attitudes when they return to the memorized scene itself. The transitions should be justified and made sense of, but may be either sudden or gradual.

(2) The performers play the scene as if they know an amazing secret that cannot be revealed. In the improvisation section, they use that secret to structure it, returning to concealment of a new secret when returning to the memorized scene.

(3) The performers play the scene in a fantasy environment, incorporating it into the scene. They then use the fantasy environment to

inform the improvisation. Each person can have a separate fantasy environment which can then be reconciled in the improvisations.

(4) The performers play the scene with a new thought or image on every line, indicated only by attitude. They then base the improvisatory section on those thoughts and attitudes.

(5) The performers play the scene as though the words were an extension which actually got into the other person's head, "penetrating" them; in the improvisation section they turn their minds into absorbing machines that suck up the words and thoughts of the other person almost before they are uttered.

(6) The performers play the scene using a prop or props in as many unusual ways as possible.

(7) The performers play the scene in a ground plan with furniture and objects, using the space and the objects in as many unusual ways as possible.

(8) The performers play the scene exploring the thoughts that the character might be experiencing besides those of the dialogue itself, then let the improvisation reveal that train of thought.

(9) The performers play the scene with the rest of the class circled around. As the scene progresses, the observers may ask questions of those playing the scene, about the character, the situation, or their feelings. The performers must stay in character, but turn to the person asking and answer it at once, then return to the action. Incorporate the questioning as part of the milieu of the scene. This idea can be extended into other forms of side-coaching; for example, half of the observers can be on one side, half on the other, and each group may act as a spur to one of the characters, giving suggestions about action or attitude: "show him how mad you are," "run at him," "kiss her," etc.

b. Solo exercises. The following exercises involve a soliloquy or monologue moving between memorized and improvised material on signal from the instructor, incorporating one of the following problems.

(1) The performer plays the scene using attitudes and moods at opposite extremes from those implied by the scene and incorporating them. In the improvised section these attitudes may be maintained or replaced by the attitudes that *are* implied by the scene. The performer returns to the memorized material and the original attitude.

(2) The performer plays the scene as if possessing an amazing secret which cannot be revealed. In the improvised sections, she or he uses that secret to inform the improvisation, returning to the memorized scene with a new secret to conceal.

(3) The performer plays the scene as if in a fantasy environment which is not commented upon, but accepted and coped with. In the improvised sections, the environment informs the improvisation.

(4) The performer plays the scene with a new image or thought on every line, indicated only by attitude. The improvised sections are based on those thoughts and attitudes.

(5) The performer plays the scene as if the words took over and did their own extensions, as if in the grip of something else which spoke through her or him. This image is exercised during the improvisation section as well.

(6) Play the scene with one or more props exploring all the unusual ways of using them. Continue the exercise during the improvisation section as well.

(7) The performer plays the scene within a ground plan with furniture and objects, exploring all the unusual ways to use the space and objects. The exercise is continued during the improvised section.

(8) The performer plays the scene as the imagined extension of another person, maintaining the extension in the improvised sections.

(9) The performer sings the scene and the improvisation as she or he imagines other characters or people observed might sing it.

3. Sung

a. Ensemble exercises. The following exercises involve a scene for two singers moving from memorized to improvised material, incorporating one of the following problems.

(1) Each performer uses moods and attitudes at opposite extremes from those implied by the scene. In the improvised section, they use the attitudes of the scene, returning to the opposites for the memorized sections.

(2) Each performer has an amazing secret which cannot be revealed. In the improvised sections, they use the secrets to inform the improvisation, returning to the memorized sections with a new concealed secret.

(3) Each performer plays the scene as if in a fantasy environment which is not commented upon, but accepted and coped with. They use the environments to inform the improvised sections. The problem is to reconcile the two separate environments. When returning to the memorized sections, the performers change the environment as well.

(4) Each performer plays the scene extending the attitudes and feelings

suggested by the music as far as possible; gentle joy becomes ecstasy. For the improvised sections, they play the opposite extensions; gentle joy becomes raging bitterness. They should incorporate, but play the attitudes even if they cannot incorporate.

(5) Each performer has a new thought or image on each phrase, but it is apparent in attitude only. The improvised sections are based on those thoughts and images.

(6) Each performer sings in stream of consciousness style during the improvised sections, dealing with the unspoken things in the scene. These may be treated as asides.

(7) Each performer plays the scene with props, exploring all the unusual ways they can be used to express the scene. The exercise continues during the improvised sections.

(8) The performers play the scene within a ground plan with objects, exploring the space and objects in both usual and unusual ways to express the scene and the improvised sections.

b. Solo exercises. The following exercises involve an aria or song moving between memorized and improvised material, incorporating one of the following problems.

(1) The performer plays the scene using moods and attitudes at opposite extremes from those implied by the scene, and, in the improvised sections, using moods and attitudes *like* those of the scene.

(2) The performer plays the scene with an amazing secret which cannot be revealed. In the improvised sections, she or he uses the secret to inform the improvisation, returning to the memorized sections with a new secret.

(3) The performer plays the scene as if in a fantasy environment which cannot be revealed, but must be coped with. Let the environment inform the improvised sections, changing the environment again for the return to the memorized sections.

(4) The performer plays the scene with a new image or thought on every line, but it is apparent in attitude only. The improvised sections are based on those thoughts and images.

(5) The performer plays the scene with one or more props, exploring as many unusual uses as possible to express the scene. The exercise continues during the improvised sections.

(6) The performer plays the scene in a ground plan with furniture and objects, exploring the space and objects in usual and unusual ways to express the scene. The exercise continues during the improvised sections.

(7) The performer plays the scene as though the words and music took

over and did their own extensions, using her or him as an instrument. The exercise continues during the improvisation.

(8) In the improvised sections, the performer speaks or sings in a stream of consciousness style, dealing with all the unspoken things in the scene. These may be treated as asides by each of the characters.

Stylizing

1. Warmups (sung or spoken)

a. Echo game. The performers let an aria or soliloquy phrase grow out of an abstract vocal sound, accompanied by an abstract physical movement, in the manner of someone in class, or someone observed outside of class, or of a character under study.

b. Aria or soliloquy phrase with extension-implosion-compression-naturalization-internalization in the manner of someone observed, or a character under study.

c. The performers sing the soliloquy lines and speak the aria lines.

d. Sound and motion in the manner of someone observed. The sound should be abstract, growing into an aria or soliloquy phrase and reverting to the abstract. The physical motions should be abstract.

e. Character walks and physicalizations in the manner of someone observed or a character under study. The performers repeat an aria or soliloquy phrase, attending to the centers of energy, the physical use of space, and gestural characteristics.

f. The performers make physical and facial character masks based on background music from the opera or the period in question.

g. The performers pass sung or spoken gibberish around the circle in the manner of the characters whose arias, soliloquies, or scenes are being used.

h. The performers sing ritual duets in the manner of people observed or characters under study. They use soliloquy or aria phrases as a B section; the physical motions remain abstract.

2. Spoken

a. Ensemble exercises. The following exercises involve scenes moving between memorized and improvised material with the problems below. The improvisation may be in English or gibberish. All of these exercises may be performed with the ABA, ABC, ABAC structure discussed previously.

(1) Scene with background music, drawn from the period of the play or improvised, defining style.

(2) Scene in the spoken manner of people observed. The physical manner follows from the music of the language.

(3) Scene in the physical, gestural, and facial manner of someone observed.

(4) Two other people manipulate those playing the scene. The performers incorporate the manipulation into the style of the people they are impersonating.

(5) The performers play the scene as nearly like themselves as possible, then as unlike themselves as possible, moving from one to the other on signal from the instructor. It can be done with one person doing like, the other unlike, or in unison.

(6) Each person moves from the most artificial, formal style to the most naturalistic style. Or one person can adopt a natural style, the other artificial. Make certain your models have some basis in actual observation.

(7) The performers play the scene in the manner of other characters from the same play or other plays.

(8) The performers play the scene in imagined, artificial styles, but make sense of the style if possible.

(9) The performers play the scene as the imagined extension of other people. Relate the styles of the characters to each other as well as to the scene itself.

b. Solo exercises. The following exercises involve a soliloquy or monologue moving between memorized and improvised material, in the style of someone observed. Be sure to specify the qualities intended so that the projection can be evaluated. The performer incorporates the problems below.

(1) Soliloquy with physical masks, centers of energy, idiosyncrasies, postural emphasis, and the like

(2) Soliloquy with use of space: rhythms, speed, size, etc.

(3) Soliloquy with gestural characteristics, explored by using all five gestural categories in the manner of the character being impersonated

(4) Soliloquy with facial masks and tics

(5) Soliloquy with vocal characteristics

(6) Soliloquy with emotional tone

(7) Soliloquy with an abstract ritual solo, gibberish, or sung gibberish used in the improvisational section.

(8) Soliloquy with another member of the class providing a mirror for incorporation. The reflector, of course, is already performing in the manner of someone else and should incorporate the initiator's movements into that style.

(9) Soliloquy with manipulation and incorporation as in exercise (8) above

(10) Speak the soliloquy, but on signal sing it improvisationally, moving back and forth between singing and speaking on successive signals. Add to this the basic assignment of moving between the memorized words and improvised words.

(11) Soliloquy in the performer's own manner, and then as much unlike as possible. Class validation or disagreement is important. Incorporate the opposites. Both the memorized and the improvised sections should deal with both styles.

(12) Soliloquy in the most formal, artifical style imaginable, then in the most naturalistic style imaginable. Both memorized and improvised sections should deal with both styles. Incorporate.

(13) Both soliloquy and improvisation sung as others might sing it, characters from the play, from other plays, or people observed might sing it.

(14) Soliloquy and improvisation as the imagined extension of another person.

3. Sung

a. Ensemble exercises. The following exercises involve a duet moving between memorized and improvised material, with attention to the following style problems, *as observed in actual practice by other people or performers*. These problems may be separately assigned to each performer utilizing the ABA, ABC, ABAC structural patterns. Or, one member of the duet may be assigned the problem while his partner relates to what he plays.

(1) Duet with physical masks, centers of energy, postural statements

(2) Duet with use of space: speeds, rhythms, sizes

(3) Duet with gestural characteristics

(4) Duet with facial masks, tics

(5) Duet with mannerisms, idiosyncrasies

(6) Duet with emotional tone—that system of feeling underlying all specific attitudes

(7) Duet with language nuance, sensual words, nonverbals

(8) Duet moving between singing and speaking. In the spoken section, either memorized or improvised words may be used.

(9) Duet moving from the memorized duet to an abstract ritual duet as the accompanist continues with the memorized score.

(10) Duet with each performer singing in the manner of other characters from the same opera or other operas in the memorized section. In the improvised section they sing in the manner of the characters who do belong in the duet. Or both character types may be used in each section.

(11) Duet with each performer in his or her own manner, then as much unlike as possible. Both the like and the unlike manners should be used in the memorized and improvised sections.

(12) Duet with each performer using as formal and artificial a style as possible, then as naturalistic a style as possible. Both styles should appear in the improvised as well as the memorized sections.

(13) Duet in a series of styles selected from the following list: classical renaissance, baroque, eighteenth-century court, nineteenth-century romantic melodrama, twentieth-century expressionism, nineteenth-century heightened realism, twentieth-century naturalism, Greek statuesque, nineteenth-century operetta, twentieth-century cabaret, twentieth-century musical comedy. Each style selected should be played in both the memorized and the improvised sections.

(14) Duet as an imagined extension of another character from the opera or from another opera. The exercise continues in the improvised sections.

b. Solo exercises. The following exercises involve an aria moving between memorized and improvised material, in the style of someone observed, with attention to the following problems:

(1) Aria with physical masks, centers of energy, postural characteristics

(2) Aria with use of space: rhythms, speeds, size

(3) Aria with gestural characteristics

(4) Aria with facial masks, tics

(5) Aria with mannerisms, idiosyncrasies

(6) Aria with emotional tone underlying all specific attitudes

(7) Aria with use of language nuance, sensual words, nonverbals

(8) Aria with mirror and incorporation

(9) Aria with manipulation and incorporation

(10) Aria with movement from the style of the character impersonated to the performer's own style and back again

(11) Aria with movement from singing to speaking and back. The music

remains with the aria score. Words may be either English or gibberish in the improvised section.

(12) Aria with movement from singing to improvised abstract ritual solo
and back

(13) Aria in the performer's own style, then as much unlike as possible.
Both like and unlike should be used in the memorized and the
improvised sections.

(14) Aria in as formal and artificial a style as possible, then in as naturalistic a style as possible. Both styles should be used for both improvised and memorized sections.

(15) Aria in the manner of another character from the same opera, or
from another opera.

(16) Aria as an imagined extension of another character from the same
opera or another opera.

Coordinating

1. Warmups

The following exercises will draw upon memorized scenes, solos, duets,
trios, and arias.

a. Echo game. Begin with an improvised abstract phrase which transforms
to a memorized aria phrase. Make a progression in attitude at the same
time.

b. Sound and motion. The performers move between abstract sound and
naturalistic motion to an aria phrase with ritualized motion. They pass
on, mirror, and transform the sound and motion.

c. Sung or spoken gibberish. The performers move between the manner of
a character from the opera and the manner of someone from the group.

d. Mirror. The initiator makes a physical and attitude progression; the
reflector responds with an aria phrase and extension, then an abstract
phrase and compression.

2. Spoken

a. Ensemble exercises

(1) Shakespeare game moving from the actual scene to an improvised
conversation in sung or spoken English or gibberish and back to
Shakespeare.

(2) Scenes played using ABA, ABC, ABAC, or $A_1A_2A_3$ structures
for moving between memorized and improvised material, with the

shifts signaled by the instructor. Two or more of the following problems should be incorporated.

(A—memorized, B—improvised, C combines improvised and memorized material, $A_1 A_2 A_3$—improvised variations on memorized lines with paraphrase extensions.)

Attitudes: A—first person assigned, second person picks up
B—second person assigned, first person picks up
C—logical extension by both performers of the preceding material
$A_1 A_2 A_3$—first person initiates, second person relates. second person initiates, first person relates, etc.

Personal experience passed as in Attitudes, above

Physical masks, centers of energy, or magic garment extensions passed as in Attitudes, above

Use of space passed as in Attitudes, above

Use of gestures passed as in Attitudes, above

Use of props: real, imaginary, real/imaginary combinations, passed as in Attitudes above

Use of scored and improvised background music. The performers shift in mood, tone, and rhythms with music

Style: In the A section, in the manner of other characters from play; in the B section, as extensions of those characters. This can be done as in pickup-exchange sequence, as in Attitudes, above

Verifiable tasks

Facial masks passed as in Attitudes, above

Addition of a nonspeaking person whom the performers incorporate and interrelate to the scene

b. Solo exercises. The following exercises involve a soliloquy moving between memorized and improvised material in one of the following structures: ABA, ABC, ABAC, $A_1 A_2 A_3$ (A, memorized; B, improvised; C mingles memorized and improvised; $A_1 A_2 A_3$, improvised variations on memorized lines, paraphrased extensions) with two or more of the following problems:

(1) Soliloquy with assigned attitudes: (In $A_1 A_2 A_3$—let attitude evolve)

(2) Soliloquy with personal experience. The improvisation becomes an extension of the personal experience.

(3) Soliloquy with physical masks, centers of energy extensions, or magic garment extensions in assigned sequence

(4) Soliloquy with facial masks. Assigned and improvised sequence
(5) Soliloquy with use of space and objects. Assigned and improvised sequence
(6) Soliloquy with use of gesture: Stress the *kind* of gestural work to be done, use the three categories (Indicating, Reacting, Describing), but define them in terms of speed, rhythm, intensity, scale, etc.
(7) Soliloquy with use of real props used in ways other than those implied by their basic function, then used in a way suggested by their basic function.
(8) Soliloquy with use of scored and improvised background music
(9) Soliloquy with use of language — two categories and two specials (nonverbals, sensual words, significant pauses) assigned — two categories and two specials improvised.
(10) Soliloquy with stylization: in the manner of a character from an opera, then in the manner of an imagined person. In the third section the two are combined.
(11) Soliloquy with assigned, verifiable tasks.
(12) Soliloquy with a silent person entering the scene. Both performers should incorporate.

3. Sung

a. Ensemble exercises
(1) Worlds in collison, with the addition of improvised sequences between the actual scenes: thus, a duet, an improvised sequence, and a new duet followed by another improvised sequence. See p. 199 for detailed description of the form.
(2) Scenes played using the following problems in ABA, ABC, ABAC, or $A_1 A_2 A_3$ form (all with assigned exchanges and third section improvised extension). Instructor signals progression.
(a) Physical masks, centers of energy, or magic garments
(b) Facial masks
(c) Attitudes
(d) Personal experience
(e) Use of space and objects — in usual and unusual ways
(f) Use of props — in usual and unusual ways
(g) Use of language nuance within context of music
(h) Stylization: in manner of characters and imagined characters
(3) With verifiable tasks
(4) With nonspeaking persons added to the scene. The performers should incorporate them.

b. Solo exercises. Aria, with following problems using ABA, ABC, ABAC, or $A_1 A_2 A_3$ structures. A, assigned; B, assigned; C, A_1, improvised extension.

  (1) Aria with physical masks, centers of energy, or magic garments

  (2) Aria with facial masks

  (3) Aria with use of space and objects

  (4) Aria with use of gesture: All three categories (Indicating, Describing, Reacting) are used

  (5) Aria with use of props in usual and unusual ways

  (6) Aria with attitudes

  (7) Aria with personal experience – B extension

  (8) Aria with stylization: in the manner of observed character and imagined character consecutively

  (9) Aria with language nuance

 (10) Aria with assigned verifiable tasks

 (11) Aria with one or more silent characters. The performer incorporates them.

Notes

Notes

Preface

1. Under the term *music-theater* I include opera as well as all other performance events in which music, words, and action interact to form a dramatic event in which music is the primary articulator.

2. We will use the term *singer-actor* throughout the book to remind ourselves of the dual nature of the aesthetic task required of the performer.

3. Of the 45 productions by the Minnesota Opera Company through the 1975-76 season, 33 were operas composed in the twentieth century, 17 were world or American premieres, and 13 were especially commissioned for production by the Minnesota Opera Company.

4. For example, the University has always allowed me complete freedom in teaching a course called "Acting for Music-Theater," which has never been taught in the same way twice and which has served as an invaluable testing ground for new concepts in performance.

Chapter 1

1. Peter Paul Fuchs, ed., *The Music Theater of Walter Felsenstein* (New York: W. W. Norton and Co., 1975), p. 125. As Felsenstein has pointed out, the separation of the operatic form into music and theater is not inherent in the form. The dichotomy of "music" and "stage" has been produced artificially; it does not emerge naturally from any of the great masterworks. Artificial or not, however, the dichotomy exists and, as we will see, it can be a creative stimulus if integrating the opposites is conceived as the task rather than either ignoring the opposition or defending the status quo.

2. One can hear the sniffs of disdain from parts of the operatic world at the comparison of Wagner and Sondheim, but such sniffing is part of the problem. Both men are men of words *and* music, and both attempt to deal with new levels of sensibility in the genre of music-theater. For sheer musical and verbal intelligence, there are not many twentieth-century opera composers who can play in the same league as Sondheim. And Sondheim was reviewed for the first time in *Opera News* as an opera composer of the work *Pacific Overtures*.

3. The fact that concerts, musical comedy, and theater peices with incidental music will all benefit from the same training which creates total music-theater is a serendipitous by-product.

4. The late Sir Tyrone Guthrie was the first to make this stirring and absolutely truthful claim for the powers of opera.

5. Compare this with Felsenstein's analysis: "The complete mastery of an operatic role—beginning with the singer's discovery of his own vocal function in the role, through learning the control he needs for the stage and realizing the full extent of his task, to the process of rehearsing, and at last the readiness to perform—requires an amount of time which no theater has available, not even the Komische Opera." Fuchs, *The Music Theater of Walter Felsenstein*, p. 38.

6. The operatic bum, like the tennis or beach variety, is one who ekes out a living from the form with a minimum commitment to the art and a maximum commitment to the social and managerial hierarchy surrounding the art.

7. It *is* hard work. And it is especially gratifying when a singer comes up after a short four-week course involving the exercises in this book and says, "This proves to me that real learning has to be fun. I learned an incredible amount, it was hard work, incredibly hard work, and yet it was a pleasure."

8. Fuchs, *The Music Theater of Walter Felsenstein*, p. 32. As Felsenstein has put it, "Whatever different opinions may be entertained concerning the contemporary interpretation of opera, no doubt exists that the focal center is the singing human being."

9. Jack Fincher, *Human Intelligence* (New York: G. P. Putnam's Sons, 1976), p. 143.

10. Even the titles are misnomers. The director of music does direct the music, but the director of the stage actually directs the drama, the theater of the music-theater partnership. At the Metropolitan Opera, of course, the stage director merely refurbishes the work of previous drama directors. The terms *regisseur* and *producer* are equally misleading. There is no accurate American title for the function of the operatic-stage director.

11. The number of stage directors who have misplaced aspirations as conductors is more limited, *not* because of their more generous nature, but because the technical skills for conducting are not so easily acquired or faked as those in the area of stage direction. Those of us who have worked in both areas know that you can fake one as easily as the other—it simply takes a little more background to do so in conducting, and the fakery is not as easily recognized as such by the man in the street.

12. It was while directing the Aspen training program that I realized for the first time the absolute necessity for the dual-director approach to training. No matter how dedicated one is to unification, one needs the loyal opposition, whether the field is music or theater or even, as in my case, music-theater. Total commitment to one end of the spectrum combined with genuine willingness to cooperate with another person equally committed to the other end is a *sine qua non* for any opera training program. So is the other person. At Aspen there was no other person.

13. Fuchs, *The Music Theater of Walter Felsenstein*, pp. 38-39. Felsenstein's comments about this dual relationship are instructive and challenging: "It goes without saying that the responsible artistic direction of an ensemble must be in the hands of either a theater-conscious conductor or of an extremely musical stage director; both of them, and only in conjunction with each other, are the guiding power. Yet the focal point of the operation must be the singing actor. Only the stage director who recognizes this commandment and obeys it will escape the temptation to stage himself rather than the work; and the conductor who must force himself to obey it rather than feel it within himself,

may be able to unleash virtuoso sound effects, but he will never really belong to the music theater. In my opinion there is no stage director of exactly the type the conductor would wish for, and no conductor whom the stage director finds entirely unobjectionable. But if these men are qualified to practice their profession, are loyal to the theater and at the same time feel a kinship with their ensembles, only one basic element is needed for the possibility of a creative collaboration: the profound knowledge of the work that is necessary for a faithful interpretation. This means that neither of the men may assume he knows the work well enough to be able to dispense with a joint analysis just because he has conducted or staged it before. Since it is impossible to know every detail of the composer's intentions in a masterwork, the chance of new discoveries — depending on the maturity and experience of the interpreter — is always a rewarding prospect. If either the conductor or the stage director is teamed up with a partner who has never done a particular work before, this will give him the opportunity not only to let his associate profit from his own experience but also to use the other's fresh, uncluttered viewpoint in order to recognize and correct some errors in his own interpretation. In the joint struggle of the conductor and the stage director to make the work their own, there may be some violent and yet fruitful altercations. Enmity will not result from this unless vanity and the craving for recognition are stronger than creative concern." Fuchs, *The Music Theater of Walter Felsenstein*, pp. 38-39. A superbly honest analysis of the situation, and a challenge to all directors and conductors who must struggle together for the sake of music-theater art.

14. *Ibid.*, p. 44. Here again, Felsenstein's comments on the singer's training and the resultant demands on the stage director are of interest: "We can all agree on one point; only very rarely has a singer had the kind of training required for contemporary music-theater production."

Chapter 2

1. And although some voice teachers will say, "If your voice is good enough, you won't need the other skills," this eliminates the 95 percent of all singers whose voices are excellent but not of the superstar-name-their-own-terms variety. Surprisingly, or perhaps naturally, however, even this super 5 percent very often demonstrate a full range of music-theater skills and commitment.

2. It should go without saying that the development of the music-theater artist is a lifelong *process*, and not a static goal to be attained at some given point.

3. One of the amusing exceptions proving the rule is the story of a superb concert singer who had performed a concert version of Cherubini's *Medea* in Italian. She was coaching it again for a later performance when the conductor remarked on the intensely moving way she had conveyed Medea's grief at the thought of killing her children. "Killing her WHAT?!!" exclaimed the offended singer. Although she had not done her dramatic homework, her musical sensitivity and emotional instincts had created an experience which, though having nothing to do with the *facts* of the drama, had the power to fill the drama in a convincing way. The projected energies were specific, if not factually accurate, and the music converted them to its advantage. This is a point we will discuss at length below.

4. Fincher, *Human Intelligence*, pp.195-196.

5. Although this subject could be pursued at greater length, a final observation is of interest. In my experience left-handed (right-brain dominated) singers and musicians are considerably more intuitive and more imaginatively free than singers and musicians as a whole. It may be that the left-handed musician has already dealt with the problem of life

as a right brain dominated, imaginative, creative process and when she or he turns over the musical processes to the left brain, this imaginative grasp of life is not relinquished. The right-hander, however, has already subordinated the imaginative-creative impulses to the logic and order of a left brain view of life, and to relinquish control of the musical faculties to the left brain as well simply enforces an already existing process of control over the other right brain functions.

6. Stanislavski was a veritable demon concerning the need for rooting out all tensions, no matter how small or seemingly insignificant. "Do not force or do violence to your feelings if your soul does not catch fire. The most dangerous thing you can do now is cripple your faculties by overloading them beyond your strength – that leads to hysteria and muscular cramps resulting from over-tenseness. Make this a rule: *The more dramatically powerful a scene is, the greater the call on your inner forces, the freer your body must be.* While you are singing watch your hands with special care: no clenched fists, no twisting of fingers. If you ball your fists, you are done for because you will have shut in your temperament, driven it deep inside. . . . One should not stand on the stage firmly on both feet as if at attention (note classic statues in this regard) that there must not be the slightest tenseness in one's neck (God forbid that one should raise one's shoulders while singing). Besides, we were told, if one's elbows or wrists are tense, he is practically nailed down, and that's the end of his creative powers." Konstantin Stanislavski and Pavel Rumyantsev, *Stanislavski on Opera* (New York: Theater Arts Books, 1975), p. 36.

7. This has been verified by the dozens of young singers who nod sadly and emphatically when the topic is discussed.

8. The approach can be used for singers, or singer-actors of almost any degree of ability. The important thing is to understand the crucial differences between the forms, and how to deal with them.

9. Peter Brooks's highly stimulating book, *The Empty Space* (New York: Atheneum, 1968) contains the following pregnant but unfulfilled paragraph on music, theater, and opera: "Closely related to this (the separation of 'eternal truths from the superficial variations') is the conflict between theater directors and musicians in opera productions where two totally different forms, drama and music, are treated as though they were one. A musician is dealing with a fabric that is as near as man can get to an expression of the invisible. His score notes this invisibility and his sound is made by instruments which hardly ever change. The player's personality is unimportant; a thin clarinettist can easily make a fatter sound than a fat one. The vehicle of music is separate from the music itself. So the stuff of music comes and goes, always in the same way, free of the need to be revised and reassessed. But the vehicle of drama is flesh and blood and here completely different laws are at work. The vehicle and the message cannot be separated. Only a naked actor can begin to resemble a pure instrument like a violin and only if he has a completely classical physique with neither paunch nor bandy legs. A ballet dancer is somewhat close to this condition and he can reproduce formal gestures unmodified by his own personality or by the outer movement of life. But the moment the actor dresses up and speaks with his own tongue he is entering the fluctuating territory of manifestation and existence that he shares with the spectator. Because the musician's experience is so different, he finds it hard to follow why the traditional bits of business that made Verdi laugh and Puccini slap his thighs seem neither funny nor illuminating today. Grand opera, of course, is the Deadly Theatre carried to absurdity. Opera is a nightmare of vast feuds over tiny details; of surrealist anecdotes that all turn round the same assertion: nothing needs to change. Everything in opera must change, but in opera change is blocked" (pp. 16-17). Brooks's statement is both accurate and depressing. He did not,

however, take the next step: to note the existence of a third form—music/drama (using his terminology). If this third form is acknowledged as a separate and independent entity, the need for change from a music-dominated version of opera to one in which a new aesthetic prevails, drawn from both of the parent forms, might become evident to all concerned. At least in this way it takes the form of a request to share and create anew rather than a demand that one form or the other give up its taste and sensibility.

10. During the preparation of this book, *The Music Theater of Walter Felsenstein* was published, as was *Stanislavski on Opera*. The number of useful books in the field is greater by two, for both books have important messages for all of us who are concerned with the singer-actor.

11. In preparing my dissertation on *The Director and the Mozart Operas*, I was not only allowed to fend almost totally for myself, but there was also virtually no criticism of the point of view it contained. This is not a condemnation of my very competent and concerned advisors, but simply another indication of the virginity of the territory.

12. His special work on opera had not been published at that time and his teachings were (and are) being used for singers directly from his acting texts without the special qualifications he made when working with singer-actors in the Bolshoi Studio.

13. Even Felsenstein's terminology can be confusing in this respect. He will use "realistic," "convincing," "truthful," and "believable" in describing the ideal music-theater production, and still allow room for strongly stylized fantasy. It is obvious that all of those words are subjective to some extent, and their meaning depends upon an outside observer for validation.

14. Every American production of Shakespeare has to cope with the twin poles of honesty and artificiality, plain talk and rhetoric, and because these opposites are seldom reconciled on a training level, they remain unreconciled in performance.

15. I could have said "by the way you sang it," but that would have placed an even phonier connotation on what is being said for those whose Gielgud-hating hackles have long since arisen.

16. It was a vastly exciting experience to attend *America Hurrah* (produced by the Open Theater in 1965), and to recognize the same kinds of experimentation we had been developing in seeming isolation in our opera workshops in Minneapolis. This book owes an additional debt to the Open Theater and to Joe Chaikin for the special influence passed on from that group by Paul Boesing. Paul became a member of the Minnesota Opera Resident Ensemble after leaving the Firehouse Theater (which was also strongly influenced by the Open Theater through Paul and other members of the Open Theater who came to Minneapolis in the late 60s to help make the Firehouse one of the country's most important experimental theaters). He passed on a number of exercises from the Open Theater experience which were modified and adapted and have become basic to our training for music-theater.

17. One of the best books available, Strickland's *The Technique of Acting*, was published in the early 50s and, as the title suggests, deals with technique. As a result, the book is out of print, and no one uses it. A pity.

18. Whenever a writer needs an example of the artificial or the unbelievable, opera can always provide it; witness this statement of Daniel Hoffman's from *Poe Poe Poe Poe Poe Poe Poe* (New York: Doubleday, 1973): "For years I thought *Lenore* ridiculous. . . . Now when I read *Lenore* I no longer think, Who can suspend disbelief in such incredible language? No, I imagine the stage of the Met, murky in a dull amber light, and a scene in an unwritten opera by Berlioz" (p. 67). Now, presumably, *Lenore* is no longer ridiculous, but simply like a Met production. Whatever that does for *Lenore*, it does little for opera.

19. It is refreshing to note, however, that there is today a movement toward a more

natural performance feeling about the stylization of ballet, an attempt to integrate the opposites of the formal and the natural within the context of the balletic form.

20. It is shocking how many young singer-actors have had this essential relationship between external (sensory) and internal (feeling) process cut off by the meaningless repetition of bad technique imposed upon them by well-meaning teachers. Actors, on the other hand, have had the same process cut off by an equally well-meaning insistence that they "do nothing without feeling it first," a certain way to promote inhibition and ensure that nothing will be done.

Chapter 3

1. Although innumerable exercises have been developed in preparing the singer to perform traditional music, far fewer have been developed in the area of contemporary music, where classical techniques are not always sufficient.

2. Robert Pirsig, *Zen and the Art of Motorcycle Maintenance* (New York: William Morrow, 1974) pp. 73-74.

3. Although one might object that written-spoken drama has no place in music-theater training, it has become a truism in the past decades that any sequence of sounds can be perceived as music, and therefore any sequence of spoken words can be perceived as musical, even though they are not sung in the traditional sense. One cannot speak without pitch, rhythm, volume, and speed, and anything possessing these qualities can be perceived musically. It is a question of degree: totally random sounds approach the traditional definition of noise (although they may still be perceived as music by our structure-imposing minds) and the most natural kind of conversation approaches what we traditionally assume is nonsinging. But pursuing the aesthetic of opposites, we can see that the most realistic form of spoken drama is vitalized by its possession of form, given in part by the playwright, and in part by the actor's spoken organization of sound and meaning, which has both the formal properties of music and the natural qualities of speech.

4. The fact that singer-actors sometimes have to speak lines, that they often do it rather badly and therefore need the training that this view provides is merely another serendipitous by-product of our investigation of the music-theater territory.

5. To my knowledge there has been only one professional production of a totally improvised opera, but I hope that there will be many more.

Chapter 4

1. The assumption is not valid in the majority of cases, but it is hoped that the interaction of this and similar training programs with the work of voice teachers throughout the country will create a more unified concept of singing-acting which posits the free, healthily produced voice as the essential base of music-theater.

2. I have encountered literally dozens of young actors who have damaged their voices badly in just this way. Unfortunately, because such damage involves both technique and vocal production, it has been largely ignored until the last decade in America. But unless the *basis* of the error is recognized, good technique will not overcome what is essentially a mental error about what acting is and what it is to communicate feeling.

Chapter 5

1. Stanley Keleman finds this set of opposites in the child's process of growth, moving between a concentration on one's self and a concentration on others: "As he (the child) develops . . . he begins to expand and extend himself away from the mother. He extends

himself and reconnects, extends himself and reforms his relationships and his self . . . he becomes a living example of *the paradox of individuality and connectedness.*" (My italics.) Stanley Keleman, *Your Body Speaks Its Mind* (New York: Simon and Schuster, 1975), p. 36.

2. In a play like *Travesties*, in which the opening monologue is the length of an average aria, the achievement of the actor in sustaining it is a staggering phenomenon. John Wood's performance of this monologue was an incredible risk, and yet the same time-sustaining demand is made constantly in opera—with the help of the music, of course.

3. One young singer who happened to have powerful if somewhat fixed focus sighed with relief when I discussed this topic. She had, it turned out, developed the habit of focus through a desire to avoid looking at her parents and teachers during recitals. Instead, she fixed her gaze on a light in the back of the hall and sang to it. The reason for the fixed quality of the focus became clear, and also the fact that she had a useful, if rudimentary tool with which to work. It was, incidentally, a great relief to her to learn that it was not only OK, it was a Good Thing.

4. Although this aria has a built-in vision upon which to focus, all arias are potential visionary experiences.

5. Rodin's *Thinker* characterizes perfectly the natural inclination of the man in deep thought: head down and resting on the hand. But the "natural" is not necessarily the most useful in music-theater.

6. The fact that a lowered focus may feel more comfortable to the singer-actor—since it is physically and psychologically protective and is the first step in a move toward the fetal position—does not mean that one should encourage it. The need of Instant Comfort is the plague of teaching and stylized art, and in the theater especially, naturalism and instant comfort are often mistaken for each other. What is comfortable may not be useful and what is useful may not at first be comfortable.

7. One should never forget that what we judge in condemning the stylistic conventions of another era is not the full-fledged reality of the original convention, but a parodistic, third-rate hand-me-down many times removed from the original. Brando's original performance is no more conveyed by the imitation than is the vitality of a genuine nineteenth-century operatic acting style by its pallid and mechanical descendants.

8. It is especially in auditions that the young performer can use the concept of the aria experience. By evoking the total experience of the song, the voice, which in isolation might not be capable of carrying the entire burden, is enhanced by support from its cohorts.

9. Eugene Herrigel, *Zen in the Art of Archery* (New York: McGraw-Hill, 1964) pp. 87-93.

10. At least Aristotle thought so. And despite centuries of criticism, his elevation of plot as the primary element of drama is still valid. Those who fail to integrate plot and character as they follow the "What happens next?" impulse do not prove plot to be secondary, any more than those character sketches that lose their narrative way prove that concern with character is a secondary concern. In either case, audiences have given their answer time and again by showing greater concern for *what* happens next than for *who* happens next. This is not intended as an anti-intellectual slam, but simply as a statement of fact. Most people would rather watch a situation comedy than see Laurence Olivier and Katherine Hepburn act (and act magnificently) in a romantic drama of character. This was the actual situation on American television in 1975. Perhaps it is best to regard plot and character as another set of opposites that must partake of each other for maximum vitality.

11. Among the exceptions to this general rule is the moment in *Otello* when Otello strikes Desdemona in the presence of the Venetian Ambassador. Time freezes, and in Felsenstein's magnificent production, the lighting assists the communication of this fact by isolating, one by one, the commenting observers of the shocking act.

12. This odd and wonderful turnabout occurs in *The Marriage of Figaro* in the third act aria of the Countess. The words themselves might very well be taken in a single melancholy mode, but Mozart will not have it so and gives the aria one of the most exquisite progressions in all opera. It is, in fact, the turning point of the piece.

13. This is the Baroque method as opposed to the causal articulation of drama first developed by Mozart. See Joseph Kerman's *Opera as Drama* (New York: Random House, 1956) pp. 52-78.

Chapter 6

1. To date, the only completely improvised professional opera of which I am aware was produced by the Minnesota Opera Company. The words, the music, and the action were all completely improvised. It was a unique and unclassifiable experience, very popular with the audience and taxing in the extreme for the singers. It was one of the best training experiences I have ever encountered and should be pursued as both an educational and an entertainment effort.

2. An important point here is that we did not wait to try something physical or verbal until we "felt" it, i.e., knew how it worked. We felt it *with* our bodies, *with* our voices, coordinated the problems *as* we actually worked with them, not intellectualizing in advance, but coping in *Gestalt* with the whole blooming, buzzing, stumbling chaos. Eventually we quit stumbling, but had we waited to "feel it," or refused to try it unless it felt natural, we would still be crawling.

3. The pleasant difference is that we can learn to break in new styles more and more quickly as we practice, whereas the length of time to break in a pair of shoes remains constant.

4. *Homo ludens* and *homo faber* are another set of opposites that are very much a part of our work. Irwin Thompson sees the life of man as an alternating cycle moving from one to the other and back again. He would not disagree, I am sure, that these opposites, particularly in an artistic endeavor, must constantly partake of each other. Our work must involve play on its highest level, and our play must have all the singlemindedness of work.

5. Stanley Keleman has discussed two types of personalities which give another view of this concept: "the self-extender and the self-collector. These correspond roughly to the extravert and the introvert. The extender reaches out into the world and needs constant approval. He keeps pushing out and expanding, and tends to be aggressive and dominant in his sexual patterns. The self-collector creates very strong boundaries and allows the world to come to him. He needs little validation from other people. He enjoys his sensations and does not try to overwhelm." Sam Keen, *Voices and Visions* (New York: Harper and Row, 1976), p. 169. These concepts are discussed more completely in Mr. Keleman's book. The two impulses clearly need integration within the individual, to create a balance of the inner and the outer.

6. This should not be confused with the concept of implosive breathing often used in teaching the process of singing. In that case the concept is used to encourage good use of air. If the singer associates increasingly energized singing with an increased use of air, he will encounter immediate difficulties. The ratio of the quantity of energized singing sound to the amount of air used to produce it is almost inverse and is certainly not one-

to-one. The concept of air imploding rather than exploding during singing often helps a singer realize and develop this seemingly irrational concept.

7. See below, page 115.

8. The remark about Olivier's performances "endangering his role" springs to mind in this connection. There is always something "beyond" the performance itself which makes the performance seem transcendent. Whether this transcendence exists in fact or by implication is less important than the fact of its existence in the minds of the beholders.

Chapter 7

1. One critic's reaction to the Minnesota Opera Company's production of *The Newest Opera in the World*, a piece that was totally improvised, musically and dramatically, each evening, yet created a story line which lasted two hours or more in performance.

2. We have found, however, that members of that same *Newest Opera* cast have returned to the exercises again and again, and never fail to learn from them on both traditional and improvisational levels.

3. An example of the extraordinary mental constipation that can afflict critics when confronted by improvisation in a music-theater context can be found in a review of *The Newest Opera In the World* which faulted the performance because a scene *in the style of Mozart was not as good as a scene Mozart would have written himself.*

4. This is less the case with actors. With them, one often feels the need for greater discipline and wishes that they could execute technically without first having to summon it up from their bowels. The actor is the singer's opposite on the music-theater continuum of discipline-freedom.

Chapter 8

1. Although gibberish is a fairly common acting exercise, sound and motion is derived from Open Theater and Joseph Chaikin. It is described in detail in Robert Pasolli's *The Open Theater*. Unlike a great many other acting exercises, however, the sound and motion is uniquely suited to the problems of music-theater, and can be used for exercising a great many music-theater techniques.

Chapter 9

1. Stanislavski and Rumyantsev, *Stanislavski on Opera*, p. 75.

Chapter 10

1. It is suggested that the instructor stick with gibberish until it is totally comfortable. Although the class may express a desire to improvise in English, it is invariably much more difficult and inhibiting than is gibberish and can impede many of the exercises rather than aiding them.

2. In all these exercises, the focus, the sense of actually seeing and communicating with another person, event, or idea, should be primary.

Index

Index

241

Naturalism: confusion about, 26; in operatic acting, 30; and extension, implosion, 89; in performance, 233-34; and instant comfort, 235
The Newest Opera in the World, 237
Nonverbal sounds, 136

Open Theater, 27, 233, 237
Opera: training programs, v-vii, 14; demand on performers, vi; essence of high emotional situations, vii; therapy, vii; training for directors and conductors, viii; supermarket training, 17; direction, literature on, 25; as a third form, 232-33; and the ridiculous, 233
Opera News, 229
Operania: disputed territory, 4-5; cold war, 47
Operatic bum, 230
Operatic cookbook, 17
Operative words, 136
Opposites: integration of, vii; synthesis of contraries, 6; theory of, 27; discussed, 37; listed, analyzed, 38-39; law applied to energizing, 52; applied to characterization, 54; self and character, 61; used in practising isolations, 65; in dealing with time extension, 68; actual and imagined subject matter, 72; lyric expansion, narrative development, work, play, 89; attitude choices in arias, 95; blending by Toscanini, 95; exercise vs. performance, 102; improvisation as integrator of, 106-7; solo-ensemble, 117; synthesis in training, 122; life and performance, 130; attitudes in scenes, 214, 216; attitudes in soliloquies, 215, 217; in American Shakespeare, 232; and development of children, 234-35; *homo ludens, homo faber*, 236; actor freedom vs. singer discipline, 237
Opposition needed in training, 230
Overload principle, 96-99

Pacific Overtures, 229
Performance transcendence, 237
Personal experience exercise, 140
Personal growth, 112

Phrasing of language, 136
Physical masks, 124-25
Physical readiness, 139
Pirsig, Robert: on romantic and classic modes of understanding, 36; restatement of view, 97
Play attitude, essential to growth, 99-100
Popping, 144
Prima donna encouragement, 21
Process vs. product, 102
Progression: avoidance in opera, 78; dramatic, 78; in music-theater, 79; varieties of, 80; exercised with attitudes, 80-81
Prop creation: and transformation, 155; with gibberish commentary, 156; to create characters, 157; with sung gibberish commentary, 158; with double props, 186; with aria phrases, 214

Question-asking: in music-theater, 86; of your character, 90; for evaluation, 113; for aria preparation, 183-84; for stimulating imagination, 184-86; for role preparation, 194-95

Ratio factor, 93-94
Readiness, and emotional stress, 58
Realism, confusion about, 26
Reich, Wilhelm, 57
Response to music: in gesture, 128; with masks, physical, personal experience, 141; warmup variations, 147; through focus, 147; with gibberish poem and attack, 148-49; phrasing to music, 151; with physical projections, 171-72; physical phrasing of arias, 181; in creating characters or environments, 186, 191; memorized and improvised, 214
Ritual duets: discussed, 119; with attitudes, 142; with nonritual sound, 144; with attack, 147; with sung gibberish, attitude and attack, 150; with three-part form, 152; with three attitudes, 152; sung, in ABA form with attitudes, 154; sung in ABA form using styles, 162; sung in ABC form variations, 163; with coordinating combinations, 164-65; sung, with coordinating combina-